A history of
Aerial Warfare

A history of
Aerial
Warfare
John W R Taylor

BOOK CLUB ASSOCIATES London

endpapers
Pilots and personnel of No. 1 Squadron, R.A.F., with
their S.E.5a fighters, at Clairmarais airfield, near St
Omer, France, July 1918.
title page
Vickers Virginias approaching Weybridge airfield.

This edition published 1974 by
Book Club Associates
By arrangement with the Hamlyn Group

Published by
The Hamlyn Publishing Group Limited
© Copyright The Hamlyn Publishing
Group Limited 1974

Printed in Great Britain by
Jarrold and Sons Ltd, Norwich

Colour Illustrations

Contents

'. . . our Ship descending out of the Air to the Sails of Sea-Ships . . . it may over-set them, kill their men, burn their Ships by artificial Fire-works and Fire-balls.'
Francesco de Lana-Terzi, 1670

The ultimate weapon: a Minuteman intercontinental ballistic missile inside its underground silo launcher, protected from enemy attack and held at almost instantaneous readiness for firing.
U.S. Air Force

Introduction

In what period of history did the story of aerial warfare begin? The earliest man-to-man combats in aircraft took place in 1914, at the start of the First World War; but the Italians had used aeroplanes and airships to make reconnaissance flights, to drop bombs, and to scatter propaganda leaflets over their opponents, in North Africa, three years earlier.

If one is prepared to accept a tethered, unarmed observation balloon as an instrument of aerial warfare, the clock must be turned back past the nineteenth century to 1794, a mere eleven years after a man first left the ground in a vehicle of this kind. The ascent by Captain Coutelle at Fleurus, in June 1794, certainly represented the first use of a man-carrying aircraft during a battle; but far more sinister operations by 'lighter-than-air' military craft had been envisaged in the previous century by—perhaps surprisingly—a Jesuit priest named Francesco de Lana-Terzi. We can read of his ideas and conclusions in contemporary English, thanks to the publication of a translation of his writings by Robert Hooke.

Remembered as the inventor of hairsprings for watches, Hooke had dabbled with aircraft models, embodying wings and springs. Father de Lana considered that a simpler method of getting air-borne had been made possible by the recent invention of the air-pump in Germany. He proposed raising a boat-shaped carriage into the air by the lifting power of four large globes of very thin copper from which all the air had been extracted by a pump. The addition of a mast and sail would then produce the first flying boat.

De Lana was correct in deducing that, in theory, such globes would weigh less than the surrounding air they replaced, and would therefore float on it, as a ship floats on water. In practice, he soon discovered that if he made the globes from metal which was sufficiently thin for the scheme to be practicable, they would collapse when the air-pump got to work. On the other hand, if he built them strongly enough to avert collapse, they would be too heavy.

To explain away this inherent snag, he wrote in the *Prodromo*, a scientific treatise published in 1670: 'God would not suffer such an invention to take effect. . . . For who sees not that no City can be secure against attack, since our Ship may at any time be placed directly over it, and descending down may discharge Souldiers; the same would happen to private Houses, and ships on the Sea: for our Ship descending out of the Air to the Sails of Sea-Ships. . . . it may over-set them, kill their men, burn their Ships by artificial Fire-works and Fire-balls. And this they may do not only to Ships but to great Buildings, Castles, Cities, with such security that they which cast these things down from a height out of Gun-shot, cannot on the other side be offended by those from below.'

As the conceiver of 'so Diabolical an Engine', de Lana foresaw how years of development might make war more terrible rather than peace more pleasurable. His fears were justified long after his death. Within fifty years of the first flight in an aeroplane, the old Jesuit's predictions were fulfilled in the devastating Japanese attack on Pearl Harbor, which cost the aggressors so little; in the German skyborne assault on Crete; and in the relentless destruction of Germany and Japan by the huge bomber forces of the Allies.

Was de Lana expressing a belief or making an excuse when he commented that 'God would not suffer such an invention to take effect'? As we study the growth of air weapons from their frail childhood to a maturity in which they could destroy all life on our planet, it is a question that we might answer in a hundred different ways. Perhaps, after all, in His infinite wisdom, God thought it best that we should have the choice of keeping or rejecting—through the pressure of a single finger on a firing-button—the most precious gift He could bestow upon us as human beings. How we respond will affect us all, whether we call our God Jehovah, Allah, Manitou or by another name, or even if we accept no god at all. Only those who believe that all men are made in God's image, and are capable of thinking and acting nobly, may feel that the allocation of such a fearful responsibility was just.

February 1974   JWRT

Full Circle

Unlike Father Francesco de Lana-Terzi, whose seventeenth-century writings foreshadowed a world threatened by air power, the brothers Wilbur and Orville Wright had a happier view. After making the first officially recognized flights in a powered aeroplane, on 17 December 1903, they spent a further year improving the design and then offered it to the U.S. War Department. In doing so, according to the editor of their letters, the Wrights 'sincerely believed that the aeroplane could play a major part in preventing war, because it would enable each side to know what the other was doing and thus make it more difficult for either to gain an advantage'.

Their beliefs proved correct for a decade. Then the fighter aircraft was evolved to hamper the work of the unarmed reconnaissance types whose crews were seeing too much. Other fighters began to escort the reconnaissance aircraft, which themselves acquired defensive armament. This led to the great aerial dogfights of the First World War. Before long, bombers joined in, to attack the airfields from which the reconnaissance and fighter squadrons were operating; and by 1918 the combat pilots were being so glamorized by the Press that the key importance of the reconnaissance units was often forgotten.

Two decades later, the Second World War heightened the disparity, as German dive-bombers blasted a path for the Wehrmacht through Poland and western Europe, as Royal Air Force fighters turned the tide of war by their victory in the Battle of Britain, and as the Allied bomber offensive ground Germany towards defeat. Only the still small voices of skilled analysts suggested that the Luftwaffe lost the Battle of Britain because its air reconnaissance was so poor, whereas the Allies won the later air battles to liberate Europe because theirs was so good. One or two of the onlookers in Germany may have recalled ruefully that it was a former Commander-in-Chief of the Wehrmacht, Colonel-General Baron von Fritsch, who had predicted in the late 1930s that 'the next war will be won by the military organization with the most efficient photographic reconnaissance'.

A fresh appreciation of the importance of reconnaissance was born out of the post-war manœuvrings of East and West. 'Peace through fear' became the order of the day, based on the deterrent power of long-range nuclear-armed bombers and missiles. Periodically, one side would test the other's will power or fighting strength by provoking incidents of the kind which precipitated the Berlin Airlift and the Cuban missile crisis; or would even carry brinkmanship as far as engaging in a long and bloody (but always short of nuclear) war in a perimeter land such as Korea or Vietnam.

When an American U-2 spy-plane was shot down in the heart of the Soviet Union, on May Day 1960, nobody could doubt any more the lengths to which the super-Powers were prepared to go to discover their opponents' secrets, or to catch a glimpse of troop movements that might herald another 'Korea' or something worse. After the U-2 incident had brought such trespassing into the open, promises were made that overflights of certain specified major countries would be discontinued. It was not too painful a concession, as aircraft in the class of the U-2 were clearly too vulnerable to risk any longer in such areas, whereas reconnaissance satellites— offering, it was believed, invulnerable targets— were being designed, built and put into day-to-day service.

Before long these robot eyes in the sky were telling the military Chiefs of Staff in Washington and Moscow most of what they needed to know about activities on the other side of what had become a rather rusted 'Iron Curtain'. When the Russians demonstrated their ability to intercept and destroy satellites, it seemed likely to be only a matter of time before such internationally illegal spying activities were brought to a violent end. Instead, when the United States and the Soviet Union concluded an agreement to limit their deployment of intercontinental ballistic missiles and anti-missile defences, the spy satellites were designated as the official observers charged with the duty of checking that neither side broke the agreement.

So reminiscent of *Alice in Wonderland* had international relations become by then that no

The first aeroplane built under military contract: Orville Wright flying the tail-first biplane which he demonstrated at Fort Myer, with such tragic results, in 1908.
U.S. Air Force

one appeared to consider it extraordinary that spying had been declared not merely respectable but the prime means of guaranteeing peace– provided the spies were motivated by on-board computers rather than human brains. It was a situation which Capitaine Coutelle, the first military airman, could never have imagined in his wildest eighteenth-century nightmare. Yet there is a close parallel with his time, for reconnaissance is once again–but for wholly different reasons–the only active military operation being conducted as full-scale day-to-day routine.

The wheel of aerial warfare might be said to have turned full circle, but nothing is really the same except the basic mission. In 1794 the aerial reconnaissance vehicles were possessed by only one side, and Coutelle knew that he would never be allowed to keep an airborne watch on enemy forces without his balloon being regarded as a tempting and highly inflammable target for their ground fire. Undeterred by such thoughts, he had agreed readily to supervise activities at the aeronautic school which members of the French Academy, led by the distinguished chemist Guyton de Morveau, proposed setting up near Paris at Meudon.

Fifty young military students were sent to the school for training, and a balloon 32 feet in diameter was constructed for their use. Its support equipment would hardly have gladdened the heart of anyone concerned with modern logistics. The American balloonist John Wise, in a book entitled *A System of Aeronautics, Comprehending its Earliest Investigations* (Philadelphia, 1850), described the improved technique devised by de Morveau to ensure enough hydrogen to keep the balloon fully inflated and ready for use whenever the weather permitted.

Six iron cylinders were fixed by masonry in a simple kind of furnace, each of their ends projecting and covered with an iron lid. Two sets of metal tubes were also inserted into these lids, one for conveying in the water, and the other for carrying off the gas which was formed from the water. The cylinders being charged with iron turnings, and brought to a red heat, the humidity of the water was instantly converted into steam, whose expanded particles were soon decomposed, by the oxygen uniting with the red-hot iron, forming an oxide of iron, while the hydrogen was thus formed, and forced out by its own pressure from the other tube; and from thence it passed through a washer of limewater, to make it deposit its carbonic acid gas, that might adhere to it, when it was perfectly pure and ready for the balloon. By this method

they procured, at a very moderate expense, a quantity of gas sufficient to inflate a balloon 32 feet in diameter, which holds 17,000 cubic feet, in the space of four hours.

How, one wonders, did the generals in charge of the French Revolutionary armies view the prospect of adding such a vehicle to their front-line forces? Instant intelligence could hardly be provided by a device which required completion of a major building project and four hours of inflation before it could be used. This may help to explain the reception given to Coutelle when he reported to the Field Headquarters of General Jourdan's Army of the Sambre and Meuse, with a small demonstration balloon. In his subsequent report, he wrote:

I arrived at Beaumont [in Belgium] covered with mud; for I was obliged to go eighteen miles without drawing rein, by such bad roads that artillery would have sunk to the axle-trees. The officer to whom I reported could not understand my mission, and still less an aerostat [balloon] in the middle of the camp. He threatened to have me shot, as a suspicious character, before listening to me. . . . The army was at Beaumont, eighteen miles from Maubeuge, from which post the enemy were only one league, and could attack at any instant. The General made me observe this, and ordered me to return and report it to the Committee [of Public Safety]. I arrived in Paris after spending two and a half days on this expedition.

Life was clearly going to be tough for the world's first military airmen. Coutelle advised that balloons intended for front-line use should be large enough to carry two people, one to observe and the other to direct operations. Experiments with a large balloon at Meudon showed that at least twenty ground personnel were needed to hold it down when inflated. On the credit side, this balloon retained its ability to raise two men, all the instruments of observation and the necessary ballast after two months of inactivity, without any need for gas replenishment.

What might be termed the first production line of military aircraft was thereupon established, producing the balloon *Entreprenant* for the Army of the North, the *Celeste* for the Army of the Sambre and Meuse, *Hercule* for the Army of the Rhine and Moselle, and *Intrepide* for the Army of Egypt. Each comprised a varnished silk envelope, a basket and a restraining net which covered the top of the envelope and was attached to the two ropes by which the balloon was tethered. In the field the ropes were normally held by ground personnel; at Meudon a windlass was used.

Observation was conducted with the naked eye and with the aid of a spyglass or telescope. Messages were passed to those on the ground by means of flags and signals attached to the sides of the car. The balloonists received instructions from signals stretched on the ground. Their usefulness was dependent to a degree on wind direction, for when the enemy were downwind the observers, while safely out of reach, could be far in advance of their own ground forces.

Coutelle was gazetted as Brevet-Captain commanding the Company of Aérostiers in the Artillery Service, attached to the General Staff. Soon he was heading north again, in advance of his thirty-man company and their balloon. On arrival at Maubeuge, he organized the construction of a kiln and the collection of firewood. Impatient at having to wait for some action, Coutelle and his little party asked permission to join in an attack on a particularly troublesome Austrian outpost. At the cost of three casualties, the Aérostiers gained the status of real soldiers.

A few days later the main party arrived with the balloon, the fire was lit in the kiln, and the balloon was filled in less than fifty hours. This was considered first-class progress, and General Jourdan immediately ordered Coutelle up 'to examine the works of the enemy, his position, and his forces'. Once again we can quote part of his own report of this:
We observed his daily progress, till, on the fifth day, a 17-pounder, masked in a ravine within

easy distance, fired at the balloon as soon as it rose above the ramparts. The ball passed over our heads, the second was so near I thought the aerostat was perforated, and the third fell below us. When I gave the signal to haul down, my company did it with such vigour that only two more shots could be fired; next morning the piece was no longer in position.

As a result of these early observation ascents, Jourdan was persuaded to take advantage of Coutelle's airborne reconnaissance capability during the battle of Fleurus, on 26 June 1794. The balloon was marched to the area of battle fully inflated, at such a height above the road that cavalry and other military traffic could pass beneath, and was restrained by ten men on each side of the road holding specially attached individual ropes. Coutelle modestly makes no comment on the part he played in the battle, but historians record that the information which he signalled to Jourdan proved to be a material factor in the far-reaching victory which the French forces gained over the Allies. The achievement was repeated during the subsequent battle on the Ourthe, near Liége, when the French defeated the Austrians.

above and opposite, bottom
Thaddeus S C Lowe supervises the inflation of the observation balloon *Intrepid* during the Civil War battle of Fair Oaks. Smoke and dust from the battle obscure the horizon.
U.S. Air Force

opposite, top
Captain Coutelle's ascent in the observation balloon *Entreprenant* during the battle of Fleurus, 26 June 1794, represented the first operational use of an aircraft in war.
Royal Aeronautical Society

This engraving from *le Monde Illustré* shows the balloon *Armand-Barbès* leaving Paris on 7 October 1870. Its three occupants included Minister of the Interior Léon Gambetta who, after arriving at Tours, organized an army to relieve the besieged capital. Before this could be done, the French surrendered. The second balloon in the picture is the *Georges Sand*, carrying two U.S. arms dealers named May and Reynolds.

During these subsequent operations there was a sequel to Coutelle's exchanges with the 17-pounder gun at Maubeuge which reflected an aspect of war now gone for ever. Quoting Coutelle's report again:

I received the order to reconnoitre Mayence, and I posted myself between our lines and the place, within easy distance of its guns; the wind was strong and so I rose alone [to reduce the weight to be lifted]. I was at 700 feet above the ground when three successive squalls knocked me to the ground with such force and rapidity that thirty-two men at each rope were dragged some distance. The enemy did not fire. A General and some of the Staff came out of the town, waving white handkerchiefs, which I signalled to our headquarters, and our General went out to meet them. When they met, the Austrian General said: 'General, sir, I beg you to let that brave officer descend, before he perishes in this high wind. It would be tragic if he fell victim to anything but the fortune of war. It was I who fired on him at Maubeuge,' Later the wind fell. I was able to ascend again, and on this occasion, without a spyglass, I could count the cannon on the ramparts and see the people walking in the streets.

It says much for the leadership in ballooning which France had shown up to this time that no other army formed a balloon corps. Even in its most primitive form, aerial warfare was already affecting morale. Enemy soldiers were dispirited whenever they caught sight of a balloon and knew that their every move would be reported. French soldiers learned to appreciate the value of balloons so much that during the wearisome moves from point to point, when the Aérostiers' ground personnel could not leave their ropes, they found refreshments prepared for them and were often brought wine by the infantry.

Unfortunately, as in more recent years, this enthusiasm did not extend to the highest levels of government. The Emperor Napoleon regarded all forms of ballooning with a superstitious dread. This was said to date from 3 December 1804, when the huge, brilliantly lit balloon launched from Paris to mark his coronation was carried by the wind all the way to Rome. There, before ending its journey limply in Lake Bracciano, it is said to have bumped against various edifices, and to have deposited on Nero's tomb the laurel wreath with which it had been surmounted. Napoleon took this as a personal affront and as a warning.

None the less, this particular incident could not have precipitated the demise of the Aérostiers, which had occurred five years earlier in 1799. Quite probably Napoleon was disenchanted with their performance when Coutelle had been ordered to Egypt in the previous year. Much of the Aérostiers' equipment had been lost in the naval battle of Aboukir Bay. Their usefulness, in Napoleon's estimation, was limited to occasional ascents to demonstrate to the Arabs the superiority of European science over that of ancient, degenerate Egypt.

Had the world's first 'air force' achieved anything in its brief life? The answer, surely, must be that its equipment and operational techniques were eventually copied and then improved upon by other military organizations in places as far away as the United States.

It must have been clear from the start that better, more mobile gas-producing equipment had to be perfected before the balloonists could become a recognized adjunct to any army dispatched beyond the borders of its homeland. The balloon itself was to undergo virtually no change throughout the whole of the nineteenth century, and the observation and signalling methods used by the original Aérostiers could hardly be improved until the invention of wireless.

This should not imply that spherical balloons were in any sense ideal vehicles. In one of his reports Coutelle commented that 'rocking is troublesome, and increases with the force of the wind, sometimes preventing the use of glasses; but I must remark that one can see the movements of infantry, cavalry, and artillery with the naked eye.... One has also to become accustomed to the noise the balloon makes after the wind has blown one side concave, and it assumes again with rapidity its globular form, due to the elasticity of the gas. I am not aware of any accident from this cause. During one reconnaissance on the banks of the Rhine, ague seized me for the first time, followed by a violent fever from which I nearly died. . . . The aerostat commanded by Captain Hammond was riddled by bullets near Frankfurt. . . .'

Little wonder that when, in England in 1803, General John Money wrote his *Short Treatise on Balloons in Military Operations*, the only response it provoked from the authorities was to the effect that 'as we have done very well hitherto without them, we may still do without them'. Yet, had the British Government taken more seriously the proposals for 'Operation Catamaran' put before it in 1799 by one Charles Rogier, dancing master of Chelsea, the history of war might have been revolutionized by advancing the coming of the Missile Age by nearly 150 years.

Details and coloured drawings of Rogier's daring scheme remained hidden inside huge reference tomes in the Royal Library at Windsor until 1972, when permission was given by Her Majesty Queen Elizabeth II for their reproduction. They showed how Rogier proposed launching a night attack on the enemy Combined Fleets, blockaded in harbour at Brest, with up to 1,000 pilotless balloons, each 32 feet in diameter and carrying 8 cwt of spiked rockets, shells and other weapons.

After a careful check of wind speed, it was intended to set a clockwork time-fuse on each balloon and then release it to drift over the enemy fleet. At the appropriate time, the clockwork was intended to light matches that would first fire all the weapons and then set fire to the gas in the balloon's envelope, causing the whole flaming mass to be dumped on the heads of the unsuspecting enemy.

Rogier left nothing to chance. Anticipating that the enemy might fire anti-aircraft rockets against the balloons if they spotted an incoming raid, he designed the craft so that a hit would cause them to drop vertically on the rocket-launchers and their crews. In fact he had devised his own surface-to-air rocket defences before working out details of the balloon bombers, to guard against the possibility of an attack by the French Aérostiers on the British Fleet.

Unhappily, Their Lordships of the Admiralty did not take kindly to the military genius of the Chelsea dancing master. However, more than 1,500 miles to the east, Tsar Alexander I seems to have been more enterprising. An authoritative history of Napoleon's ill-fated expedition to Russia tells how, when French troops entered Moscow in 1812, they found in the Castle of Voronzoff a huge balloon packed with many thousands of pounds of gunpowder. According to General Count Philip de Segur: 'This prodigious winged aerostat was constructed by command of Alexander, not far from Moscow, under the direction of a German artificer. Its task was

Reacting quickly to the ability of the postal balloons to overfly the Prussian troops surrounding Paris in 1870, Krupps, the famous armament manufacturers, produced this anti-aircraft gun.

13

to hover over the French army, to single out its chief, and destroy him by a shower of balls and fire. Several attempts were made to raise it, but without success, the springs by which the wings were to be worked having always broken.'

Not until the nineteenth century neared its mid-point did aerial warfare take another small but positive step forward. In 1849 the Austrians decided to test the effect of a 'flying-bomb' attack against Venice, whose citizens were barricaded on their islands in rebellion against rule from Vienna. A large number of hot-air balloons were made, each comprising a paper envelope from which was suspended a 30-lb bomb fitted with a time-fuse–features reminiscent of Charles Rogier's 'Operation Catamaran'.

Few of the aerial missiles launched against Venice fell on the city; those that did caused more panic than casualties. Even worse, the scheme backfired, for a sudden change of wind direction soon had the Austrians in retreat, chased by their own bombers.

By comparison with these small-scale but exciting events, the remainder of the century was rather dull, although important technical progress was made. This became evident on 14 November 1862, when Captain F Beaumont of the Royal Engineers gave a talk at Chatham on 'Balloon Reconnaissances as practised by the American Army.'

Beaumont had spent some time with McClellan's Federal forces, and had been able to observe the work of the Balloon Corps of the Army of the Potomac, headed by a civilian balloonist named Thaddeus S C Lowe. Formed in September 1861, this corps comprised one Chief Aeronaut (Lowe), one Captain Assistant Chief Aeronaut and fifty non-commissioned officers and privates; two balloons, each drawn by four horses; two gas generators, each drawn by four horses; and an acid cart drawn by two horses.

This, clearly, was a far more mobile unit than Coutelle's Aérostiers, with their very static kilns. The generator carts simply housed a container in which hydrogen could be generated by the action of cheap, easily transported dilute sulphuric acid on any pieces of iron that were available, including the tyres from broken wheels and old shot. The gas was passed through a pair of lime-filled purifiers and into the balloon, which could be airborne within three hours of reaching its operational base.

The official *History of the United States Air Force 1907–1957* comments briefly that: 'During the Richmond campaign of 1862 the Corps operated frequently over the lines, and its observations were of value to Union commanders. Some of Lowe's balloons were deployed in the west as well. The Confederacy used a few balloons, but there is little mention of them after May 1862. Changes in Union Army commands in 1863 brought in generals who were not interested in the balloon, and Lowe's corps was disbanded in June of that year.'

So died America's first air force. It did, however, pioneer one significant activity that the official history was remiss in overlooking. During Captain Beaumont's talk at Chatham, he recalled: 'I once saw the fire of artillery directed from a balloon. This became necessary, as it was only in this way that the picket, which it was desired to dislodge, could be seen. However, I cannot say that I thought the fire of artillery was of much effect against the unseen object; not that this was the fault of the balloon, for, had it not told the artillerists which way the shots were falling, their fire would have been more useless still.'

Useless or not in 1862, artillery spotting was destined to be one of the most vital of all duties for aerial observers.

Meanwhile, balloons were used for the first demonstration of yet another application of flight in support of military operations. The year was 1870, the place Paris. The French capital was surrounded by Prussian troops and completely isolated from the rest of the nation, or so the Prussians thought. In fact, there were in the city six more or less airworthy sporting balloons and a similar number of the world's most experienced aeronauts. This fortunate coincidence led to a situation, on 23 September, in which the besiegers had to watch helplessly while a balloon ascended from Paris and sailed calmly over their heads with a load of dispatches which showed that the capital was far from defeated. The balloon's occupant, Jules Durouf, landed safely at Evreux, about sixty miles from Paris, at the end of an uneventful three-hour flight.

When. Gordon Tissandier followed him in another balloon, the infuriated Prussians fired at it with their muskets, but without effect. Within a week, two more aeronauts had flown out safely and Paris felt that it had established the world's first airline operation, especially when V.I.P. passengers and letters began to be carried. Unfortunately, it was an airline that could offer only a one-way service–downwind– and few of the homing pigeons also carried out of Paris found their way back with messages.

None the less, it was a gallant effort. When the original batch of balloons had nearly all left, work was started on constructing more of them in the spacious buildings of the Gare d'Orléans. Inflation was no problem, as sporting balloons had been using town gas for nearly fifty years. The Paris balloons were inflated at the Villette gas-works and normally took off at night to reduce the hazard from ground fire, after the *Daguerre* had been shot down on 12 November.

The problem of finding crews for the new balloons seemed to be solved when somebody suggested conscripting acrobats from the Hippodrome. These men certainly had no fear of heights, but showed a more healthy respect for Prussian guns. On several occasions they used their professional skills to valve out sufficient gas to bring the balloon near to the ground, while still within the city walls. They then shinned down a rope to the ground; after which the lightened balloon shot off, carrying its deserted passengers and mail on a voyage to a mystery destination.

Before long, sailors replaced the acrobats, and the service became more disciplined, although it was never entirely predictable. For example, when a sailor named Prince left in the balloon *Jacquard*, he announced 'I am going to make an immense voyage. They will talk of my flight.' The poor fellow spoke truly. The south-easterly wind was so strong that his balloon was spotted next day near the Lizard, in Cornwall. He dropped his dispatches, which were picked up safely. The balloon then rose and was last seen disappearing in the direction of America.

Despite such incidents, the operation was a great success, though it could do nothing to save Paris from her enemies. By the time the final

sortie was flown, on 28 January 1871, carrying news of the armistice, at least sixty-four balloons had left the city, of which fifty-seven reached friendly territory in safety. Crew and passengers numbered 155, and an incredible total of some 3,000,000 letters were air-mailed to the outside world. Replies, intended for the pigeon post, were photographed on microfilm – another idea that was to be resurrected many years later to save valuable aircraft space in time of war.

Meanwhile, across the Channel in England, a chain of events had started which was eventually to have a profound influence on the future development of aerial warfare. The first links in the chain seemed far from auspicious. Yielding to pressure that it ought to be showing some interest in ballooning, in 1862 the War Office had commissioned Henry Coxwell, one of Britain's leading aeronauts, to make a series of ascents at Aldershot. The purpose was to show

When the Balloon Post was inaugurated, there were only six airworthy sporting balloons in Paris. Sixty-four were flown out of the city during the siege, the others having been produced on assembly lines like this one in a Parisian railway station.

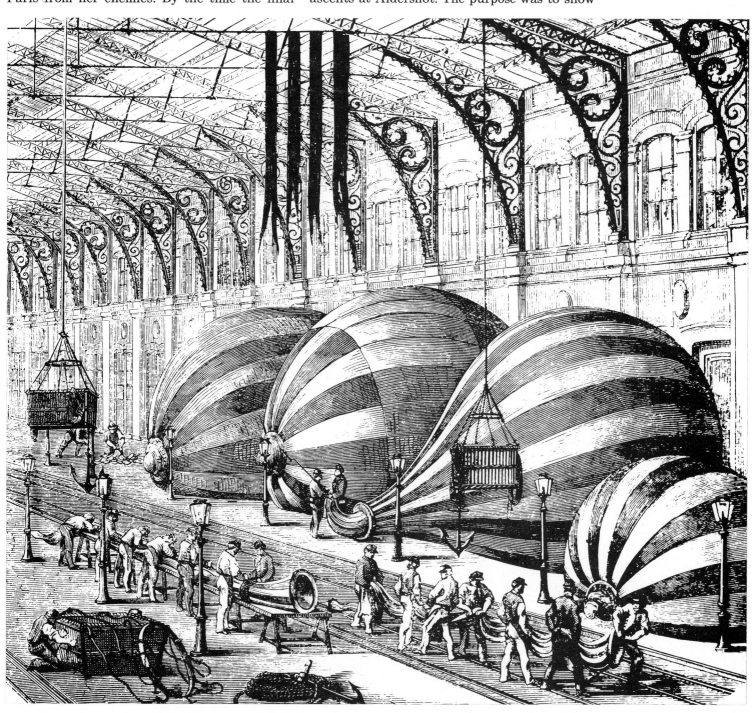

15

how captive balloons might be useful for reconnaissance and signalling, and even for ·the dropping of aerial torpedoes on enemy forces— a technique that Coxwell had first demonstrated in Berlin in 1848.

His passengers included Captain Beaumont, whose visit to Thaddeus Lowe's American Balloon Corps has already been mentioned. This officer's enthusiasm was not shared by his superiors, and the disenchanted Coxwell went back to Germany, where the start of the Franco-Prussian War in 1870 found him instructing balloon detachments at Cologne.

Not until eight years later did the British Army deign to carry out further experiments with balloons, at Woolwich Arsenal. Two years later, a balloon section was allowed to participate in manœuvres at Aldershot. In 1882, after further trials, the Balloon Equipment Store was transferred from Woolwich to the School of Military Engineering at Chatham, where a small balloon factory, depot and training school were established. Finally, in 1884, three balloons, two officers and fifteen other ranks from this unit

went to war with the British Army, just 101 years after a man had first become airborne in a balloon.

Their destination was Bechuanaland, where dissidents had raised a republican flag at Mafeking. Order was restored without a shot being fired, giving the balloon detachment little opportunity of proving its worth. The best move it made was to give a joy-ride in the largest of its aircraft to a local chief named Montsiou, who commented afterwards: 'If the first white men who came into this country had brought a thing like that and, having gone up in it before our eyes, had then come down and demanded that we should worship and serve them, we would have done so. The English have indeed great power.'

Perhaps it was as well he remained ignorant of the fact that the two smaller balloons lacked the power to lift even one man off the ground in the rarefied atmosphere of Mafeking, high above sea-level. Even more important, from the viewpoint of British prestige, was that people like Montsiou knew nothing of progress being made in Germany.

The First Zeppelins

The first experiments in aerial warfare, involving the use of balloons, had spanned more than a century. Mobility had improved enormously in that time, particularly when, in the latter part of the nineteenth century, gas could be compressed into easily transportable cylinders instead of needing to be generated in front-line areas; but major drawbacks remained. In particular, there seemed to be no way of preventing the hazardous instability of a spherical balloon in anything but calm conditions.

Clearly, too, there would be an immense improvement in utility if the balloons could be freed from their tethers, with the assurance of returning to their base after flying over enemy positions. This implied some form of propulsion and control, and seemed far from any likelihood of achievement. Primitive forms of airship, with elongated envelopes and steam or electric propulsion, had been moving slowly and briefly through the sky, notably in France, since 1852; but these represented no improvement over balloons in terms of reliability and practical value.

The first major advance came when the problem of stability for tethered balloons in windy conditions was overcome by the invention of the sausage-shaped *Drachen* or kite balloon. Who invented it is a matter of controversy, and irrelevant. There is no disputing that it was perfected by August von Parseval, a German officer, and H B von Sigsfeld, whose prototype made a highly successful appearance at German Army manœuvres in 1897. In addition to its elongated envelope, this balloon was fitted with tail fins to keep it pointing steadily into wind. From that moment the life of a military balloonist became far less hazardous and unpleasant. The kite balloon went on to become a standard front-line observation platform for both sides in the First World War, and a very effective anti-aircraft barrage balloon in the Second World War. Little changed to the present day, it remains of value as a jumping-point for parachute-training and for specialized tasks such as providing an aerial station for radar development.

In modern terminology such duties belong to the passive side of aerial warfare; in other words, the vehicles involved might be shot at, but will not normally hit back. The airship was regarded differently from the start. An immense, elongated gas-bag gave it great lifting capacity, for men, guns, bombs or anything else. Its ability to fly anywhere, once the control and propulsion problems had been solved, offered a wide variety of new military applications; and its ability to climb to great heights made it invulnerable to anything but extreme bad weather – or so it seemed.

The key to efficient propulsion had come with the perfection of the petrol engine. Here, at last, was the lightweight, high-performance power plant that designers of both the lighter-than-air and heavier-than-air categories of aircraft had sought for generations. Within the space of a few years, at the turn of the century, it made possible both the small airships on which Alberto Santos-Dumont became the idol of Paris, and the tail-first 'stick-and-string' biplane *Flyer* on which Orville and Wilbur Wright made the first officially recognized controlled, powered, and sustained aeroplane flights on 17 December 1903.

'Controlled' needed to be interpreted a trifle loosely. Orville's first flight consisted of a switchback succession of shallow climbs and dives which ended when one dive stuck his nose into the sand at Kill Devil Hill, Kitty Hawk, North Carolina. 'Sustained' also had to be regarded relatively. That first flight lasted just twelve seconds and covered 120 feet, which is much less than the wing span of a modern four-engined airliner. But there was no doubt concerning the meaning of 'powered'. The four-cylinder petrol engine, built by the Wrights themselves with the help of a mechanic named Charles E Taylor, gave an average 12 hp for a weight of less than 200 lb including radiator, tank, water coolant and fuel. It enabled the Wrights to build a sturdy aeroplane, weighing no less than 605 lb without a pilot. Total cost, including rail fares to and from Kitty Hawk, was under $1,000.

By 1905 the brothers had improved the design of their *Flyer* to such an extent that they decided

Drachen (kite) balloon being prepared for operational use in Tripoli during the Italo-Turkish War of 1911–12. *Italian Air Ministry*

from making progress, they ended with the feeling that people were interested only in stealing and copying their design. So they decided to become more secretive and simply to sit back and wait for somebody to accept their price, which they had agreed should be $200,000. In a letter to their friend, the engineer and glider-builder Octave Chanute, Wilbur wrote, on 10 October 1906: 'We do not believe there is one chance in a hundred that anyone will have a machine of the least practical usefulness within five years. If our judgement is correct, undue haste to force a sale would be a mistake.'

This time their judgement was not correct. Less than three years were to elapse before a Frenchman would cross the Channel in a machine that would make the Wright *Flyer* look truly the original prototype of all aeroplanes, which it was. Only until 1909 would the Wright, in its various improved forms, reign supreme.

Its makers may have believed that its reconnaissance capability would make land warfare impossible. Their counterparts in Germany were thinking in terms of gigantic craft that would make aerial warfare more terrifying, in the service of Kaiser Wilhelm II.

That the Germans placed most faith in lighter-than-air craft at this period reflects no lack of imagination or technical expertise. The electrically powered airship *La France*, built by Charles Renard and A C Krebs in 1884, had made seven flights within a year, the first of them a twenty-three-minute circular flight of five miles during which a speed of 14·5 mph was attained. Added to the fact that both Daimler and Benz had built practical petrol engines in 1885, giving aircraft-designers the lightweight power plant which they had awaited for a hundred years, it was logical to combine the navigable airship with the petrol engine as the quickest and surest method of producing a really useful flying machine.

Even Wilbur Wright is reported to have said at the end of 1901 that eventually man would fly in a powered aeroplane, but that it would not be in the lifetime of Orville and himself. He could not foresee that within only two years they would solve the stability problems they were encountering with their gliders, and also produce a suitable power plant for an aeroplane.

Airship development in Germany went far from smoothly at first. On 14 June 1897, Dr Wölfert's pioneer Daimler-engined dirigible fell flaming to the ground during its first test flight, near Berlin, killing the designer and his assistant.

Meanwhile the aristocratic Graf (Count) Ferdinand von Zeppelin, a retired Lieutenant-General in the Kaiser's Army, had been discussing with the Prussian General Staff his ideas for a mighty, invulnerable fleet of aerial battleships. His interest in aerial warfare dated from his first ascent in a Federal Army balloon during the American Civil War; but his own concepts for military aircraft were very different from such

to seek some financial reward for six years of work. On 19 October they offered to build an aeroplane for the U.S. War Department. The reply to their letter, signed by Captain T C Dickson, said: 'It is recommended that the Messrs Wright be informed that the Board [of Ordnance and Fortification] does not care to formulate any requirements for the performance of a flying-machine or take any further action on the subject until a machine is produced which by actual operation is shown to be able to produce horizontal flight and to carry an operator.'

On 5 October they had made their best flight to date, covering $24\frac{1}{5}$ miles in 38 minutes 3 seconds.

Unable to convince their own Government that they had produced a practical aeroplane, they switched their sales drive to Europe. Far

frail and tethered bubbles of gas. The basic idea was for a rigid airship, consisting of an aluminium cylindrical structure covered with fabric, which would serve as a prime mover towing two unpowered sections of similar construction, each carrying 1,100 lb of bombs.

Zeppelin's ideas were rejected in favour of a simpler type of one-piece all-metal airship designed by David Schwarz. A prototype had already been built in Russia, but it had collapsed before leaving the ground. Schwarz died before the improved second version was completed. It was an impressive cylindrical craft, made of thin aluminium sheet, braced internally by steel wires and powered by a 12-hp Daimler engine which drove four propellers, two for propulsion and two for directional control. Soon after its initial ascent near Berlin on 3 November 1897, something went wrong with the belt-drive to the propellers and, after drifting four miles, the airship made a heavy landing and was broken up by the wind.

Except for a token payment of 6,000 marks (about £2,600 in 1974 monetary values) from the Kaiser, in recompense for time spent on preparing his proposals, Zeppelin had received no official help up to this time. In 1898, after the influential Union of German Engineers had declared that his ideas showed great promise, he was able to form a company to build a prototype of his great airship. To house it he erected a floating workshop/hangar/office on Lake Constance, influenced like other pioneers by the mistaken idea that a landing on water would encounter fewer obstructions and be somehow 'softer' in the event of trouble.

Known as the 'LZ1', the first Zeppelin airship was designed in detail by an experienced balloon engineer named Theodor Kober, with the assistance of the young E H Ludwig Dürr, who was destined to be responsible for all the later Zeppelins. Construction began in 1898, when Graf von Zeppelin was already in his sixtieth year.

By comparison with anything that had preceded it, LZ1 was immense. Its length of 420 feet would make even a modern 231-foot Boeing 747 'Jumbo Jet' airliner look small, and its structure was so well conceived that later Zeppelins were little different in their essentials. In the first volume of *The War in the Air*, Sir Walter Raleigh described it as a pencil-shaped rigid structure, with a diameter almost exactly one-eleventh part of its length. He continued:

The framework, built of aluminium, consisted of sixteen hoops, connected by longitudinal pieces, and kept rigid by diagonal wire stays. Before it was covered it resembled a vast bird-cage, and looked as frail as a cobweb, but was stronger and stiffer than it looked. It was divided by aluminium bulkheads into seventeen compartments; of these all but the two end compartments contained separate balloons or gas-bags. Two or three of these might collapse

without completely destroying the buoyancy of the ship. The whole structure was covered with a fabric of rubberized cotton. A triangular latticed aluminium keel ran along below, to give strength to the ship, and to furnish a passage-way from end to end. At points about a third of the way from either end of the ship spaces in the keel were made for the two cars, in each of which was a 16-hp Daimler motor driving two small high-velocity propellers, one on each side of the ship. The lateral steering was done by a large vertical rudder, placed aft. The longitudinal balance was controlled in several ways. In this first ship a heavy sliding weight suspended under the keel was moved at will, fore and aft. This was superseded in later ships by four sets of elevating planes, two sets in the fore-part and two sets aft.

Twice during assembly of the LZ1 the floating hangar broke from its moorings, delaying completion by six months and costing an ill-afforded 100,000 marks to repair. At last, on 2 July 1900, after twelve hours of inflation from 2,200 cylinders of hydrogen, the 399,000-cubic-foot monster left the hangar and made its first twenty-minute flight with a five-man crew commanded personally by the old Count. Controllability was poor, due in part to distortion of the structure in flight; three months later and after two more flights, during which a maximum speed of 17·5 mph was attained, Zeppelin had to admit the LZ1 was a disappointment. In any case, there was insufficient cash left in the company's funds for a refill of hydrogen, which would have cost 8,000–10,000 marks. The company went into liquidation and LZ1 was broken up.

Ferdinand von Zeppelin was not a man to accept defeat. He acquired all the assets of the former company for 124,000 marks and set about finding ways of financing construction of a stronger airship. He first approached Carl Berg, the industrialist who had pioneered the early commercial production of aluminium and who had helped with the design of both the Schwarz

Zeppelin LZ4, first flown on 20 June 1908, had a length of 446 feet and was powered by two 105-hp Daimler engines. It demonstrated the potential of large airships with a famous flight over the Alps.

In the First World War, as anti-aircraft defences improved, it became necessary for the German Zeppelins to fly at ever-increasing height during their bombing raids. When clouds hid the target from view, a crew member could be lowered through them in a gondola of this type. With an unobstructed view of the target, he could then direct bombing operations by radio.

airship and LZ1. Berg agreed to provide the structural members of the new LZ2 on credit. Daimler provided on loan two of their latest engines, which weighed no more than the 14-hp version but gave 80 hp. The German War Ministry offered to supply the necessary hydrogen for inflation at no cost. Zeppelin obtained 8,000 marks from a public appeal, 124,000 marks from a lottery, 50,000 marks from the German Chancellor's Fund – and found the remaining 218,000 marks himself.

As LZ2 emerged from its hangar, on 20 November 1905, it made a fine sight. But before it had been extracted completely it was damaged and had to be eased back inside for repairs. When it did make its first flight, on 17 January 1906, engine failure necessitated a forced landing away from base, and LZ2 was wrecked by strong winds as it lay at its overnight moorings.

The Zeppelin story continued doggedly through that first decade of the twentieth century – in a succession of lotteries, airships, minor successes and major setbacks. The old man must have felt that his troubles were over when LZ3 flew so well that it earned a Government contract worth 400,000 marks for the construction of LZ4, with the promise of a further 2,150,000 marks to purchase both airships if the new one proved capable of covering at least 700 kilometres (440 miles) in a non-stop twenty-four-hour flight.

On 1 July 1908 the LZ4 made a spectacular twelve-hour flight over Switzerland, causing great excitement in the streets as it passed majestically over Lucerne and Zürich and then cruised over the Alps in perfect weather. Five weeks later, before it could complete the official twenty-four-hour test, it was destroyed by fire when its hydrogen ignited after a forced landing. Casualties were limited to two slightly injured crew-members.

This time Zeppelin shared his frustration with millions of his fellow Germans, who were so impressed with the potential of airships and the indefatigable determination of their creator, now seventy years old, that they made spontaneous donations to a kind of 'Save the Zeppelin' fund. Here, in the formative years of air power, was proof that public support for military aviation could always be expected when it was most needed – a realization that was later to find expression in campaigns like the British 'Spitfire Fund'. In Germany in 1908, the donations from the public eventually reached an incredible 6,125,000 marks. The money was used to form a trust which, in turn, put up three million marks to establish a new company, the Luftschiffbau-Zeppelin GmbH at Friedrichshafen.

When the Crown Prince of Germany flew in the rebuilt LZ3A, and the Kaiser personally decorated Count von Zeppelin with the Order of the Black Eagle, nobody could doubt any longer that the giant rigid airship was accepted as a success. The German Army took delivery of the LZ3A in 1909, redesignating it ZI. One month later this airship was followed by ZII, built under the works number LZ5 as a replacement for LZ4. It is interesting to note that the official acceptance flight of ZI, by a crew under Major Sperling, was the first flight of a Zeppelin captained by anyone other than the Count himself.

To repay and further encourage public interest, it was decided also to set up a network of Zeppelin passenger-carrying services, operated by a company named DELAG, the German Airship Transport Company. The first airline of any kind, anywhere in the world, DELAG was to carry about 10,000 fare-paying passengers on 1,600 flights totalling nearly 3,200 hours between 22 June 1910 and 31 July 1914, without killing any of them, although several airships were lost. This remarkable achievement, in an era when the heavier-than-air aeroplane was still finding its wings, was not attained cheaply, as it is believed to have produced an operating loss of well over 2,000,000 marks. However, its worth in terms of public interest, and as a means of training crews for military airships, was incalculable.

Military Zeppelins fared less well than their civilian counterparts in terms of casualties among those who flew in them. This was particularly true of German naval airships. The L1 crashed on 9 September 1913, with fourteen fatalities; L2 caught fire in flight one month later, at the cost of twenty-eight lives. As a result, when the First World War began on 4 August 1914, the German Army had a fleet of six Zeppelins and a wooden Schütte-Lanz, whereas the Navy had only the L3. To strengthen this fleet, two of the DELAG passenger Zeppelins were taken over by the Army and one by the Navy.

Looking back, it is clear that these eleven rigid airships represented the most formidable weapons of air power then available to any nation on earth. Few of the aeroplanes pressed into service by military air services up to that time carried any form of armament, apart from the crews' personal weapons. Even the airships operated by other countries were mostly small non-rigid 'blimps' of limited operational value. The first military Zeppelins, ZI and ZII, had quickly convinced the German Army that aircraft with a maximum speed of less than 45 mph were useless except for local flying, over land, in fair weather. Most flights encountered wind speeds of over 20 mph at cruising height, and the speed of non-rigid airships could easily be reduced to a farcical degree when flying into a head-wind of this magnitude.

Even the new, bigger and faster rigid airships presented problems. Loss of the naval L1 had revealed for the first time a hazard to which they were particularly susceptible. Fortunately for the peace of mind of their crews during prolonged operations, the true seriousness of this particular phenomenon could not be foreseen at the time.

Only in retrospect could Peter W Brooks comment in *Historic Airships*:

Caught in a squall, L1 was lifted far above her pressure height. (The height at which the gas containers are fully distended and above which gas must be allowed to escape.) The resulting loss of gas and a subsequent down-draught then combined to carry her uncontrollably into the sea. The same sort of accident was to be repeated again and again through the story of the rigid. In some cases structural failure, usually from rapid ascent or turbulence, occurred before the airships involved hit the surface. On the evidence of 40 years and nearly 80,000 hours of rigid airship flying, the strong up- and down-draughts commonly associated with cold fronts and thunderstorms represented a quite insurmountable hazard to large airships and were probably responsible for the loss of most rigids

Extracting Cody's British Army Aeroplane No. 1 from the airship shed at Farnborough. When fitted with the biplane tail shown here (folded sideways to reduce the overall length of the aircraft for storage), the machine flew 400 yards at a height of 10 feet on 22 February 1909.
Flight International

destroyed in flying accidents. Of the 20 rigids destroyed in fatal flying accidents (other than those lost by enemy action) it appears that well over half were lost from this cause, or from associated phenomena such as lightning strike or static discharge.

Such irremediable shortcomings, coupled with the destructive power of aeroplanes firing incendiary ammunition from machine-guns, were to bring the reign of the big military rigid airship to an early end. Ironically, the usefulness of the smaller, non-rigid blimps was to continue for more than forty years afterwards, initially in Britain and then in the United States.

The beginnings of the British chapter of the story reflect characteristics that have not changed to this day—the daring and brilliance of individuals and the vacillation of Governments, particularly when a decision involves the commitment of public money in a time of peace. One effect of such policy is reflected in the familiar remark that, in war, Britain loses every battle but the last. A more studied and consistent policy towards air power might have eliminated the need for some of the lost early battles in two world wars.

We left the British Army demonstrating its sporting traditions by giving joy-rides to African chiefs at Mafeking. After the establishment of the Balloon Section of the Royal Engineers, in 1890, the approach became more professional. By 1894 the balloon factory had been transferred to the heart of 'army country' in South Farnborough, Hampshire. After moving to a better site, in 1905, it expanded rapidly in size and importance, becoming successively H.M. Balloon Factory in 1908, the Army Aircraft Factory, the

Royal Aircraft Factory and, finally, the Royal Aircraft Establishment, which remains in the forefront of world aviation and air-power research centres to this day.

In its years as the Balloon Factory, it cannot be said to have advanced greatly the science of aerial warfare. The need for improvement was made apparent by experience in the South African War of 1899–1902. Four balloon sections saw action against the Boers, achieving their best results when directing the fire of British artillery at Magersfontein and during the Battle of Lombard's Kop. This did not prevent many field commanders considering balloons a nuisance, with their cumbersome wagons of hydrogen cylinders and other equipment. In any case, in battle the hard-pressed and by no means air-minded gunners often failed to keep an eye on the signals being waved furiously at them by the balloonists until it was too late for the information to be of any value.

Seeking something better than balloons, Colonel J L B Templer, Superintendent of the Balloon Factory, went to Paris in January 1902 to study the airships being flown by Santos-Dumont. Although convinced of the value of such craft for military reconnaissance and more aggressive duties, it was to be five years before he could wheedle sufficient money out of the Government to complete an airship.

No greater success attended his efforts to foster aeroplane development at Farnborough. Templer was far-sighted enough to believe, at a time when most other people doubted, that the Wright brothers had produced a practical aeroplane and had flown it satisfactorily. He sent one of his associates, Colonel J E Capper, to invite

Wilbur and Orville to continue their experiments in Britain. Reluctant at first, the patriotic Wrights were eventually so disappointed with their own Government's attitude that they put up a succession of proposals in 1906–8, only to be rejected twice by the British War Office and once by the Admiralty.

The happy outcome of this official disinterest was that it compelled the Factory to rely on its own resources and talent. It began to develop non-rigid airships of its own design, and to experiment with wireless telegraphy in order to replace the unsatisfactory signalling techniques employed by balloonists when observing artillery-fire.

Nulli Secundus, first of the Farnborough-built airships, which flew for the first time in September 1907, was 'second to none' in little but name. It was about 120 feet long, less than 30 feet in diameter, and was powered by a French-built Antoinette engine developing 50 hp. At least it was a start; and when the little airship chugged to London at its maximum speed of 16 mph on 5 October, circling St Paul's and manœuvring over the gardens of Buckingham Palace, it made headline news. Few of its admirers cared to remember that a head-wind brought the return journey to a premature end over the Crystal Palace, where its crew decided to land, deflating *Nulli Secundus* five days later for return to Farnborough by road.

Several other blimps were built in the Factory, but the best of the six airships in service with the Navy at the outbreak of war in 1914 were a non-rigid Astra-Torres that had been bought from France and a semi-rigid Parseval of German design. The Parseval, designed by the inventor

of the *Drachen* balloon, was so good that eighteen were completed in Germany between 1909 and 1913. In their homeland they were considered inferior to the Zeppelins, but one was sold to the Austrian Army, two to Russia, one each to the Turkish and Japanese armies, and two to Italy, in addition to the British Admiralty aircraft.

Use of the Astra-Torres and Parseval airships over the Channel from 10 August 1914 convinced the Admiralty of the value of such craft for maritime patrol, and about 150 more non-rigids of various types were delivered to the Royal Naval Air Service during the First World War, together with nine large rigid airships. The earliest of the latter, R.9, was not actually the first rigid built for the Admiralty, which had ordered a naval airship from Vickers Ltd at Barrow-in-Furness in 1908.

The arguments of those who had advocated construction of such a craft were persuasive. By comparison with the aeroplanes with which the War Office was then dabbling, an airship could remain on patrol for much longer periods, could carry wireless (which was then heavy and cumbersome), could remain stationary while on reconnaissance, could lift a much heavier load, and could offer far more roomy and comfortable accommodation for its crew. The Admiralty allocated £35,000 for what was designated R.1 in the Navy Estimates of 1909–10; in the words of Sir Walter Raleigh:

For two years public curiosity was kept alive on a diet of conjecture. A good part of this time was taken up in improvements and modifications of the design of the ship. When at last in May 1911 the shed was opened and the huge airship was brought out to her mooring mast in the dock,

J W Dunne's Gnome-engined D.8 tailless V-wing biplane. Its inherent stability was demonstrated dramatically by Commandant Felix in 1913. During a flying meeting at Deauville, while flying alone, he astonished the crowd by leaving the cockpit and walking on the lower wings.
Royal Aircraft Establishment

*those who had expected a larger and better
Zeppelin seemed justified in their belief. The
ship was 512 feet long and 48 feet in diameter,
with a blunt bow and pointed stern. Her capacity
was approximately 700,000 cubic feet. The
framework was of a new alloy called duralumin,
nearly as strong in tension as mild steel and not
much heavier than aluminium. . . . The ship was
fitted with two Wolseley motors of 180 hp each,
and with a whole series of vertical and
horizontal rudders. She was popularly called
the* Mayfly.

She never did fly. At first her sturdy structure
proved too heavy to be lifted by the gas she
contained. After modification she broke her back
en route to the mooring mast.

Farnborough's efforts to get into the aeroplane business had fared no better. They could
be said to date from 27 January 1894, when
Captain B F S Baden-Powell (whose brother
formed the Boy Scout movement) demonstrated
at Pirbright army camp how kites could be used
instead of a balloon to lift a man into the air.
Such devices had been used in the Far East for
centuries, but this represented something new
in the Western World, offering interesting
possibilities, except in the absence of any wind.

Baden-Powell ascended first under a single
monoplane kite and then under a train of them.
Meanwhile, in Australia, Lawrence Hargrave
had invented the box-kite, combining great
strength with high lift to an unprecedented
degree. It inspired the entry on to the aviation
scene of one of the most remarkable characters
ever to have graced it.

Samuel Franklin Cody has become such a
legendary figure that he is best introduced in the
words of aviation historian Charles Gibbs-Smith,
who has made a close study of his achievements.
In *Aviation: an Historical Survey from its Origins
to the end of World War II*, he comments: 'Cody
was an attractive and flamboyant expatriate
American (naturalized here in 1909), an expert
cowboy, marksman, theatre showman, and friend
– but not relative – of Buffalo Bill Cody. He was
one of the valuable curiosities of aviation, with
no technical training but great energy, common
sense, and considerable originality, who contributed to aviation history more by his courage and
enthusiasm than by any real innovation or
advance, except in the realm of the kite.'

Few people would argue with that assessment.
None the less, Cody was a key figure in the
development of British military aviation in the
decade before the First World War. After selling
a number of his Hargrave-type man-lifting kites
to the Balloon Factory, he was appointed Chief
Instructor in Kiting in 1906. The disciplined,
formal military acres at Farnborough were soon
invaded by a sergeant-major's nightmare – a man
with flowing hair and goatee beard, wearing a
huge stetson hat, pistols hanging from his belt
like a cowboy, and riding a richly saddled white
horse. Despite his appearance, the Chief In-

structor in Kiting soon gained the respect and
affection of those with whom he came in contact.

In 1905 he evolved from his kites a biplane kite-
glider which he flew successfully at Farnborough.
Of particular note is that it was controlled by
ailerons, first used in the previous year by
Esnault-Pelterie in France, instead of by the
warping wing tips that were to remain standard
until the war years. Two years later, Cody fitted
a 12-hp Buchet engine to one of his kites and flew
it as a pilotless aeroplane. He then obtained War
Office permission to build a full-size version of
the same thing at the Balloon Factory; the result
was the famous British Army Aeroplane No. 1,
first of a series of Cody bamboo biplanes, massive
and rugged as the man himself yet astonishingly
successful.

Completed in the spring of 1908, this big
biplane remained grounded for lack of an engine,
which neither Cody nor the Factory could afford.
Its designer spent his time helping with re-
building of the *Nulli Secundus* airship, in which
he had accompanied Colonel Capper, now Superintendent at Farnborough, on its epic flight to
London. When the modified and redesignated
Nulli Secundus II proved a failure, he was
allowed to transfer its engine to his aeroplane.
On 16 October 1908 he made a flight of 1,390 feet
at a height of 50–60 feet over Laffan's Plain,
Farnborough. It was the first officially recognized flight by a powered aeroplane in Britain.

Meanwhile, another Farnborough protégé,
J W Dunne, had been making progress with a
series of unique gliders and powered aeroplanes
of tailless V-wing configuration. The main aim
of designers at that period was to achieve such
perfect stability in the air that their aircraft
could be flown 'hands off' while they made their
observations of the ground and wrote notes
describing what they saw. Dunne believed that
his strange-looking craft would make this possible, and eventually proved it. By then, however,
he had to do it without financial aid from the
Government.

The reason was that in April 1909 the War
Office discovered to its horror that it had spent
no less than £2,500 on aeroplane experiments,
and decided to call a halt to such extravagance
(despite the knowledge that Germany was spending £400,000 on military flying in that year).
Having progressed so far, both Dunne and Cody
decided to continue on their own. Cody must
have derived particular satisfaction from the
fact that when the Government held important
military trials in 1912, to give British designers
an opportunity to compete against the best
aeroplanes available from overseas, the latest
version of his great biplane won convincingly
and carried off £5,000 in prize-money.

This merely showed the fallacy of such contests, as the Cody aeroplane was clearly useless
to military pilots, especially if they lacked the
designer's great strength. Cody himself was
killed in the following year.

The start of aerial bombing: Lieutenant Gavotti, flying an Etrich Taube, attacks Turkish ground forces with $4\frac{1}{2}$-lb bombs at the oasis of Taguira on 1 November 1911. By Kenneth McDonough.

right
Operation Catamaran:
Charles Rogier's plan for
attacking the French and
Spanish Combined Fleets in
Brest Harbour in 1799. He
suggested launching up to
1,000 pilotless balloons from
British ships stationed
upwind of Brest. Each
balloon was intended to
have a diameter of 32 feet,
giving it the ability to lift
about 900 lb of spiked
rockets, shells and other
weapons. On arrival over
the target, a clockwork
mechanism (pre-set in
accordance with measured
wind speed) was intended to
open a valve at the top of
the balloon. Loss of gas
would cause the balloon to
lose height over the enemy
ships. At the same time, a
central fuse was intended to
ignite three banks of spiked
rockets, and the clockwork
mechanism was arranged to
open doors to release the
shells or bombs. Finally, the
fuse was intended to ignite
the main volume of gas in
the balloon, causing the
whole contraption to fall,
blazing, on to the target.
*Reproduced by gracious
permission of Her Majesty
The Queen*

below
German Naval Zeppelins
leaving their base for a night
attack on England during
the First World War. Note
the observer's gondola,
forward of the control car.
By Kenneth McDonough.

Aerial Cavalry

It would have been a grave injustice had the first aeroplane bought for military use been anything but a Wright biplane. Persistent lobbying by President Theodore Roosevelt, coupled with reports concerning flying activities in Europe, at last persuaded the U.S. War Department to test the substance of the Wright brothers' claim that they could deliver a practical aeroplane.

In a true democratic gesture, it advertised on 23 December 1907 that it was inviting tenders for an aircraft capable of carrying two persons at a speed of at least 40 mph for 125 miles. Two months later, it accepted three bids, including one from the Wrights for $25,000. Only their contract produced an aeroplane.

Interest in military ballooning had been spasmodic in the United States, and had been kept alive mainly by individual enthusiasm. Since 1898 the former balloon detachment of the Signal Corps had virtually ceased to exist; but an Aeronautical Division was established by the Corps on 1 August 1907 to 'take charge of all matters pertaining to military ballooning, air machines, and all kindred subjects'. The officer in charge was Captain Charles de F Chandler, and this embryo air force was allocated two enlisted men, a corporal and a first-class private.

While awaiting its promised aeroplanes, the Signal Corps revived its ballooning activities, with particular reference to the improved techniques made possible by aerial photography and wireless. It added to its strength a small non-rigid airship, built by Thomas Baldwin for $6,740. Powered by a 20-hp engine built by Glenn Curtiss (America's greatest aviation pioneer, after the Wrights), it was 96 feet long, carried a crew of two on an open girder slung under the envelope, and had an endurance of two hours at a maximum speed of 20 mph. After acceptance at Fort Myer on 12–15 August 1908, it was used for the next year on training and exhibition flights.

Hopes that an aeroplane would also be available during this period were to be sadly dashed. Wilbur Wright had left for France in May, to demonstrate the brothers' latest biplane to a syndicate that was interested in putting the design into production. The importance of the trip was underlined by the fact that Charles and Gabriel Voisin had already set up the world's first aeroplane assembly line in France. They were building machines like that on which the British-born Henry Farman had won the 50,000-franc Deutsch-Archdeacon Prize for the first pilot to make a flight round a one-kilometre circuit at Issy-les-Moulineaux, a suburb of Paris, on 13 January 1908.

By 6 July, Farman had succeeded in flying 20 kilometres (12·4 miles) in 20 minutes 20 seconds, piloting an improved version of the same aircraft. The Wrights, who had done no flying since 1905, began to realize that they had underestimated European designers. Their secrecy had, paradoxically, helped the opposition. Unable simply to copy Wright designs, or to embody the Wrights' ideas in their aircraft, the Europeans had evolved configurations that would eventually leave the tail-first Wright biplane behind. By fitting wheels, and dispensing with the need for catapult-assisted take-off, as used by Wilbur and Orville since 1904, they achieved from the start a go-anywhere capability that the Wright *Flyer* lacked.

However, when Wilbur began demonstrating his biplane in France, it was clear that it still outclassed all opposition at that period. Never had the Europeans seen anyone flying with such confidence and for so long. Even kings and princes, including Edward VII of Britain, made the pilgrimage to the flying-fields at Le Mans and Paris to see him fly. So did the unknown A V Roe, who travelled by bicycle as he could afford nothing else; he was soon to establish himself as Britain's greatest aeroplane pioneer.

At Fort Myer, Wilbur's 'kid brother' made an equally good start to his demonstrations. The new 30-hp Wright engine proved so reliable that on 12 September 1908 he remained airborne for over one and a quarter hours. The old prone piloting position of the original *Flyer* had given way to two side-by-side seats on the leading-edge of the lower wing of both this aircraft and the one taken to France. During retraining at Kitty Hawk this had enabled Wilbur to carry Charles W Furnas, a mechanic from his home-town of

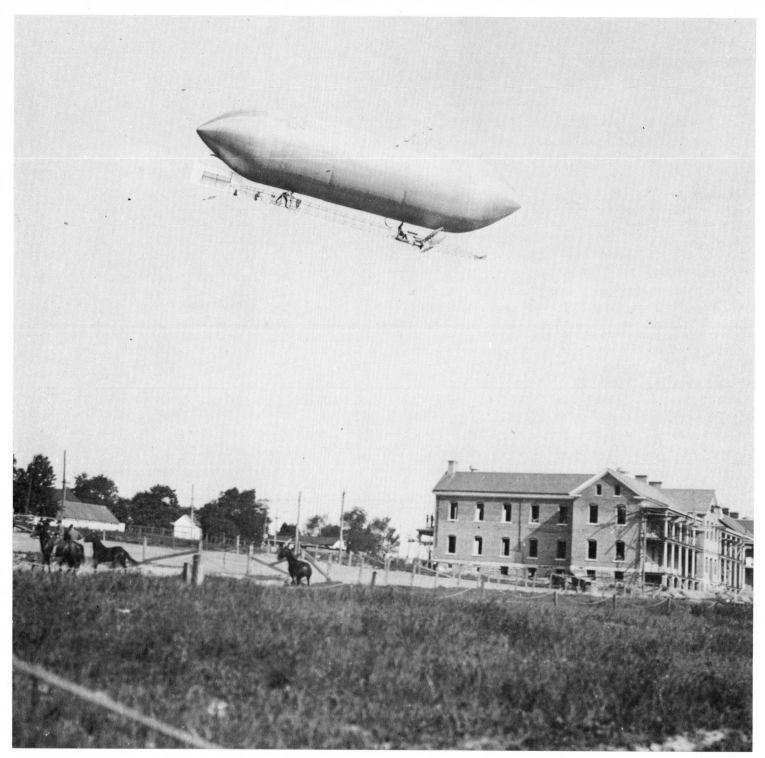

The Baldwin airship in flight over Fort Myer in the summer of 1908, carrying two members of the Signal Corps.
U.S. Air Force

Dayton, for a twenty-eight-second flight as the world's first aeroplane passenger.

Orville now felt no qualms about taking a succession of Signal Corps officers with him during his demonstrations at Fort Myer. One of the officers, on 17 September, was Lieutenant Thomas E Selfridge, who had been associated with Alexander Graham Bell and Glenn Curtiss in the first successful aeroplane experiments in the United States after the 1903–5 work by the Wrights.

In May 1908 Selfridge had been the first U.S. Army officer to make a solo flight in a powered aeroplane when he flew the *White Wing*, which had been developed by Bell's Aerial Experiment Association. The flight with Orville was to be his last. During the fourth circuit of the flying-field,

at a height of about 125 feet, a crack in one blade of the starboard propeller led to vibration which eventually caused the propeller to break loose and to cut through one of the tail support wires. The biplane dived to the ground, severely injuring Orville and fatally injuring his passenger.

Nine months after this setback, the Wrights returned to Fort Myer with a replacement aircraft differing little from its predecessor except in having a slightly reduced wing area and higher undercarriage. This time all went well. During the first official test, on 27 July, with Lieutenant Frank P Lahm as passenger, Orville set a new world record for a two-man flight of 1 hour 12 minutes and 40 seconds. In the final cross-country speed test, over a five-mile course

Members of the
Aeronautical Division of the
U.S. Army's Signal Corps
with an observation balloon
at Fort Myer, Virginia in
the summer of 1908.
U.S. Air Force

between Fort Myer and Alexandria, Orville and his passenger, Lieutenant Benjamin D Foulois, averaged 42·5 mph, earning a bonus of $5,000 to add to the contract price of the aircraft.

The Army accepted the aircraft and designated it the Wright Model A on 2 August. The Washington *Evening Star* preferred to call the aircraft 'Aeroplane No. 1, Heavier-Than-Air Division, United States Aerial Fleet'. It was to be a long time before the 'Fleet' reached a battleworthy status.

Under the terms of the original contract, Wilbur Wright trained Lieutenants Lahm and Frederic E Humphreys to fly the Model A. After logging about three hours each, they were proclaimed to be pilots on 26 October 1909. On 5 November they crashed the aircraft; soon

afterwards they were posted back to their regular jobs. For a time after the crash the 'United States Aerial Fleet' had neither pilots nor an airworthy aeroplane. The first of a succession of repairs made the Model A available to Lieutenant Foulois, who taught himself to fly by means of a correspondence course from the Wrights and a little help with his landings from an instructor.

Not until March 1911 did Congress make available the first $25,000 of a $125,000 appropriation for Army flying, enabling the Signal Corps to take delivery in the following month of a Curtiss Model D 'pusher' and a Wright Model B on wheels. The Model A was placed in honourable retirement in the Smithsonian Institution, where it can still be seen in the U.S. National

Air and Space Museum, side-by-side with exhibits
that range from the original Wright *Flyer* to
spacecraft.

When Captain Chandler was reappointed
Chief of the Aeronautical Division in 1911, he
also took charge of the flying school at College
Park near Washington DC. His instructors
included Lieutenant Henry H (Hap) Arnold, who
was destined to be the great wartime leader of
the U.S. Army Air Forces during their supreme
testing time thirty years later.

Even in the early, formative years before the
First World War, Americans showed an eager-
ness to forge an effective air weapon that went
far beyond the capabilities of their primitive
aeroplanes. As early as 30 June 1910, Glenn

Curtiss made the first recorded bombing trials,
flying his pusher biplane at a height of 50 feet
and dropping dummy bombs on the shape of a
battleship outlined with flags on Lake Keuka,
New York. Live bomb-dropping dates from
7 January 1911, when Lieutenant Myron S
Crissy and Philip Parmalee made initial trials
from a Wright biplane at San Francisco.

To improve accuracy, a former Army officer
named Riley Scott invented a bombsight which
showed great promise when tested in 1911. When
the U.S. War Department showed no interest, he
brought it to Europe, where he won the Michelin
prize for bomb-dropping at an international
contest held on 11 January 1912.

Scott was not the only U.S. citizen to contribute

to the eastward transatlantic 'brain drain' in the interests of air power. The future possibility of air combat had first been demonstrated by a U.S. Army pilot, Lieutenant Jacob Earl Fickel, when he fired a rifle from a single-seater Curtiss biplane at a target in Sheepshead Bay, New York on 20 August 1910. When Samuel Neal McClean invented and Colonel Isaac N Lewis improved a lightweight, low-recoil machine-gun, this represented an ideal weapon with which to take the idea of air fighting an important step further. A Lewis gun was strapped in front of the right-hand (passenger's) seat on a Model B Wright, so that it could be fired forward and downward between the gunner's legs. With Lieutenant Thomas de Witt Milling at the controls and Captain Chandler manning the gun, the first firing trials were made on 2 June 1912. The results were so good that ten more guns were requested for intensive testing. The Army Ordnance Department replied that this was not possible as the Lewis gun had not been adopted as a standard weapon.

Isaac Lewis thereupon sailed to Europe and formed a company in Belgium to produce and market the gun. Thus he was able later to supply the Allies with an air-to-air weapon of the greatest importance during the First World War.

There had already been many experiments in fitting both guns and bombs to aircraft in Europe, but the bombs were clumsy, hand-made and often hand-dropped devices, while the usual Vickers and similar belt-fed heavy machine-guns had severe limitations for firing from the open, dusty, windy aircraft of the time.

One of the most difficult problems was to devise a method of firing a machine-gun from an aircraft of sufficient speed to catch others in the air or to avoid being shot down itself by ground fire. In general, design had progressed much more rapidly in Europe than in the United States. Most aircraft built for military use now had proper cockpits for the crew, open at the top but enclosed on all sides. Some still retained pusher propellers behind the wings, a feature going back to the original Wright *Flyer*. On these, with the crew in a nacelle forward of the propeller, it was comparatively easy to mount a forward-firing gun controlled by the observer in the front cockpit; but there were snags.

The load that could be lifted by the light, frail, low-powered aircraft was often so small that the addition of a gun left no chance of carrying other equipment or bombs, or even sufficient fuel for a worthwhile endurance. When the gunner stood up to fire the gun, the extra drag imposed by his body reduced even further the pathetic top speed. The demonstration of how a heavy gun could be mounted on the nose of a 50-hp two-seater, on the Voisin stand at the 1910 Paris Air Show, produced a comment from one knowledgeable visitor to the effect that he could not wait to see what happened when it was fired from aircraft capable of 50 mph. Perhaps wisely, it never was.

In other respects French military aviation

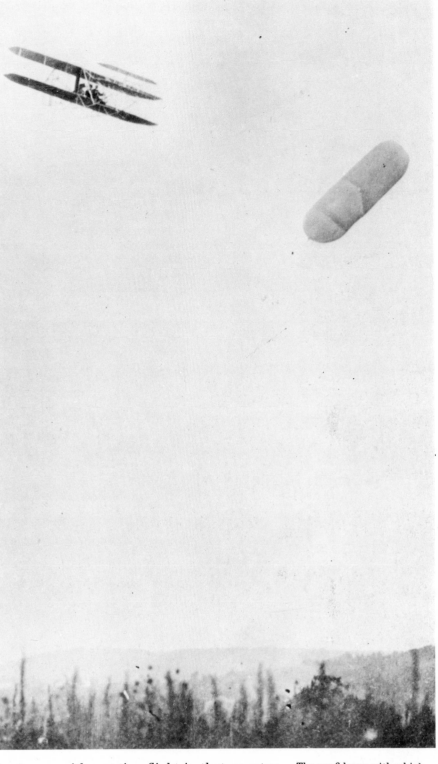

kept pace with sporting flight in that country, which had led the world with events like the first great Aero Show, which took place in the Grand Palais in Paris in 1908; the first Flying Meeting at Rheims in 1909, in which most of the world's leading pilots competed; and a succession of flights to stir the imagination and arouse the interest of the public, like Louis Blériot's crossing of the English Channel on 25 July 1909. It mattered little that he had become lost at one stage, and made it to a heavy landing at Dover only because a fortuitous shower of rain cooled his overheating engine.

By the end of 1910, there were thirty-nine military pilots and twenty-nine military aircraft in France. The aircraft were of Blériot, Breguet,

The confidence with which the Wrights were flying by 1908 is well shown by this rare photograph of Orville flying high over Fort Myer, with a passenger, during the acceptance trials which were to end so disastrously. *U.S. Air Force*

Farman, Voisin and Antoinette design, and their quality is indicated by the fact that, in October of the following year, five French manufacturers felt able to enter aircraft for the most exacting official test that had been held up to that time. The test called for a circular flight of 300 kilometres (186 miles), starting and finishing at Rheims. The aircraft were to carry a load of 300 kilograms (661 lb) exclusive of fuel. The three prize-winners were all tractor designs (i.e. propeller at the front), and two of them were monoplanes; but the French military services continued to prefer pusher biplanes.

The great advantage possessed by French manufacturers was the availability of lightweight, efficient aero-engines. The first real breakthrough had come in 1908, when Laurent Seguin and his brother had built the prototype of an entirely new internal-combustion engine which they called the 'Gnome'. Based on the rotary layout invented by Lawrence Hargrave in Australia twenty years earlier, this consisted basically of five cylinders which rotated round a stationary crankshaft, so that the engine acted as its own flywheel and solved the problem of cooling the cylinders without the complication and weight of a water-cooling system.

Although made of steel, the prototype Gnome gave 34 hp for a weight of only 112 lb. It proved outstandingly reliable and smooth in operation, at the cost of two basic shortcomings. Lubrication was by castor oil, which was flung out of the valves in a constant spray as the engine rotated, giving the windscreen and pilot of a tractor-type aircraft a liberal coating (and smell) of castor oil by the end of each flight. Also, as rotary engines increased in size and power, the gyroscopic effect reduced manoeuvrability, making turns against the direction of the engine particularly difficult. None the less, the Gnome and other rotaries like the le Rhone were the engines with which civil and military flying achieved its greatest successes throughout much of the decade up to the end of the First World War.

The only power plants to rival them for much of this period were the fairly conservative six-cylinder Mercedes and Daimler-Benz engines fitted to German military aircraft. Rated at about 100 hp in 1913–14, these sturdy engines enabled German pilots to set some impressive duration and altitude records which should have alerted the French and British air services to the kind of opposition they could expect when the war started. Fortunately for them, the War Ministry in Berlin, dazzled by the capability of Count von Zeppelin's big airships, had been late in appreciating the value of aeroplanes for Army support.

The German General Staff had been more perceptive. In 1912 they had decided that aeroplanes were superior to small non-rigid and semi-rigid airships, and had initiated a replacement programme that would make available a total of fifty-seven field aviation units by 1 April 1916, plus a smaller number of units to be based at fortress towns and military bases. The target date was selected as being the earliest by which Germany would be fully prepared for a major war. On mobilization, it was planned to form an additional 46 units to work with the artillery attached to each infantry division of the Army.

The Germans were determined to make up rapidly for a late start. Their aircraft industry already included companies producing aeroplanes under names that were to become all too familiar to the Allies in the war that everyone knew must come – Albatros, Aviatik, Gotha, LVG, and of course Fokker, run by a young Dutchman who had found it easier to sell aeroplanes in a more militaristic country than his own.

Germany, like France, was thus well served by a soundly established industry, capable of expansion to produce the vast quantities of aircraft that would be needed in the future war. What of the third of the major European Imperial Powers, Britain?

Development of aeroplanes specifically for military use had ended with the suspension of Cody's and Dunne's activities at Farnborough in 1909. There appeared to be a slight change of heart in October of the following year, when it

Lieutenant Myron S Crissy, the first man to drop a live bomb from an aeroplane, on 7 January 1911. He was flown by Wright demonstration pilot Philip O Parmalee (right).
U.S. Air Force

was announced that the scope of the Balloon Section of the Royal Engineers was to be extended 'to afford opportunities for aeroplaning'. Nobody was quite sure what this meant. It certainly brought no immediate change in the day-to-day activities of the Balloon Factory at Farnborough, which was now divorced from the Balloon School and headed by Superintendent Mervyn O'Gorman. Fifty men and fifty women were employed there, in one small machine shop, one shed for making balloons, and an airship shed.

O'Gorman decided it was time to begin some serious aeronautical research and development. In January 1910 he appointed Frederick Green, from the Daimler Company, as Engineer in Charge of Design. Towards the end of that year, Green met at the Aero Exhibition in London a young man named Geoffrey de Havilland, who had designed and built two aeroplanes and had flown the second of them, which was fitted with a 45-hp engine of his own design. De Havilland had run out of money and wanted a job. On Green's recommendation, O'Gorman offered to buy the de Havilland 2 aeroplane for £400 and take on its builder as a designer and test pilot. Seldom has any organization made a better deal.

During the month that this young man joined Green's staff, the War Office sent to the Factory for repair a non-standard Blériot monoplane that was known, with some justification, as the 'Man-Killer'. Here was the opportunity for which the design team had been waiting. After inspecting the aircraft, they requested official permission to rebuild rather than repair it. The unsuspect-

ing War Office agreed, and what had come to the Factory as a tractor monoplane emerged eventually as a tail-first pusher biplane. Apart from the 60-hp ENV engine, no vestige of the original Blériot remained.

In the following April, a similar thorough 'repair' transformed a Voisin pusher biplane into a neat tractor biplane. Even the original 60-hp Wolseley engine disappeared this time. Its replacement was an eight-cylinder Vee Renault of similar power, which ran so quietly by comparison with the usual rotaries that the aircraft was soon known as the 'Silent Aeroplane'. Its official designation was B.E.1 (Blériot Experimental No. 1), signifying a tractor layout as used by the Frenchman. Factory-designed pusher biplanes were to be designated F.E. for Farman Experimental, with S.E. standing for Scout Experimental and R.E. for Reconnaissance Experimental.

The B.E.1 was to be the forerunner of one of the most tragically famous families of military aircraft in flying history. The chain of events which shaped its future began on 1 April 1911 when the Balloon Section of the Royal Engineers was expanded into an Air Battalion, comprising a Headquarters at South Farnborough, No. 1 (Airship) Company, also at Farnborough, and No. 2 (Aeroplane) Company at Larkhill on Salisbury Plain.

At last the Army was to get some aeroplanes of proven and practical design. By the summer of that year it had six Bristol Boxkite biplanes (four with 50-hp Gnome engines and two with 60-hp Renault), a very tired Henry Farman pusher biplane (50-hp Gnome), a much-restored Howard Wright biplane, and a Blériot XXI monoplane (70-hp Gnome) owned privately by one of the pilots.

The qualifications for the latter were interesting, and reflected the view that aeroplanes would never be of any military use except as 'aerial cavalry' for reconnaissance. A would-be pilot had to possess an Aviator's Certificate, previous experience in aeronautics, good map-reading and field-sketching ability, not less than two years' service and an aptitude for mechanics; he also had to be a good sailor.

It is easy to smirk at such demands in a modern air-conditioned, computerized, supersonic age; but were they so stupid? The aeroplanes of the period were very light and seldom stable, and there was no proof that this would not cause airsickness akin to seasickness. Map-reading and sketching were obvious assets to a reconnaissance pilot lacking both camera and radio. Mechanical aptitude was equally useful at a time when engine failures and forced landings were to be expected. The main snag, in the absence of official flying training establishments, was the need to have gained an Aviator's Certificate, as this restricted the field to those with sufficient cash to pay for flying lessons. Even this requirement was made less tough by the fact

left
The first man to fire a rifle
from an aeroplane, on 20
August 1910, was Lieutenant
J E Fickel. He sat on the
wing leading-edge of a
Curtiss pusher biplane
piloted by Charles Willard.
U.S. Air Force

below
On 2 June 1912, Captain
Charles de F Chandler fired
this Lewis machine-gun in
flight, from a Wright Model
B piloted by Lieutenant
Thomas de Witt Milling.
U.S. Air Force

that a pilot accepted for service had £75 of the
money he had spent on his training reimbursed
by the War Office.

The keenness of the men of the Aeroplane
Company of the Air Battalion, and the in-
adequacies of their aircraft, were soon demonstrated. When the Army's autumn manœuvres
were cancelled in 1911, the Company requested
permission to test its potential by flying to the
air bases that had been specified for the exercise,
at Hardwicke, near Cambridge, and Thetford in
Norfolk. The result was a near-disaster. Two
pilots wrote off their aeroplanes completely;
another crashed two aircraft on successive days.
Only two completed the round trip unscathed.

A decade later, when the first international
airlines began operating in Europe, pilots who
followed railway lines between London and Paris
referred to this as 'navigating by Bradshaw'. On
his way north in August 1911, Lieutenant Connor
of the Air Battalion did so literally. Until he
crashed on high ground near Oxford, he found
his way with the aid of a map torn out of a copy
of *Bradshaw's Railway Guide*. The only instruments fitted to his aircraft were a revolution
counter and a compass.

Captain Brooke-Popham, accompanied by
Captain Burke, had also hoped to reach Oxford
on the first day; but his ancient Farman had a
top speed of only 30 mph in a dead calm. Faced
with a slight head-wind, he could get no farther
than Wantage before dark – and nobody then
flew by night. When the two men resumed their
slow progress next morning, an engine failure

soon entailed a forced landing and a broken tail skid, which a local coachbuilder took nearly all day to patch together.

It was wasted effort. Another forced landing, occurring almost immediately after take-off, caused more serious damage. A few miles away, Captain Massy had got no more than fifty yards before wrecking his aircraft when resuming his journey after a precautionary landing in bumpy weather. Like Connor he escaped injury because the stick-and-string aeroplanes of the time could land slowly, in almost any reasonable field, and had the habit of simply collapsing around their pilots in a crash, except at the end of a steep dive.

One of the other pilots, Lieutenant Reynolds, had a more exciting time. In a subsequent report,

above
By comparison with the later 'chicken coops' the original 80-hp Voisin Type L bombers were quite trim. The 130 lb of small bombs were placed on the cockpit floor until the time came for the observer to drop them overboard.

right
The Voisin IV, of 1915, was produced in two operational versions. The IV LB was a bomber; the IV LBS was a fighter with a 37-mm Hotchkiss cannon mounted on the nose. Both versions were powered by a 120-hp Canton-Unné engine, which gave them a maximum speed of 74 mph.

quoted in volume one of *The War in the Air*, he wrote:

That evening, soon after seven o'clock, I started again. It was warm and fine but rather suggestive of thunder; the air was perfectly still. I scarcely had occasion to move the control lever at all until I got to Bletchley, where it began to get rather bumpy. At first I thought nothing of this, but suddenly it got much worse, and I came to the conclusion that it was time to descend. A big black thunder-cloud was coming up on my right front; it did not look reassuring, and there was good landing ground below. At this time I was flying at about 1,700 feet altitude by my aneroid (worn around the neck), which had been set at Oxford in the morning. I began a

above
The quietness of the engine of the B.E.1, by comparison with the then-popular rotaries caused it to be known as the 'Silent Army Aeroplane'.
Ministry of Defence

left
Dual-control arrangement on a biplane used in 1915 for flying training at the Wright brothers' school, Dayton, Ohio. Until such installations became standard, pupils learned the 'feel' of the controls by placing their hands on those of the pilot – leaning over his shoulder to do so on tandem-seaters. Pupil Breadner (*left*) went on to become an Air Marshal in the Royal Canadian Air Force.
Canadian National Defence

glide, but almost directly I had switched off, the tail of my machine was suddenly wrenched upwards as if it had been hit from below and I saw the front elevator go down perpendicularly below me. I was not strapped in, and I suppose I caught hold of the uprights at my side, for the next thing I realized was that I was lying in a heap on what ordinarily is the undersurface of the top wing. The machine in fact was upside-down. I stood up, held on, and waited. The machine just floated about, gliding from side to side like a piece of falling paper. Then it over-swung itself, so to speak, and went down more or less vertically sideways until it righted itself momentarily the right way up.

Then it went down tail-first, turned over upside-down again, and restarted the old floating motion. We were still some way from the ground, and took what seemed a long time in reaching it. I looked round somewhat hurriedly; the tail was still there, and I could see nothing wrong. As we got close to the ground the machine was doing long swings from side to side, and I made up my mind that the only thing to do was to try and jump clear before the crash. In the last swing we slid down, I think, about thirty feet, and hit the ground pretty hard. Fortunately, I hung on practically to the end, and, according to those who were looking on, I

did not jump till about ten feet from the ground.

There were to be many amazing escapes in the next decade and a half, before military pilots were issued with parachutes as a normal item of equipment. But no survivor's story gives a better description of the ordeal of a crash in a slow aircraft without an enclosed cockpit or safety-belt. Lieutenant Reynold's story gives a hint of the courage demanded by the first generation of military pilots of all nations, and fosters a healthy respect for the handful of Italian pilots who were the first to go into action in the aeroplanes of 1911.

On 29 September 1911, Italy had declared war on Turkey, following the latter's refusal to agree to the Italian military occupation of Tripolitania and Cirenaica. The Italian Expeditionary Force sent to North Africa included an aeroplane section consisting originally of Captains Piazza and Moizo, Major Falchi, Lieutenants Rossi and Gavotti, with two Blériot XIs, two Etrich Taubes, two Henry Farmans and three Nieuports. Undeterred by thoughts of the effect that the hot climate might have on the wooden structure, low-powered engines and handling qualities of these types, the section was ready to start work on 22 October, only two days after the last of the expedition's equipment had been landed.

The distinction of making the first operational flight in history in a military aeroplane went to Captain Piazza, who carried out a one-hour reconnaissance of the Turkish positions between Tripoli and Azizia in one of the Blériots. On the same day Captain Moizo became the first pilot to sustain damage in action, when his Nieuport was holed in several places by ground fire during a reconnaissance of an oasis at a height of 650 feet. His one broken wing rib was soon repaired, and on the 25th Piazza and Moizo achieved an important success when they observed three advancing columns of Turkish and Arab troops, totalling some 6,000 men. Thanks to the pilots' reports, the Italian ground forces had plenty of time to set their defences in order to meet the threat.

As the campaign developed, history was made by this small force almost every day. On 26 October, Lieutenant Gavotti, in an Etrich, and Captain Piazza played an important part in directing the fire of mountain artillery and the big guns of the battleship *Carlo Alberto* during the battle of Sciara-Sciat, in which the Turks were estimated to have lost 3,000 men. It was no easy task. Flying above the line of fire, the aircraft were subjected to shock waves from the 'friendly' shells passing beneath them, as well as to hostile fire by the enemy; but neither was hit.

Bombing from an aeroplane on active service

above
Captain Piazza standing in front of the Blériot monoplane in which he made the first operational flight in a military aeroplane, on 22 October 1911, during the Italo-Turkish War in North Africa.
Italian Air Ministry

opposite, top
One of the Type P semi-rigid airships, each of which was 207 feet long. It was used for reconnaissance and light bombing during the war of 1911–12. A 120-hp Clement Bayard engine gave it a top speed of 35 mph when carrying a crew of five.
Italian Air Ministry

opposite, bottom
Captain Montù, with two grenades strapped to his chest, prepares to take off on the rear seat of Lieutenant G Rossi's Farman for a bombing and reconnaissance flight on 31 January 1912.
Italian Air Ministry

41

dates from 1 November 1911, when Lieutenant Gavotti took off in an Etrich, carrying four 4½-lb Cipelli bombs in a leather bag, with the detonators in his pocket. Circling above the Turkish encampment at Ain Zara, he took one of the bombs on his knees, fitted the detonator and dropped it overboard. Having observed what he described as 'the disastrous results' of his attack, he then dropped the other three bombs on the oasis of Taguira. The mission involved a total of about sixty miles of flying in an aircraft with a maximum speed of 56 mph. Those 18 lb of bombs can be regarded as the first weapons to point the way to the future possibilities of air power.

For the record, the first official communiqué reporting operations by military aeroplanes was issued from the Italian Headquarters at Tripoli on 5 November. It stated: 'Yesterday Captains Moizo, Piazza and De Rada made an aeroplane reconnaissance, during which De Rada tested successfully a new Farman military biplane. Moizo, after locating the position of the enemy's battery, flew over Ain Zara and dropped two bombs into the Arab encampment. He found that the enemy were much diminished in numbers since he saw them last time. Piazza dropped two bombs on the enemy, with effect. The object of the reconnaissance was to discover the headquarters of the Arabs and Turkish troops, which is at Sok-el-Djama.'

By the end of November the work of this first small expeditionary air force had been so impressive that two more Italian sections, made up of eight pilots with four Blériots, three Farmans and a Deperdussin, were dispatched to North Africa. But Piazza remained the pace-setter. On 10 January 1912 he made the first air-drop of propaganda leaflets, inviting the Arabs encamped at Fonduk-Ben Gasur to desert the Turks and to give themselves up to the Italians. On 24 and 25 February he brought back the first wartime reconnaissance photographs taken from an aeroplane, showing Suani-Beni Adem, near Zanzur.

Lighter-than-air units of the Italian forces were also able to show their capabilities in 1912. The airships P2 and P3 made many reconnaissance and light bombing sorties, demonstrating the superior payload capacity of such craft on 19 April, when Commandant Sulsi took a ciné-film of the enemy camp from the P3. Kite balloons were also flown over land and from pontoons, for visual observation and filming of enemy dispositions and movements.

These very successful air operations continued throughout the remaining months of the campaign, which was to lead to Italian colonization of Libya for three decades In the following year, the various nations involved in the Balkan War made use of observation balloons and aeroplanes, with varying success. In Mexico an attempt was made by a French mercenary pilot to drop 9-lb bombs on the Government cruisers *Tampico* and *Guerrero*, at Guaymas, in support of the Army of General Obregon. The bombs missed their target, but the ships withdrew to safer waters.

Meanwhile, an incident in Morocco had set in motion a chain of events which was to have a major influence on the development of military aviation.

The incident itself involved not an aircraft but a ship. The gunboat *Panther* was the only vessel in the German Navy at that time with a battle record, having sunk what was described as a revolutionary Haitian warship in 1903. The *Panther* was not a particularly formidable vessel, displacing 1,000 tons and carrying only light armament and 125 men; but its sudden arrival off Agadir on 3 July 1911 'to protect German interests' represented a blatant show of force. There were, in fact, no Europeans in the port, and Germany had neither interests nor commerce to protect in that part of Morocco.

The target was clearly French interests, and recent disturbances in the northern part of the country around Fez were used as the excuse for German intervention. With Britain aligned firmly by the side of France, the crisis was eventually ended; but there was no longer any doubt of German intentions, and from the autumn of that year the Royal Navy and Britain's Army began to prepare for war.

One essential was to evolve the Air Battalion into something that would bear comparison with the large, well-equipped air services already existing in France and Germany. A question in Parliament revealed that there were thought to be eleven 'actual flying men' in the Army and eight in the Navy. The latter eight existed only because a member of the Royal Aero Club, Frank (later Sir Francis) McClean, had persuaded the Admiralty to let him train the first four on his own aeroplanes.

One of the original naval pilots, a fiery little bearded Lieutenant named Charles Rumney Samson, talked the Admiralty into buying McClean's two training aircraft, and these became the nucleus of a naval flying school at Eastchurch. The Air Battalion, for its part, had two small experimental airships with well-worn envelopes, and a handful of aeroplanes that were of little use for anything but training.

Against this background, on 18 December 1911, the Committee of Imperial Defence in London appointed a Technical Sub-Committee of eight members to suggest measures by which Britain could speedily create an efficient air force. Within ten weeks its recommendations were ready. Within eight more weeks they had been approved. On 13 April 1912, the Royal Flying Corps (R.F.C.) was constituted by Royal Warrant. On 13 May it absorbed the Air Battalion and its reserve. To set it on its feet, it was allocated £308,000 by Parliament—a sum that would not buy one fighter aircraft today.

Perhaps it was as well nobody knew that the First World War was a mere twenty-seven months away.

Army versus Navy versus Air Power

The birth of the Royal Flying Corps in Britain was not universally welcomed. Many officers of the Army and Royal Navy objected to the idea of a third service, even if its stated purpose was to support and serve the land forces and Fleet in time of war. They had a sneaking suspicion that the baby would grow up into something other than the subservient supplier of 'eyes in the sky', which was all they wanted military aviation to be. They were absolutely correct—but for all the wrong reasons. Countries like Germany, which tied its forces too long to the beck and call of the older military services, were to regret it. Even the United States, retaining its overland air forces under nominal Army control until 1947, was then to initiate a 'unification' of its armed forces which appeared, to outsiders, simply to result in three services instead of the former two.

As a result of all this, military aviation, its suppliers and its leaders have never had an easy life. In Britain, the inter-service rivalries, bickerings and non-cooperation began almost as soon as the R.F.C. came into existence.

Basically, it was to consist of a Military Wing, a Naval Wing and a Reserve, with a Central Flying School at which all aircrew would receive their basic training. The Aircraft Factory at Farnborough was to be retained as sole source of supply for the aircraft to be flown by the R.F.C. Each of the main Wings was to regard itself as a reserve for the other.

The task of the Military Wing was laid down as being quite simply to provide reconnaissance services for any future expeditionary force. Sir Walter Raleigh emphasized in his first volume of *The War in the Air*, in 1922, that 'All its other and later uses were consequences of this central purpose, and were forced on it by the hard logic of events.' To meet the basic commitment, it was reckoned to need seven aeroplane squadrons (each consisting of three flights, with four aircraft per flight), and one airship and kite squadron (with two airships and two flights of kites). Two pilots were to be provided for each aeroplane, with two more in reserve to cover the inevitable risk of wartime wastage.

As the first stage in implementing this policy, the Military Wing was put under the command of Captain F H Sykes, who as a General Staff officer had spent a considerable period in 1911 visiting French military and civil aerodromes, and attending a military aeroplane competition held at Rheims. The impressive progress he had witnessed was reflected in the chain of recommendations which had led to the formation of the R.F.C. Now, his first task was to reorganize what he had inherited from the Air Battalion, Royal Engineers.

No. 1 Squadron of the Military Wing was the former airship company at Farnborough. Its commander, Captain E M Maitland, was almost alone among British pilots of the time in preferring lighter-than-air craft. No. 2 Squadron was formed under the leadership of Captain C J Burke at Farnborough, where the equipment composed one B.E., one Breguet and two Bristol Boxkites. To keep the newly posted pilots occupied, they were sent up for hours in the baskets of tethered balloons, from which they practised the art of aerial observation by sketching the streets of Farnborough, counting the cows on the common, and learning to describe what they observed. To complete the force, the former aeroplane company on Salisbury Plain was redesignated No. 3 Squadron.

Until the Central Flying School became fully organized at Upavon in Wiltshire, it was decided to continue accepting only pilots who had been trained privately, and to offer only advanced training at C.F.S. What would be termed operational conversion today, on to first-line aircraft, was to be handled by the squadrons of the Military Wing and the Naval Flying School.

The Naval Wing Headquarters was established at Eastchurch, in Kent, alongside Commander C R Samson's pioneer Naval Flying School. With the connivance of the First Lord of the Admiralty, Winston Churchill, this branch of the R.F.C. at once proceeded to go its own independent way. Instead of having its pilots trained at Upavon, it continued handling the entire flying syllabus at Eastchurch. Unwilling to believe that the Royal Aircraft Factory, so long a source of

supply for the Army, could possibly know the types of aircraft needed by the Navy, it decided to buy its aeroplanes from Britain's struggling private manufacturers, laying the groundwork for a thriving and imaginative industry that was to be the saviour of Britain's air forces in the coming war.

It did not even retain the official designation of 'Royal Flying Corps, Naval Wing' for more than a few weeks. Instead, it became the Royal Naval Air Service, first by popular use and finally, on 1 July 1914, by official proclamation. For better or worse, Britain now had two separate air services, doing virtually everything differently and independently. The Military Wing recognized this by becoming, simply, the Royal Flying Corps.

The R.F.C. spent the last two pre-war years learning to work with and for the Army, to the best of its ability. Foreigners, and 'those web-footed people' down at Eastchurch, could play with machine-guns and bombs as much as they wished. The job of the R.F.C. was to find a steady, unarmed aeroplane on which its pilots could accompany the Army wherever it went, as all-seeing aerial cavalry.

The leaders of the Corps had very definite ideas on the type of aircraft they wanted. Of those available in 1912 there was nothing more suitable, and well tested, than French aircraft like the pusher biplanes designed by Henry and Maurice Farman, and the latest, improved Blériot XI with an 80-hp Gnome engine. These would do the job admirably until the Royal Aircraft Factory had geared itself up to produce large numbers of B.E.2 biplanes, evolved from that 'Silent Aeroplane' designed at Farnborough by young Geoffrey de Havilland. The Farmans

could then continue to fly as trainers.

Britain's private companies, headed by men like Tommy Sopwith, the Short brothers, A V Roe, and Frederick Handley Page, were suggesting that they could build better aeroplanes than the Royal Aircraft Factory. To keep them quiet, the War Office arranged a series of Military Trials on Salisbury Plain, in August 1912, so that they could demonstrate the capabilities of their latest designs by comparison with the best the French had to offer. Factory designs were barred, ostensibly to prevent unfair competition from State-financed products. In fact, it would have been a waste of time, as the B.E.2 had already been chosen as the future mainstay of operational squadrons.

Nineteen aeroplanes were presented for the Trials, two of them all-British, eight British with foreign engines, and nine foreign (two of them built under licence in the United Kingdom). They comprised five tractor biplanes, eleven tractor monoplanes, two pusher biplanes and one pusher monoplane.

The competition was organized with a view to finding the best aeroplane for the primary task of providing reconnaissance for an expeditionary force. As this was regarded as the *raison d'être* of virtually all the world's military air arms at that period, the tests by which proficiency was to be determined are worth listing in detail.

The first nine requirements were constructional. In order of supposed importance, they called for:

1. Accommodation for at least one passenger in addition to the pilot, both having the best possible view of the ground in a forward arc. (This clearly favoured the more primitive open biplanes, with no protection for the crew.)

2. The aircraft should stand still on the ground with the engine running, without being held back; and the engine should be easy to start, preferably from the pilot's seat.

3. Dual controls were to be fitted.

4. The occupants were to be sheltered from the wind and able to communicate with each other. (The obvious winner here was the Avro biplane, which had a fully enclosed cabin but was clearly one of the poorest contenders for the accommodation prize.)

5. All parts of the airframe were to be interchangeable, like parts with each other and also with sample parts picked from stock.

6. Operation of the aircraft should not impose an undue strain upon the pilot. A vital consideration on active service.

7. Each aircraft had to be capable of being dismantled and transported by road, either by trolley or on its own wheels. The width, packed for road travel, was not to exceed ten feet.

8. Each aircraft was to be presented in a packing-case suitable for rail transport. The case itself to be easily taken to pieces for storage in a small space.

9. The engine should be silenced effectively. (In a pollution-conscious age it is interesting to note that the competitors were unanimous in ignoring this requirement, having no horse-power to waste on such refinement.)

above
Henry Farman biplanes of the Royal Flying Corps on the Common at Farnborough, the original home of No. 2 Squadron.

below
Second place in the Military Trials held on Salisbury Plain in August 1912 went to this 100-hp Deperdussin monoplane.

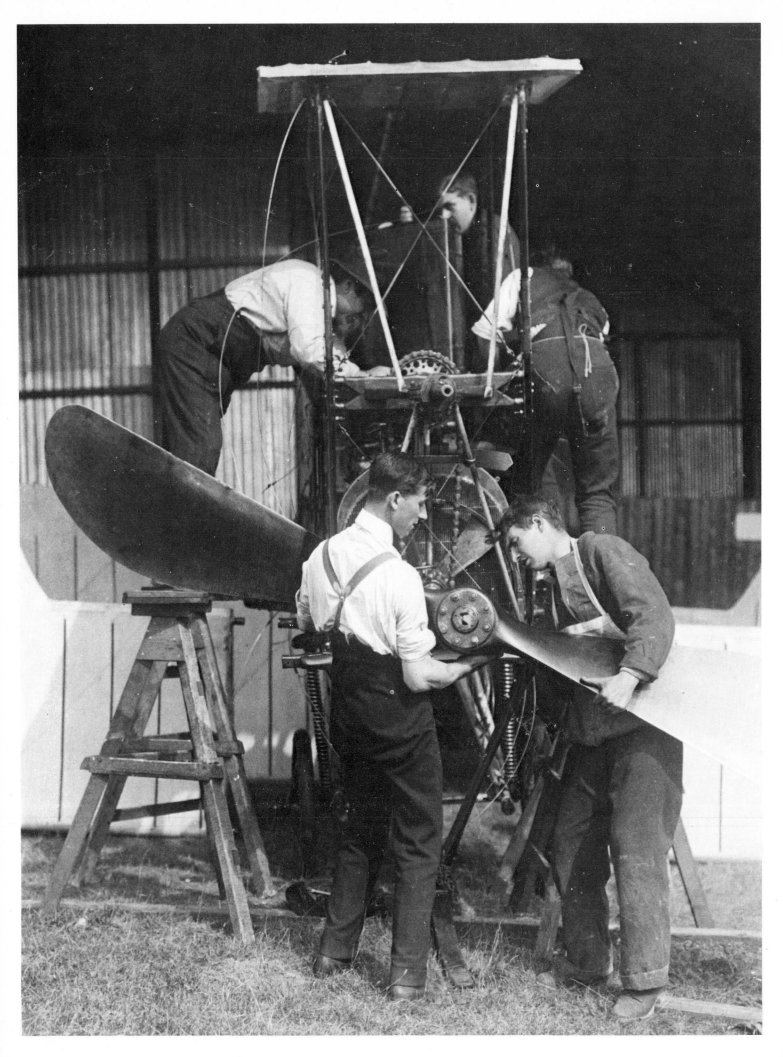

opposite page
Assisted by S F Cody
himself (*top left*), a team of
five men managed to
assemble the big Cody
'Cathedral' in 1 hour 35
minutes in front of judges at
the Military Trials.
Flight International

left and below
The first four-engined
aeroplane, pointing the way
to both the heavy bombers
and transport aircraft of the
future, was the *Bolshoi*
flown by Igor Sikorsky at St
Petersburg, Russia on 13
May 1913. It spanned more
than 92 feet and was
powered by four 100-hp
Argus engines.

On the first day, all the competing aircraft were duly deposited at the starting-line in their packing-cases. One after the other, their crews were given the signal to start unpacking them. On completion of assembly, a pilot had to take off and prove that nothing had been left undone. The time, for the purposes of the competition, counted from the word 'go' to when the aircraft left the ground.

A V Roe's enclosed biplane was the winner of this do-it-yourself aeroplane-building race, becoming airborne in a mere fourteen and a half minutes. At the other extreme, it required the furious efforts of five men for nearly nine and a half hours to get the Maurice Farman into the air. With the Avro also a clear leader in terms of comfort, it seemed to have a fair chance of ending up first; but the flying tests were to produce the worst possible winner.

An early surprise came when eleven aeroplanes passed the tough qualifying test. This called for a flight of at least three hours, carrying two people weighing not less than 350 lb, the usual instruments, and fuel and oil for four and a half hours. A height of 4,500 feet had to be attained at some stage of the flight, and at least one hour had to be spent above 1,500 feet. After that came climbing, gliding, fuel consumption, calculated range, speed, speed range, landing distance, quick take-off and rough-weather tests.

Of these speed range was adjudged most important, and eventually decided the whole contest. Cody, once considered an unnecessary expense at Farnborough, had fitted a 120-hp Austro-Daimler engine to his latest biplane, nicknamed the 'Cathedral'. This engine not only ticked over sweetly on the ground, earning valuable marks, but gave even the massive 'Cathedral' a top speed of 72·4 mph. As the biplane could remain in the air at 48·5 mph, this gave a speed range of 23·9 mph, which nothing else could match. One pilot could register only a 2·2 mph difference between his fastest and slowest speeds—reflecting, one would hope, his lack of experience rather than the actual capability of the aircraft.

Cody received £5,000, and the R.F.C. continued using French aeroplanes until it could equip progressively with versions of the B.E.2. Lest this should seem merely pigheaded in retrospect, it might be worth noting that the prototype completed some of the Military Trials tests unofficially. Its 70-hp Renault engine gave it a maximum speed of 70 mph and it could fly under perfect control at 40 mph. This bettered even Cody's speed-range performance by 6·1 mph, and it also had a better rate of climb than anything in the competition.

The first versions to enter service were the B.E.2a and B.E.2b, differing only in detail from the original B.E.1. Among the most brilliant engineers at Farnborough was a young man named Edward Teshmaker Busk, who had

above
During Army manœuvres on Salisbury Plain in September 1910, Robert Loraine, famous as both actor and pilot, flew a Boxkite equipped with air-to-ground wireless.
The Marconi Co.

opposite, top
First flying-boats to serve with the U.S. Navy were five F-boats, developed from the original Curtiss pusher flying-boat of 1912. The C-2 (later AB-2) illustrated was used by Lieutenant Commander H C Mustin for the first U.S. Navy catapult launch from a ship, the battleship *North Carolina*, on 5 November 1915.
U.S. Navy

left
Short S.27 pusher biplane in position on the take-off platform erected above the foredeck of H.M.S. *Hibernia*, prior to the Royal Review of the Fleet in May 1912.
Short Brothers & Harland Ltd

gained an Aviator's Certificate solely so that he could study stability and control problems in the air. He now turned his attention to ways of achieving complete inherent stability, and his ideas were built into the prototype B.E.2c. The wings were now staggered (i.e. the top wing was farther forward than the lower one), with ailerons instead of the usual warping tips for control. A fixed fin was added forward of the rudder, and the tail plane was lowered.

In June 1914 this prototype was flown from Farnborough to Netheravon, in Wiltshire, by Major Sefton Brancker, who was destined to become one of the great leaders of British aviation. After climbing to 2,000 feet, he did not touch the controls again until the aircraft was 20 feet above the ground on the landing approach. He spent his time en route writing a reconnaissance report on the scene that unfolded below.

Such exploits left the R.F.C. in no doubt that the B.E.2c met its requirement better than any other aeroplane in the world. Altogether, a total of 1,117 were to be delivered to this service, followed by 1,801 improved B.E.2es. The fortunes of war were to see them unjustly categorized among the most disastrous military aircraft ever built.

Meanwhile, the Royal Naval Air Service (R.N.A.S.) had been developing a variety of new and revolutionary applications of air power at sea. Like the R.F.C., it was aware of the value of reconnaissance. A fleet commander who could detect and locate precisely an enemy 'over the horizon' could begin any engagement with an immense advantage. But the advantage might be even greater if the aircraft locating the enemy could lob a torpedo at it before returning to base.

This was asking a lot of the aeroplanes of the time. Aerial bombs had progressed in some cases to a weight of 20 lb by 1913. As an alternative to being dropped by hand, they could be stowed vertically in a kind of pipe-rack attached to the side of the fuselage, and released by extracting a pin which held their tail fins in the rack. A torpedo was very different, with a weight of 810 lb (equivalent to four or five passengers) in its standard 14-inch form, requiring a special support crutch under the fuselage, and release gear.

above
Following one of his pioneer flights from a ship, Commander C R Samson walks away from the S.27 after landing ashore.
Flight International

left
To demonstrate the potential of its Boxkite biplane, the British and Colonial (later Bristol) Aeroplane Company arranged a public display of aircraft Nos. 12A and 14 (there was no 13) on Durdham Down, Bristol in November 1910. On the 15th of that month an order for eight improved military Boxkites, for Russia, represented the first Government contract ever placed for British aeroplanes.
The Bristol Aeroplane Co.

In 1911 a lightweight 352-lb torpedo had been launched from a Farman biplane by Captain Guidoni of Italy. Now, after a number of preliminary experiments, the R.N.A.S. was ready to see if a full-size 14-inch torpedo could be air-launched with any hope of hitting its target. The weapon was mounted in a crutch under the belly of a Short folding-wing seaplane with a 160-hp Gnome engine. Flown by Squadron Commander A M Longmore (one of the four original naval pilots trained by Frank McClean), this seaplane launched its torpedo successfully in flight on 28 July 1914. Early in the following year the Director of the Air Department of the Admiralty, Commodore (later Rear-Admiral Sir) Murray F Sueter, asked Shorts to design and put into production for the R.N.A.S. a more powerful seaplane which could carry a torpedo as its standard load. The result was the Short 184, with a Sunbeam engine of 225 to 275 hp.

It had proved comparatively easy to build aeroplanes able to locate and attack enemy ships; the real problem was to find a way of getting them far enough from land to do so. Once again, as in the case of military aviation ashore, the lead was to come from the United States.

On 14 November 1910, Eugene Ely, one of the new breed of professional pilots who were taking over from the pioneers, clambered on to the open seat of a Curtiss pusher biplane on board the cruiser U.S.S. *Birmingham*, anchored in Hampton Roads, Virginia. Behind him, every spare inch of space on the ship, even to the highest cross-trees, was packed with sailors hoping to see either history being made or an airman get a ducking. Ahead of the aeroplane stretched a platform, 83 feet long by 28 feet wide, sloping gently down towards the bow.

After opening up the 60-hp Curtiss engine, Ely gathered speed down the wooden ramp, but seemed to be going all too slowly as his wheels left the end. Those at deck-level lost sight of the aircraft as it dipped towards the water, and waited expectantly for the splash. Ely struggled to maintain every scrap of lift, weighing up how far he could afford to drop, to gain speed, before losing all chance of flaring out safely. He nearly left it too late. As the biplane nosed upward, its propeller sliced into the water, causing damage to the tips that might have brought disaster. Instead, the Curtiss slowly gained height and went on to land safely ashore.

The naval aircraft-carrier may be said to date from that moment. Two months later, on 18 January 1911, Ely completed his double by taking off from San Francisco and landing his Curtiss on a deck built over the stern of the U.S.S. *Pennsylvania*, which was standing 13 miles out to sea. His aircraft was brought to a halt by primitive arrester gear, consisting of a series of ropes stretched across the deck, with a sandbag at each end. When picked up by hooks on the aircraft's skids, they quickly dragged it to a halt. After spending some time on the ship, Ely took off again and returned to shore.

Although these historic flights impressed the U.S. Navy, no early attempt was made to develop further the idea of a carrier able to operate wheeled aircraft. Most people continued to feel that it was more natural for seagoing aeroplanes to be equipped for taking off and landing on water. To give them what they wanted, Glenn

Eugene Ely's Curtiss biplane leaving the U.S.S. *Pennsylvania*, 18 January 1911.

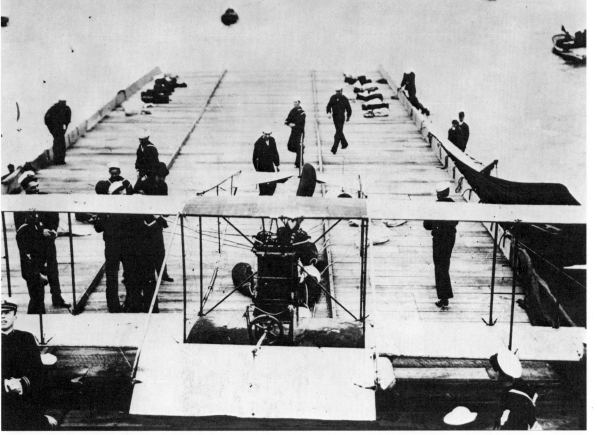

Ely's Curtiss at rest on the wooden flight deck of the U.S.S. *Pennsylvania* after his first successful deck landing on 18 January 1911. Some of the sandbag-weighted ropes which were laid on deck to drag his aircraft to a stop can be seen in this picture. *U.S. Navy*

A large proportion of the serviceable aircraft of the Royal Flying Corps converged on Netheravon in June 1914 for a month's combined training in all aspects of military aviation under active service conditions. This aerial view of the 'concentration camp' shows B.E.2s, a high-altitude R.E.5, Maurice Farmans, Blériot monoplanes, Avro 500s and Henry Farmans, lined up in front of mobile canvas 'T' hangars.
Ministry of Defence

Judging by the expression on the face of some of these British soldiers, an invitation to fly in the stand-up, open gondola of an early airship was not always accepted with relish.

Curtiss flew the first practical float-equipped seaplane on 26 January 1911; the first flying-boat, with the pilot seated inside the boat-type hull, on 10 January 1912; and an aircraft that was delivered originally as a seaplane, then fitted with retractable wheels, making it the first amphibian. Being able to travel on land, on water and in the air, it was known as the *Triad*.

On 17 February 1911, Curtiss flew one of his seaplanes out to the U.S.S. *Pennsylvania* in San Diego Bay, landed alongside and was hoisted on board by derrick. This incident–appearing to be so much simpler than building a flying plat-form over the deck, with consequent loss of fire-power from the covered-up gun-turrets–prob-ably set back development of genuine aircraft-carriers by several years. The Royal Navy, in particular, began thinking in terms of seaplane-carriers that would have to stop in order to lower their aircraft into the water for take-off and to retrieve them after flight. Such a practice took no regard of the fact that the frail, unscientific floats of the time often refused stubbornly to 'unstick' when the sea was calm and broke up when it was rough.

Despite opposition from many high-ranking

officers, who could see no use for such primitive aircraft with the Fleet, on 26 September 1910 the U.S. Navy Department had appointed Captain W I Chambers to handle all correspondence concerning aeroplanes. He was to stay in charge of naval aviation throughout its first three vital years.

It was Chambers who arranged Ely's pioneer deck-landing experiments on the *Birmingham* and *Pennsylvania*, and who then ordered a Curtiss seaplane as the first U.S. Navy aeroplane and had it flown out to the *Pennsylvania* by Curtiss, as already described. It was this seaplane, designated A-1, that became the *Triad*. On it Lieutenant Theodore G Ellyson, U.S. Naval Aviator No. 1, took off from an inclined wire on 7 September 1911, before making the first successful catapult launch, at the Washington Navy Yard, in the similar A-3. These experiments were aimed at finding ways of operating directly from a ship without the need for a flying-off deck, and the catapult was to find important future applications.

Meanwhile, the mantle of leadership in seaflying passed from the United States to Britain, thanks largely to Charles Rumney Samson.

Convinced that anything the U.S. Navy could do the Royal Navy could do better, he is said to have made a secret flight in a Short S.27 pusher biplane from a platform built over the forward gun-turret and bows of the battleship H.M.S. *Africa*, while it was moored in Sheerness Harbour in December 1911. Having satisfied himself that the operation could be effected safely, and without making anyone look foolish, he is supposed to have repeated the take-off officially on 10 January 1912, landing ashore afterwards. Whether or not the unofficial flight really took place we may never know. Like the story of King Alfred's burning the cakes, it is too good to leave out of any history of its period.

Apart from the addition of three air-bags to the main and tail skids of the S.27, to keep it afloat if it should alight on the water, it was a perfectly standard type of landplane, with a 50-hp Gnome engine and a top speed of 39 mph. Re-engined with a 70-hp Gnome, it was dispatched to add lustre to the Royal Review of the Fleet, at Weymouth, on 8 May 1912.

Lieutenant R Gregory, another of the original four Navy pilots, put up an impressive show by first dropping a 300-lb bomb from the S.27 while

'Walking' an airship like the 152-foot-long Gamma required a lot of manpower. Of interest are the swivelling propellers, devised by the British pioneer Ernest Willows and adopted later for Factory airships like the Gamma. They enabled the pilot to drive an airship up or down, without needing the huge elevator surfaces that were used to tilt the complete airship when the propellers were non-swivelling.

The extent to which Italian airships increased in size and fighting power during the First World War is emphasized by this photograph of part of the gondola of a 265-foot semi-rigid M class airship. Between the twin propeller shafts six large bombs were clutched in a vertical rack, and a machine-gun protected the airship from rear attack.
Italian Air Ministry

flying at a height of 500 feet, and then locating a submarine which was submerged to periscope depth. On the following day, the aircraft was hoisted on board H.M.S. *Hibernia*, to which the *Africa*'s platform had been transferred, and took off safely while the ship was steaming at 15 knots –the first take-off from a ship under way. Whether the pilot was Gregory or Samson is another of those questions that historians find so worrying.

Far more significant is the fact that the success of these experiments persuaded the Admiralty to convert the old light cruiser H.M.S. *Hermes* into a carrier for two seaplanes. When it entered service in late 1912, a whole new era of naval warfare began, although it was hardly apparent at the time. At the instigation of Winston Churchill, Samson bought from the Short brothers a 160-hp seaplane with folding wings, for trials on board the *Hermes*, so introducing a feature that would become standard on future seagoing aircraft.

It was no coincidence that when this 'Folder', No. 81, took part in the naval manœuvres of July 1913, it was fitted with a wireless transmitter.

Tests with wireless on military aeroplanes had been under way for years (a Bristol Boxkite with a Thorne-Baker transmitter had participated in British Army manœuvres in 1910) and promised to revolutionize artillery observation when the equipment became lighter and more reliable.

Another technical development still in its infancy was night flying; but Lieutenant R Cholmondeley of No. 3 Squadron, R.F.C. had flown safely from Larkhill to Upavon and back by moonlight, in a Maurice Farman, in April 1913. A first hint of the type of aircraft that might seek the cover of darkness for its operations had been given when Igor Sikorsky's *Bolshoi*–the world's first four-engined aeroplane–took off for the first time in Russia on 13 May 1913. Nobody could foresee then that it would become the prototype for a Squadron of Flying Ships that would make 400 raids, carrying immense loads of bombs. Perhaps it was as well, too, that nobody knew how soon the world would suffer the most fearful war it had ever known–a war in which the aeroplane would be employed as a terrible weapon of destruction.

Western Front 1914-18

It is often suggested that the First World War, advanced the progress of aviation at an incredible pace. This is not true. By the end of the war the best fighters in service could fly at 120–125 mph. The experimental S.E.4. built at Farnborough in 1914 was not only 10 mph faster than this but embodied a standard of streamlining beyond that of any wartime combat aircraft, and was built with an enclosed cockpit, which they lacked.

Strange ideas persisted throughout those four wartime years. No pilot would fly with the S.E.4's transparent cockpit cover in place, because it was considered dangerous to be shut in. Even more frustrating to designers, who appreciated the performance penalties of drag, was the general preference for biplanes, with their profusion of struts and wires, reduced field of vision and restricted arc of fire for the observer's gun, when the air forces could have been flying monoplanes.

Pre-war racing had proved conclusively that monoplanes were faster than biplanes of similar weight and power–and hence ought to have made better combat aircraft. There had been problems, certainly. Back in 1912, after five experienced pilots had been killed by the collapse of the wings of their Blériot monoplanes, the French Government had grounded all aircraft of this type in Army service until the wings were strengthened. Louis Blériot gained prestige by explaining the cause of the accidents and showing how the weakness could be remedied. Within a fortnight this ban was lifted.

A similar short-lived ban had been imposed by the Royal Flying Corps after a succession of fatal accidents to Deperdussin and British monoplanes in the summer of 1912. The resulting prejudice was to delay replacement of biplanes by cleaner, faster monoplanes in the world's air forces for more than twenty years. When, for example, Bristol produced their M.1 in 1916, showing it to have a performance and manœuvrability that would have been invaluable to pilots in France, only 125 production models were ordered and a mere handful saw service in the Middle East. The official reason for this was that the M.1 landed at 49 mph, which was too fast for a first-line aircraft.

Methods of construction changed little during the war years, although Dr Hugo Junkers and Professor Madelung of the Junkers Flugzeug-Werke in Germany developed and put into production all-metal aeroplanes with cantilever (i.e. externally unbraced) wings. Perhaps the greatest advance was in the power and reliability of aircraft engines, which made the opening up of a network of commercial air routes possible after the war. Unfortunately, the stories of combat exploits had created an impression that pilots were brave and reckless supermen, and the average man and woman could not imagine themselves as potential air travellers.

The romantic view of aerial warfare in 1914–18 is that it was waged by a twentieth-century breed of knights in shining armour, racing round the skies in brightly painted fighters and living brief, gay lives between bouts of single-handed combat. Alas, even this smacks more of Hollywood than reality. For every dashing Red Baron there were dozens of pilots and observers flying lazy circles in slow reconnaissance aircraft, reporting the accuracy of friendly artillery and being shot at by unfriendly anti-aircraft guns, which were known as 'Archies'.

Everything hostile had its slightly humorous nickname, which helped to disguise the deadly seriousness of the war the aircrew fought. The name 'Archie' had a sporty 'old pals' ring about it that may have contributed to the legend that it was more of an ever-present puff of smoke, comfortably far away, than an exploding shell that flung shrapnel in all directions. Most pilots retain memories of friends and colleagues whose aircraft were flying in formation one second and, in the next, disintegrated into an unrecognizable tangle of collapsed and burning wood, wire and canvas after a direct hit.

Such sights were fortunately still in the future as the air services deployed to perform their allotted tasks in August 1914. The two sides were evenly matched in terms of numbers of aeroplanes. The German Army Air Service had, on all fronts, a total of 258 aircraft, intended basically for reconnaissance. Together, the French and British mustered 219 aircraft on the Western Front, of which the R.F.C. contributed 63, with

Designed at the Royal Aircraft Factory by H P Folland, the S.E.4 single-seat tractor scout of 1914 was more advanced than almost any aeroplane built during the four years of war that followed. A 160-hp Gnome engine gave it a speed of 131 mph, an unclaimed world record at the time. Revolutionary features included variable-camber wings, which predated flaps, fan cooling for the engine, an advanced engine cowling, a removable celluloid cockpit cover, and accurately streamlined bracing wires.
Imperial War Museum

105 officers and 95 motor transport vehicles. An indication of the extent to which the bottom of the barrel had been scraped to produce this expeditionary air force is given by the fact that the ammunition and bomb lorry of No. 5 Squadron was still painted in the bright scarlet colour scheme of a famous sauce-manufacturer, with 'The World's Appetizer' in gold letters on its side.

To their credit, a mere five years after Blériot's first near-disastrous crossing of the English Channel, the British squadrons had all flown to France, on 13–15 August. One of the pilots, Captain (later Air Chief Marshal Sir) Philip Joubert de la Ferté, recalled many years afterwards what this involved.

With his colleagues of No. 3 Squadron, he left Netheravon for Dover on 12 August. One pilot stalled his Blériot two-seater on take-off, killing his mechanic and himself. The rest had one thought uppermost in their minds as they headed for the coast at about 50 mph in their unarmed aeroplanes. In Joubert's own words:

We had been ordered, secretly, that if a Zeppelin was seen by any of us we were, regardless of our safety, to ram it. I was proceeding peacefully twenty miles north of Portsmouth at about 3,000 feet, when my mechanic gripped my shoulder and shouted in my ear, 'Zeppelin, sir!' Shuddering with fright, I looked over my shoulder and saw one of the Spit forts lifting its head above the morning mist. In this light it looked just like an airship – but I had a lot to say to the mechanic when we landed.

After bivouacking that night at Dover, the pilots wrapped motor-car inner tubes round their waists as makeshift lifebelts and headed out over the Channel. Of the four squadrons available at this time, Nos. 2 and 4 were equipped with B.E.2s, No. 3 with Blériot monoplanes and Farman biplanes, and No. 5 with Farmans, Avro 504 biplanes and factory-built B.E.8s.

They wasted no time in flying into action. The first reconnaissance flight over enemy territory was made by Joubert in a Blériot and Lieutenant Gilbert Mappleback of No. 4 Squadron in a B.E.2 – strangely enough from the R.F.C. airfield at Maubeuge, where the first experimental

left
Because of the pre-war prejudice against monoplanes, the Bristol M.1C was given no opportunity to prove its capability in France.

below
First of the all-metal products of the German Junkers company was the experimental J.1, which flew for the first time on 12 December 1915. Unbraced (cantilever) wings gave it a very advanced appearance; it was usually known as the 'Tin Donkey' because of its overall covering of thin sheet iron. A switch was made to light alloy on later designs, usually corrugated for maximum strength.

balloon reconnaissance had been undertaken by Captain Coutelle 120 years before. Both lost their way, and eight hours elapsed before Joubert returned to Maubeuge after landing at Tournai and Courtrai to ask the way.

The pilots were not the only members of the British Expeditionary Force who made mistakes. A roar of musketry greeted two of No. 3's aircraft as they passed over a column of British soldiers on the road to Mons. Up to that moment, only the French had fired at R.F.C. aircraft. Now that the British had arrived and had displayed an equally poor standard of aircraft recognition, ground crews had to work all night painting a shield-shape Union Jack under the wings of each aeroplane. These were the first British military markings. Soon German aircraft sported black crosses, while the Allies settled on multi-

opposite, top
Among exhibits in the Swiss
Transport Museum at
Lucerne is this Blériot XI
monoplane, which belonged
to pioneer pilot Oskar Bider.
Together with its owner and
eight other pilots, it formed
the nucleus of the Swiss Air
Force in 1914.
Air BP

opposite, bottom
In the early months of 1916,
a Fokker *Eindecker*, with
synchronized machine-gun,
dives to attack a French
Voisin 'chicken-coop'.
By Kenneth McDonough.

below
Produced before the war,
this 65-mm calibre 'balloon
gun' was Krupps' twentieth-
century counterpart of the
anti-aircraft weapon devised
to shoot down the Paris
postal balloons in 1870. The
unique pivoting axles of the
wheels obviated the need for
a rotating gun mount on the
carriage.
H F King

coloured roundels for identification.

Second Lieutenant L A Strange of No. 5 Squadron resented the fact that R.F.C. aircraft were unarmed, and fitted a Lewis gun on the front cockpit of his Farman. On 22 August, he and his gunner set out in pursuit of an enemy Albatros reconnaissance aircraft which flew over Maubeuge. After forty-five minutes they had to give up what proved to be their first and last armed chase. On landing, Strange was ordered to remove the gun, which slowed further an already slow aeroplane, and his observer had to revert to the customary and quite ineffective rifle.

This did not prevent casualties being inflicted on the enemy air force. On 25 August three B.E.2s of No. 2 Squadron pursued and harassed an enemy two-seater with such persistence that it was forced down. The high-spirited Lieutenant H D Harvey-Kelly, who had been the first R.F.C. pilot to land in France, and Lieutenant W H C Mansfield landed near the enemy and continued the pursuit on foot, only to lose the Germans in a wood. So they returned to the abandoned aeroplane, removed a few souvenirs and set fire to it before returning to base.

More aggressive sorties were permitted during the British Army's retreat from Mons. Pilots making dawn reconnaissance flights filled their pockets with hand-grenades and tied larger missiles, including petrol bombs, over their flying clothing. An early success was recorded on 1 September, when two bombs dropped on columns of German cavalry converging on a cross-roads near Villiers-Cotterets caused a stampede.

Meanwhile, many hundreds of miles away on the Eastern Front, the general absence of armament on military aircraft had led to the sad loss of a pilot whose name would probably have meant little to his allies in the West, but who was now writing his name in history books for the second time.

On 27 August 1913 Lieutenant Petr Niko-laevich Nesterov of the Imperial Russian Army had been the first pilot in the world to perform a loop, in a Nieuport IV monoplane at Kiev. He was immediately put under arrest for ten days for risking Government property; but before the end of the year he was awarded a Russian Aero Club Medal for his feat, and was promoted to Staff Captain.

One day before the anniversary of his exploit, the airfield near Sholkiv in Galicia where his squadron was based was attacked by three

With their rear gunners muffled against the intense cold, Caproni three-engined strategic bombers of the Italian Army Air Service cross the Alps on their way to targets in Austria. By Kenneth McDonough.

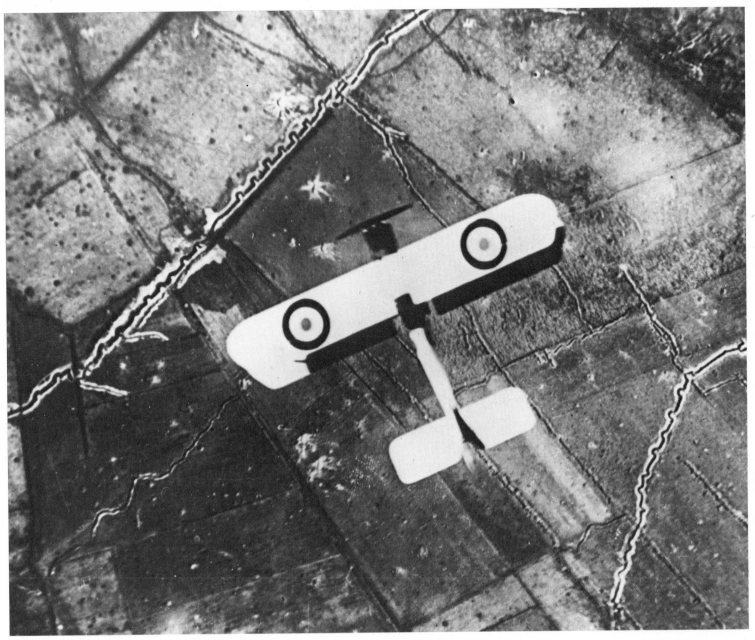

enemy aircraft led by the Austrian Baron von Rosenthal. Nesterov took off in his unarmed Morane Type M monoplane and, without a moment's hesitation, rammed von Rosenthal's aircraft. Both pilots were killed.

In retrospect, it is clear that this was the period of the war at which Germany should have thrown the full might of its Zeppelin fleet into raids on French and British cities, which would have offered no defence. Instead, the Army Zeppelins were expected to provide close support for the ground forces by attacking the Allies in front-line areas. Within a month, three of the seven Zeppelins available at the outbreak of war had been shot down by ground fire on the Western Front and a fourth over Poland in the east.

The ease with which the giant airships could have attacked Paris, and the demoralizing effect this would have had on people in the French capital, was demonstrated when the war was less than four weeks old. On 30 August a Rumpler Taube two-seater reconnaissance monoplane, piloted by Lieutenant F von Hiddessen, dropped five small bombs in the Bastille-Gare de l'Est

district, killing a woman and injuring two other people. More chilling for Parisians who remembered the siege of 1870 was a message dropped with the bombs, which said: 'The German army is at the gates of Paris. Surrender. You have no other choice.'

This was to be a rare moment of wartime glory for the bird-wing Taube, which was quickly condemned as useless for front-line duty. It had been a mainstay of the field aviation units when the war began, and Taubes flitted busily through the air as the German Army advanced through Belgium to France. A lack of efficient ground organization prevented the best use being made of the information acquired; but on the Eastern Front it was a different story.

In the last week of August, the Germans achieved the greatest victory of the opening stages of the war, annihilating two Russian corps, reducing by half the strength of three others, and capturing 125,000 prisoners and 500 guns. After what became known as the battle of Tannenberg, the German commander, General von Hindenburg, stated that success would never

From the very start of the First World War, R.F.C. reconnaissance aircraft became virtually the eyes of the Army, reporting enemy troop movements and directing artillery fire. Trenches and innumerable shell-holes are clearly visible on the ground over which this B.E.2 is flying. *Imperial War Museum*

opposite page
Flying his SPAD fighter *Vieux Charles*, the French ace Georges Guynemer (54 victories) attacks a formation of Fokker Triplanes with other members of Escadrille SPA.3, Groupe de Combat No. 12, the famous Cigognes. By Kenneth McDonough.

Designed originally by Etrich in Austria, the type of aircraft known as the Taube (Dove), because of its birdlike monoplane wings, was built by several German manufacturers. This Rumpler Taube is similar to the aircraft flown over Paris by Lieutenant F von Hiddessen on 30 August 1914.
Imperial War Museum

have been possible without air reconnaissance.

In the west, where Paris was saved by the armies under General Joffre at the battle of the Marne (6–9 September), the verdict of the Allies was similar. The first great turning-point in the pattern of the war had resulted from an Allied victory against enemy forces that had seemed irresistible. A message from Joffre said: 'Please express most particularly my thanks for the services rendered to us every day by the English Flying Corps. The precision, exactitude, and regularity of the news brought in by them are evidence of their perfect organization and also of the perfect training of pilots and observers.'

The 'backs to the wall' situation at this time gave Britain's other small expeditionary air force the opportunity for which it had been waiting. Eastchurch Squadron of the R.N.A.S., under Wing Commander C R Samson, had flown to Ostend on 27 August in three B.E.s, two Sopwith Tabloids, two Blériot monoplanes, one Henry Farman, one Bristol biplane and a Short seaplane which had had its floats exchanged for wheels. This motley force was supplemented by Astra-Torres airship No. 3, which had the merit of being the only R.N.A.S. aircraft armed with a machine-gun at that time. Back in Britain, the R.N.A.S. had 30 assorted landplanes, 31 seaplanes, 6 airships and the balance of the service's

830 personnel for all its other commitments.

On 30 August, because of the deteriorating situation in Belgium, Eastchurch Squadron had been ordered back to the United Kingdom; but Lord Edward Grosvenor had crashed his Blériot en route while landing at Dunkirk, and this delayed the whole party for three days. During that time, a telegram was received from the Admiralty notifying a change of plan. Addressed to the French Ministry of Marine, it said:

The Admiralty considers it extremely important to deny the use of territory within a hundred miles of Dunkirk to German Zeppelins, and to attack by aeroplanes all airships found replenishing there. With your permission the Admiralty wish to take all necessary measures to maintain aerial command of this region. The Admiralty proposes therefore to place thirty or forty naval aeroplanes at Dunkirk or other convenient coast points. In order that these may have a good radius of action they must be able to establish temporary bases forty to fifty miles inland. The Admiralty desires to reinforce officer commanding aeroplanes with fifty to sixty armed motor cars and two hundred to three hundred men. This small force will operate in conformity with the wishes of the French military authorities, but we hope it may be afforded a free initiative. The immunity of

The standard method of bomb-dropping in the early period of the war, before the general introduction of racks and sights, is demonstrated by this pilot of an R.N.A.S. airship.
Imperial War Museum

Portsmouth, Chatham and London from dangerous aerial attack is clearly involved.

The task of translating into action this requirement for local air and ground superiority around Dunkirk base could not have been allocated to a better man than Samson. He had already fitted a machine-gun to a motor car and gone hunting for the enemy. Now he was to be given *carte blanche* to hit the Germans in every way possible. Borrowing a couple of French machine-guns and four French artillerymen, he was able to set out with a force of four motor cars, twenty men and an escorting aeroplane, and issue a proclamation to say that he had temporarily reoccupied Lille.

Samson's armoured cars, though few in number, were soon fabled as the scourge of the enemy and a source of moral encouragement for the French. He decided that it was time for the aircraft to show their paces. This was not easy when his nominal force of three squadrons, with thirty-six aircraft, was often reduced to two or three airworthy machines.

A small detachment was sent to Antwerp with the aim of attacking the Zeppelins in their sheds at Düsseldorf and Cologne. A violent squall on 12 September tore the aircraft from their tie-downs and sent them cartwheeling to destruction. Ten days later, their replacements took off with loads of small bombs for the first British air raid

into German territory. Three of the pilots failed to find the targets, hidden under thick mist. The fourth dropped one bomb short; the others failed to explode.

Better results were achieved on 8 October, when Squadron Commander Spenser Grey and Flight Lieutenant R L G Marix left on what would clearly be the last possible attempt to damage the Zeppelin sheds, as enemy troops were about to enter Antwerp. Their aircraft were tiny unarmed single-seater Tabloids, powered by an 80-hp Gnome engine and each carrying a few 20-lb bombs. Again, Grey was hampered by mist and could only unload his bombs on Cologne Railway Station. Marix located the Zeppelins' lair at Düsseldorf, dived to only 600 feet to ensure that his bombs would not miss the target, and had the satisfaction of seeing flames shoot up 500 feet as the shed erupted with the brand-new Zeppelin ZIX inside it. His Tabloid was damaged by ground fire and had to be abandoned after a forced landing twenty miles from Antwerp. Marix arrived back at base safely, on a bicycle borrowed from a friendly Belgian.

This was the sole major combat success gained by the forty or so Tabloids built for the R.N.A.S., but the type is remembered in other ways. Before the war, a 100-hp version on floats had given Britain its first victory in the international

67

A steady increase in the number of machine-guns fitted to the F.E.2d enabled its crews to hold their own against much faster and more manœuvrable enemy fighters until the autumn of 1917. This example had a fixed forward-firing Lewis gun controlled by the pilot, and two more on free mounts

contests for the coveted Schneider Trophy and became the prototype for more than 400 Schneider and Baby seaplanes which served the R.N.A.S. throughout the First World War.

Tabloids were the first single-seat scouts (predecessors of the true fighter aircraft) to enter production and service anywhere in the world, and by February 1915 all those in Samson's force carried a Lewis gun above their top wing, firing clear of the propeller disc. More important still,

the spectacular destruction of Zeppelin ZIX convinced Commodore Murray Sueter, Director of the Air Department of the Admiralty, of the war-winning potential of strategic bombing.

He found a willing industrial partner in Frederick Handley Page, who showed him a design for a big twin-engined biplane, intended to carry six 112-lb bombs at speeds up to 72 mph. This aircraft was designed to meet an Admiralty requirement, issued in December 1914, for an

over-sea patrol bomber. Murray Sueter foresaw more exciting possibilities, and asked Handley Page if it could be scaled up into an even more ambitious 'bloody paralyser'. From this rather vague specification was to emerge the world's first heavy night bomber. While the Admiralty waited for its introduction into service, it initiated plans for a strategic attack wing of smaller aircraft that could be based well inside France, near enough to make repeated raids on

munition and industrial centres in Germany.

Meanwhile, the other combatant nations all began to show a keen interest in strategic bombing. Germany was the first, opening its long-anticipated Zeppelin assault on England on 19 January 1915. As on the British side, it was the German Naval Air Service, under the inspired leadership of Kapitan-leutnant Peter Strasser, which pioneered the air offensive. However, in spite of the scale and the effects of this and

for use by the observer. To fire the rear one backwards over the top wing, the observer had to stand on his seat, with only his feet and ankles below the rim of the cockpit. Like most First World War aircrew, he did this without the benefit of a parachute.
Imperial War Museum

subsequent raids, they were subordinated to the naval airships' main task of reconnaissance and naval cooperation over the North Sea, which they performed superbly. The constant surveillance of Allied shipping movements accounted to a large degree for any successes the German Navy achieved, and each Zeppelin was reckoned to be worth half a dozen cruisers.

There was no effective defence against air attack in early 1915. Recognizing this, a succession of international conventions had made attempts to protect civilian non-combatants by banning or limiting the practice. The limitations were relaxed progressively as the potential for air attack increased.

For example, the Hague Declaration of 1899 banned the launching of all forms of projectiles or explosives from balloons or other forms of aerial vessels. At the time, nobody had yet made a proper flight in a powered aeroplane and the first Zeppelin was only half-built. Eight years later, only twenty-seven of the forty-four nations attending the 1907 Hague Convention were prepared to renew the ban. The non-signatories included Germany, France, Italy and Russia. Britain, which had affirmed its support for the Declaration, had not then flown an aeroplane and in any case was absolved from observation of the ban if it became involved in war with a non-signatory.

opposite, top
Inside the forward control gondola of a Zeppelin. The officer at the chart table has a speaking-tube and engine telegraph system like that of a ship for communicating with the engine-room. He verbally instructs the two pilots at forward and side control wheels. The mechanic (*right*) is descending the ladder from the internal catwalk leading to all parts of the airship. *Illustrierte Zeitung*

opposite, bottom
The after engine gondola of a Zeppelin. While three mechanics attend to the engines, gunners keep a wary eye open for fighters. *Illustrierte Zeitung*

above
A Farman 5B of 1914, one of the first aircraft built for the Italian Air Service by the Fiat company.

left
Close-up of a Lewis machine-gun mounted at an angle to the fuselage of a Bristol C Scout, enabling the bullets to pass outside the propeller 'disc'. This aircraft, No. 1611, was flown by Captain Lanoe G Hawker, V.C. The sight, which assisted him to aim the gun while flying 'crabwise', can be seen on the rear centre-section strut. *T Hawker*

right
Another solution to the problem of firing a machine-gun without hitting the propeller is demonstrated by this Beardmore W.B.III carrier-borne fighter. Its Lewis gun was fixed to fire vertically upward, from below the aircraft to be attacked. The W.B.III was a folding-wing adaptation of the Sopwith Pup.

below
One of the truly great aeroplanes in the history of aerial warfare, the Fokker *Eindecker* was the first production fighter to be fitted with interrupter gear for its forward-firing machine-gun. It almost shot the Allied air forces from the air over the Western Front in ten months of 1915–16.

To the Kaiser's credit, if any credit can be given to such a man, he sanctioned his Navy's Zeppelin raids only on the strict understanding that the targets would be shipyards, arsenals, docks and other military objectives, and that London would not be attacked. With the best will in the world, an airship commander could make no such promise in the face of adverse weather, strong winds, absence of navigation aids, and the later blacking-out of lights on the ground. More often than not he was blown off course and could only guess at the identity of the dark shapes far below that felt the weight of his bombs.

None of this was much consolation for the victims of Zeppelin attack. That first raid, by L3 and L4 in January 1915, killed two people in Great Yarmouth and two in King's Lynn, and injured sixteen more. Damage was restricted to a power station and some houses, although one

74

left
A Morane-Saulnier Type N scout of the Royal Flying Corps. It had a 100-hp Le Rhône rotary engine and a forward-firing machine-gun. In the absence of interrupter gear, deflector plates were fitted to the propeller blades to kick aside bullets that would otherwise have damaged them.

below
Until effective incendiary ammunition for machine-guns became available, some aircraft, like this Farman, carried Le Prieur rockets on mounts attached to their interplane struts. On 25 June 1916, in concerted attacks on fifteen German kite balloons along the British front in France, four were destroyed by Le Prieur rockets. Three more were destroyed next day on the Second Army front.
Imperial War Museum

opposite, top
Like knights of old, the top fighter pilots of 1914–18 could often be identified in combat by their colourful mounts and the heraldry they bore. Insignia carried by this SPAD XIII was that of America's 94th Pursuit Squadron, the first to see action in France, and symbolized Uncle Sam's hat being thrown into the ring when the U.S. entered the war.
Howard Levy

opposite, bottom
Best German fighter of 1918 was the Fokker D VII. The Armistice Agreement, noting items to be handed over to the Allies, specified 'especially all machines of the D VII type'–the only time a specific type of aircraft has ever figured in such a document.
Howard Levy

bomb did fall near a wireless station at Hunstanton. In an effort to excuse the pointless attack on King's Lynn, an official German historian said that the Zeppelin had not dropped its bombs until it had come under fire from the town's anti-aircraft guns. In fact, King's Lynn was undefended and brightly lit, as the blackout had not yet been introduced.

Less than a month later, on 16 February, the L3 and L4 had to make emergency landings in Denmark when caught in a gale. All but four of the crew-members managed to jump clear before the 490-foot craft were swept away by the wind and never seen again.

Such were the risks that confronted crews of the early airships; they were part of the price of trundling over Britain at 47 mph, no more than 6,000 feet above the ground, with a typical load of five 110-lb high-explosive bombs and twenty $6\frac{1}{2}$-lb incendiaries. Effectiveness of the Zeppelins

improved very rapidly, to the extent that the L30
class of 1916 were each 650 feet long and powered
by six 240-hp Maybach engines, which enabled
them to fly 4,600 miles, with a maximum speed of
64 mph, a ceiling of 13,000 feet and a military load
capability of up to sixty bombs with a total
weight of 11,000 lb.

Unfortunately for the crews, there had been
an equally dramatic improvement in the capabilities of combat aeroplanes since the Zeppelin
offensive began, and this was to make even the
L30 class no longer good enough.

A warning of future possibilities had been
given as early as 5 October 1914, when Sergeant
Joseph Frantz and Caporal Quénault of the
French Escadrille VB24 shot down a German
two-seater, near Rheims, with a machine-gun
mounted on the nose of their Voisin III 'chicken-
coop'. The nickname of this single-engined
pusher biplane was appropriate. Thousands were
built throughout the war, as bombers and attack
aircraft with guns of up to 37-millimetre calibre.
They did good work, by day and night, but even
a steady growth of engine power from 120 hp to
350 hp could not push their maze of struts and
wires through the air at more than 84 mph, and
the bomb-load was never more than 660 lb.

That initial combat success by Sergeant Frantz
set no pattern for the future; and the first victory
of an aeroplane over a Zeppelin, which followed
on 7 June 1915, was even less repeatable.

Flight Sub-Lieutenant R A J Warneford of
No. 1 Squadron, R.N.A.S. was on his way from
Dunkirk to Berchem-Sainte-Agathe, with six
20-lb bombs hanging from his Morane-Saulnier
Type L monoplane, when he caught sight of the
LZ37 over Bruges. Despite heavy defensive fire
from enemy machine-gunners, he at once gave
chase and, after climbing to 11,000 feet, dived to
drop his bombs on the huge target beneath him.
The Zeppelin exploded in a mass of flames; its
vulnerability had been dramatically exposed.

Starting the starboard engine of one of the 269 Caproni Ca 33 three-engined bombers built in Italy in 1916–18. Defensive armament comprised a Revelli machine-gun on the front cockpit and up to three more on the rear gunner's platform behind the top wing.
Italian Air Ministry

Warneford, too, was soon in trouble, with a broken fuel-pipe. Only after he had flown back to base did he realize that he had been on the ground behind the enemy lines for thirty-five minutes while repairing the break. He received the Victoria Cross for his achievement, but his luck did not last. Only ten days after his duel with LZ37, he was killed in the simple kind of flying accident which took the lives of so many of the outstanding pilots of both sides.

In spite of Warneford's success, nobody believed that this was the best way of dealing with Zeppelins. One alternative was the steel dart or *fléchette*, about 5 inches long and $\frac{3}{8}$ inch in diameter, which had been carried in canisters and dropped from the Blériots and Farmans of No. 3 Squadron, R.F.C. since the autumn of 1914. The idea was to saturate German troop concentrations and horse-lines with as many as 250 *fléchettes* from each canister; but even in a combat area life is scattered so sparsely over the ground that results were difficult to judge, the main snag being that anything but a direct hit was a waste of effort.

Engineer Lieutenant Francis Ranken of the R.N.A.S. tried to offer better results, especially against Zeppelins, by devising a dart containing an explosive charge. Vanes, which extended from the tail of the dart on release, were intended to make it lodge on the envelope of the airship in such a way that the charge would explode inside. Like many wartime ideas, it proved better in theory than in practice, as did firework-type rockets fired from mounts on the wing struts of fighters. The real answer was a machine-gun and, paradoxically, it was the Germans who perfected

the device which was to spell doom for the Zeppelin.

All kinds of schemes had been suggested in an effort to evolve a way of firing forward from a single-seater tractor fighter. The first of these to achieve any significant success was that which gained the Victoria Cross for Captain Lanoe G Hawker of No. 6 Squadron, R.F.C. On 25 July 1915, Hawker forced down three German two-seaters during an evening patrol. He did this with a single-shot Martini cavalry carbine, mounted at an angle on the side of his Bristol Scout so that it would fire outside the propeller disc. This called for a high standard of markmanship, as the aircraft had to be flown 'crabwise' in order to line up the gun on target – and it is worth noting that each of the two-seaters claimed by Hawker carried a machine-gun.

Weapons used on British fighters in this way ranged from Lewis guns to a breech-loading duck-gun firing chain-shot. A Lewis gun on top of the upper wing was more easy to aim; but replacement of the ammunition drums was difficult until the invention of the Foster mounting. This was curved at the rear so that the gun could be pulled backwards and down until it was pointing nearly vertically. As well as facilitating loading, this enabled the pilot to fire upwards into the unprotected underbelly of his opponent, and was a favourite with the first great British fighter ace, Captain Albert Ball, V.C.

There are many stories, both true and fabled, about pilots who flew over enemy aircraft towing grapnels which tore away their opponents' wings. One authentic attack of this kind was made against an Albatros two-seater by the top Russian ace, Staff Captain Alexander A Kazakov, on 18 March 1915. The grapnel or anchor jammed as it was being unreeled, and eventually the enemy's fire became so troublesome that Kazakov rammed the Albatros with his undercarriage. The German crashed. The Russian went on to achieve a further sixteen conventional victories and a chestful of decorations, including the French Légion d'Honneur and the British D.S.O., M.C. and D.F.C.

The all-important idea of an interrupter gear that would synchronize the stream of bullets from a machine-gun, so that they would pass between the blades of a spinning propeller, came simultaneously to Lieutenant Poplavko in Russia, two brothers named Edwards in Britain, and Franz Schneider, Chief Designer of the LVG company in Germany. Only Schneider made

An early example of the family of big four-engined Sikorsky Ilya Mourometz bombers built for the Tsar of Russia's Squadron of Flying Ships. Some aircraft had an open, wire-railed promenade deck on top of the rear fuselage, on which crew or passengers could walk in flight.
Igor Sikorsky

any real progress, patenting his invention on 15 July 1913 and later fitting a synchronized gun to the prototype LVG EVI two-seat monoplane. However, when this aircraft was on its way to the front for testing in combat, in 1915, it was lost and the gun gear was forgotten for a time.

A less satisfactory version of the same kind of 'timing' gear was tested before the war by Raymond Saulnier of the Morane-Saulnier company in France. Some of the bullets from the Hotchkiss machine-gun used with his interrupter gear tended to hit the propeller blades and chew them away; so he fitted a steel plate to each blade, to deflect the offending bullets before they could leave the pilot in the embarrassing position of lacking a propeller.

On the outbreak of war, the French Government took back the borrowed Hotchkiss; but Roland Garros, one of the greatest pre-war sporting pilots, remembered the Saulnier tests when he was issued with a Morane-Saulnier Type M monoplane in a scout squadron of the French Air Force in the first months of 1915.

Although there was no question of fitting interrupter gear, it seemed worth while to see if the deflector plates would be adequate by themselves. So he obtained a set, fitted them to his propeller and set off in search of a target.

The date was 1 April 1915, and the crew of the German two-seater did not worry overmuch as the Morane closed on them. No single-seater of this kind ever fired straight ahead – none but Garros' aircraft. A stream of bullets from the machine-gun mounted above the fuselage passed through the shining propeller disc as if the blades were not there, and the German crew died without any chance of warning their friends of this terrifying new development.

Other German aircraft fell to the mystery Morane during the next two weeks. Then, on 19 April, engine trouble forced Garros to land behind the German lines. Before he could destroy the aircraft he was taken prisoner, and the enemy were astute enough to appreciate the magnitude of their prize.

Anthony Fokker was ordered to fit guns and steel deflector plates to the new *Eindecker*

(monoplane) EIs he was building for the Army Air Service. Believing he could do better, he discussed the situation with Heinrich Luebbe and Fritz Heber at his Schwerin works. Within a few days they had evolved a practical interrupter gear consisting of a simple engine-driven system of cams and push-rods which operated the trigger of a Parabellum machine-gun once during each revolution of the propeller. Generally similar to the earlier scheme devised by Schneider, it was to have a devastating effect when it reached the Western Front.

In retrospect, it is difficult to believe that a mere 425 *Eindeckers* were built and that their reign of terror lasted for only ten months. It began on 1 August 1915, when Lieutenant Max Immelmann forced down a British aeroplane that had been attacking Douai Aerodrome. It continued as Immelmann raised his tally of victories to fifteen and, as the almost legendary 'Eagle of Lille', was awarded Germany's highest decoration for gallantry, the Pour le Mérite or 'Blue Max'. The manœuvre by which he gained some of his kills – a half-loop and roll off the top, which

gained height and put him quickly on the tail of his enemy – became so familiar to other pilots, and the soldiers in the muddy trenches who watched the aerial combats in awe, that it has been known ever since as the 'Immelmann turn'. The death of this pilot, on 18 June 1916, also marked the end of the Fokker's period of supremacy.

In the month before Immelmann's first victory, the R.F.C. had fought a total of only forty-six air combats. By December 1915 that number was recorded daily. Even in its most effective EIII version, the *Eindecker* weighed a scant 1,400 lb, complete with pilot, fuel and ammunition – less than the average family car of today – and had a top speed of only 83 mph. Yet its reputation was so frightening that, on 14 January 1916, R.F.C. Headquarters ordered that reconnaissance aircraft were always to be escorted by at least three combat aircraft flying in close formation, and that a mission had to be abandoned if one of the escort became detached.

This began the practice of formation flying that has continued to this day – one of the most

The observer of an R.E.8 about to take off for a reconnaissance mission is handed a box of photographic plates by an air mechanic. The photograph was taken at an R.F.C. airfield near Arras on 22 February 1918.
Imperial War Museum

drastic changes in the history of aerial warfare and all due to one small fighter. It did not save the B.E.2c, which for a considerable period suffered a casualty-rate so high that no other R.F.C. type ever approached it. Being inherently stable, it lacked the manœuvrability to elude the Fokkers. The observer, in the front cockpit, was so surrounded by struts and wires that his gun was virtually useless. These were lessons that the R.F.C. never forgot.

The aircraft that finally outfought the *Eindeckers* were the French Nieuport Baby, with a gun above its upper wing, and the British D.H.2 and F.E.2b pusher fighters. They were followed by machines like the improved Bristol Scout, the first of a long succession of fighters with synchronized guns, and the Sopwith 1½-Strutter, which pioneered a new generation of two-seater fighters. It had been delivered originally to No. 5 Wing of the R.N.A.S. at Coudekerque in April 1916, for both fighter escort and bombing duties, and was intended also for service with No. 3 long-range bombing Wing at Luxeuil. But the R.F.C. found itself so desperately short of aircraft for the impending battle of the Somme that it appealed to the R.N.A.S. for help. The Admiralty agreed to part with large numbers of its invaluable 1½-Strutters, which gave the

Germans a nasty shock when they discovered, to their cost, that it was the first two-seater with a synchronized front gun as well as the observer's gun.

Before long the R.F.C. was following the R.N.A.S. in operating Sopwith Pup fighters; the old policy of flying only Farnborough designs had clearly gone for ever. One result was that the later twin-gun Sopwith Camel became the most successful fighter of the war, with a final count of 1,294 victories. Yet it was smaller, less powerful and slower than most modern light planes, with an engine of only 130 hp and top speed of 115 mph.

In Germany, Peter Strasser's confidence that the Super-Zeppelins of the L30 class would be able to cope with any opposition, provided he could have enough of them quickly, was not shared by all the crew-members. An operational sortie in such an airship could easily last twenty-four or thirty-six hours, in air temperatures as low as 36 degrees below zero in winter; but even flying at 13,000 feet was now no longer good enough. The aeroplane had improved its ability to kill faster than the Airship Service and its suppliers could devise ways to survive.

Five airships were destroyed by fighters based in the United Kingdom between 2 September and

right
The pilot and observer of a
Handley Page twin-engined
heavy bomber, photographed
at an airfield near Cressy,
France, on 25 September
1918.
Imperial War Museum

opposite, top
Two Handley Page O-100
heavy bombers of the Royal
Air Force (formerly
R.N.A.S.) on the airfield at
Dunkirk on 20 April 1918.
Imperial War Museum

opposite, bottom
The scale of 1914–18
bombing may have been
small by modern standards.
It is, none the less, a
sobering thought that this
large collection of 112-lb
bombs was dropped by the
F.E.2bs of No. 149 Squadron,
R.A.F. in just one night in
July 1918.
Imperial War Museum

28 November 1916, and two more fell to Britain's anti-aircraft guns. Four of them were L30 class Zeppelins, with an average of seventeen crew in each. In an endeavour to put themselves out of reach of the fighters, the Airship Service acquired new classes of 'height-climbers' able to reach 18,000 or even 21,000 feet. It was not enough. The latest Allied fighters could outfly them in every way and, firing incendiary ammunition, made life intolerable for the Zeppelin crews.

Only seven airship raids against Britain were made in 1917, and four in 1918. The end came on 5 August 1918, when Peter Strasser himself died in the L70, pride of the Airship Service. The huge size of the 'height-climbers' had made them structurally weak and difficult to handle on the ground; and they had clearly outlived their usefulness.

The eighty-eight Zeppelins built during the war had made fifty-one raids on Britain, dropping 5,806 bombs with a total weight of $196\frac{1}{2}$ tons, which killed 557 people, injured 1,358 and caused £1,500,000 worth of damage. More serious, perhaps, was that twelve R.F.C. squadrons and a large force of anti-aircraft guns and searchlights manned by 12,000 personnel were tied down on home defence duties in late 1916, when they would have been very welcome in France.

In contrast, only two Zeppelin raids on Paris were made during the war. To reach the French capital, it was necessary to battle past the entire Allied air forces on the Western Front, and one of the two airships that did attempt to do so was destroyed.

Victory over the Zeppelins did not automatically ensure the safety of those who had learned to fear their attacks; the big bomber was now ready to take over the task of strategic attack. The Voisin 'chicken-coops' had helped to point the way, but the Italians and Russians were the true pace-makers in 1915–16.

Caproni of Milan had built the prototype of a unique three-engined biplane known as the 'Ca 30', with one pusher propeller and two tractor propellers at the front of twin tail booms. When the war came, they developed from it two improved bomber versions, building 164 Ca 32s with 100-hp Fiat A.10 engines in 1915–16, followed by 269 Ca 33s with 150-hp Isotta-Fraschini V4B engines in 1916–18. These fine aircraft laid the foundations of Italy's strategic bombing force and were used by day and night. Their crew of four comprised two pilots, a nose gunner and a rear gunner who stood on a railed platform above the centre engine to man one, two or three machine-guns. These rear gunners were among the unsung heroes of the First World War, as their duty often required them to stand in that position, exposed to the below-zero cold and slipstreams for hours, on mid-winter flights that crossed the Alps twice en route to and from targets in Austria, with the ever-present possibility of attack by enemy fighters.

The big bombers were no easy targets for even a highly experienced fighter pilot. The crews of the Tsar's Squadron of Flying Ships proved this on the Eastern Front in their four-engined Sikorsky Ilya Mourometz bombers. About eighty

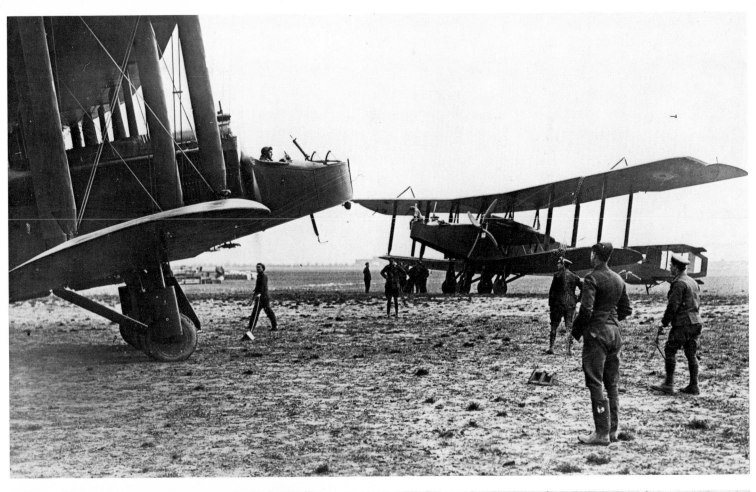

above
First British aeroplane designed especially for day bombing, the D.H.4 was the best aircraft of its type used by any First World War air force. Most production models had a Rolls-Royce Eagle engine of 250 or 375 hp. This gave them a speed of 119–143 mph and, coupled with an armament of three machine-guns, enabled the D.H.4s to outfly and outfight most of the opposition. Two 230-lb or four 112-lb bombs could be carried.

right
This 920-lb bomb was the largest carried by an Ilya Mourometz. Standing between the two officers to the left of the bomb in this photograph is the aircraft's designer, Igor Sikorsky. He left Russia during the Revolution and resumed his aviation activities in the United States, where he became the 'father' of the modern helicopter.
Igor Sikorsky

of these giant aircraft were built, of which half served operationally, the others being used for training. The first multi-engined heavy bombers to serve with any air force, they made some 400 raids in 1914–17, losing only one aircraft to enemy fighters in the process. This was, perhaps, not surprising as each of these 97–101-foot-span aircraft bristled with up to seven machine-guns, in addition to carrying a ton of bombs. Their appearance may have been primitive, but the genius of Igor Sikorsky–the future 'Father of the Helicopter' in America–was shown by the self-sealing fuel-tanks of the Ilya Mourometz and experiments in armour protection for the crews.

Heavy bombers were no new thing, therefore, when Germany began developing twin-engined Gotha and Friedrichshafen aircraft to take over strategic attack from the Zeppelins in 1916–17, with the much larger Staaken 'Giants' to follow. The British habit of referring to all enemy long-range bombers as 'Gothas' in 1917–18 did less than justice to the Staakens, of which about thirty-five were built. All were used operationally, without loss, some in raids over France and the United Kingdom. The R.VI version spanned $138\frac{1}{2}$ feet, weighed $11\frac{1}{2}$ tons, and could fly for seven to ten hours with a crew of seven. It had four defensive gun positions and internal stowage for eighteen 220-lb bombs. Its power plant comprised

four 240-hp Maybach or 260-hp Mercedes engines in tandem pairs.

In the west, the unit responsible for bomber attacks on England was Bombengeschwader 3, based on two airfields in Belgium. Its thirty Gotha G IVs were each powered by two 260-hp Mercedes engines, enabling them to fly at 15,000 feet when carrying six 110-lb bombs. At such a height, and in the absence of an air-raid early-warning system, they could reach their target, spend time dropping their bombs, and be on their way home before defending fighters could climb to attack them.

The first attacks mounted by the Gothas did not penetrate as far as London. Shorncliffe and Folkestone bore the brunt of the bombing on 25 May 1917, when twenty-one aircraft succeeded in killing ninety-five people and injuring 195 more. Seeing the raiders escape, apparently unscathed, produced severe criticism of Britain's defences, and the morale of the public was badly jolted by the thought that further attacks were inevitable. R.N.A.S. and R.F.C. pilots did their best to intercept the enemy from home bases and from Dunkirk. Not until after the war was it learned that one Gotha had been lost over the Channel and another had crashed in Belgium on its return flight.

The second raid, on 5 June, was made by

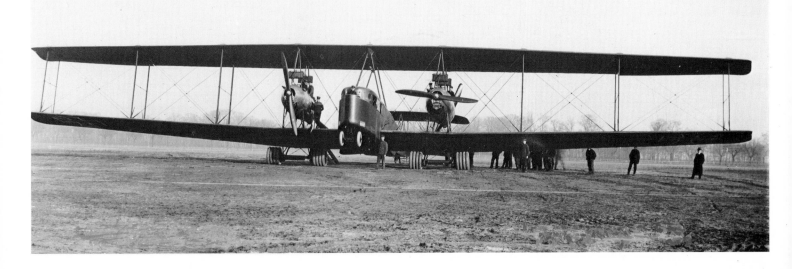

Known affectionately as the 'Harry Tate', after a contemporary music-hall artist, the Factory-designed R.E.8 replaced the B.E.2 as the standard British reconnaissance, artillery-spotting and infantry-contact patrol aircraft in the latter part of the war. Maximum speed with a 150-hp R.A.F. 4a engine was only 103 mph, but the R.E.8 could remain airborne for 4¼ hours.

This famous photograph of the Albatros D.IIIs of the Richthofen 'Jasta' was taken from the pocket of a dead member of the squadron. April 1917 was the heyday of these 'Vee-strutters'. They soon met their match in the Sopwith Triplane and Spad VII, and subsequently were completely outclassed by the Camel and S.E.5.

twenty-two bombers against Shoeburyness and Sheerness. One was shot down by anti-aircraft guns.

London's turn came on 13 June, when fourteen Gothas from an initial force of eighteen flew over the capital in broad daylight, in perfect formation, dropping seventy-two bombs around Liverpool Street Station and smaller numbers elsewhere. In terms of casualties – 162 dead, 432 injured – it was to prove the worst raid of the war; but nobody knew that at the time, and there was a public outcry when all the Gothas escaped, although ninety-two British pilots had taken off in pursuit.

There was only one more daylight raid on the capital, on 7 July, followed by three directed against other targets in south-east England. By then the defences had become so well organized that Bombengeschwader 3 had to seek the cover of darkness for its operations. Between 2 September and the end of that year, it mounted fifteen night raids, of which nine penetrated to London. The German crews had every right to feel safer, as it had always been considered too hazardous to fly single-seater fighters at night. When the assault continued into 1918, two pilots of No. 44 Squadron, flying Camels, eliminated this feeling of security from enemy minds by shooting down

America's most successful fighter pilot of the First World War was Captain 'Eddie' Rickenbacker, who was credited with twenty-six victories. He is seen here with one of the 'Hat-in-the-Ring' Spad XIIIs of the 94th Aero Squadron, with which he served throughout his eight months of combat flying.
U.S. Air Force

a Gotha in flames. Within four months, on the night of 19–20 May, the defences were able to claim seven of the forty-three aircraft dispatched against London and Dover.

The Germans had had enough. Aeroplane raids on Britain ceased from that moment. The Zeppelins were withdrawn after the disastrous night of 5 August, and an official statement was issued by the German High Command to the effect that all bombing of London and Paris was to be stopped 'for military and political reasons'. If the politicians supposed that their act, resulting from the defeat of both their airships and their bombers, would persuade their enemies to follow suit, they were sadly mistaken.

Aeroplane attacks on Britain had killed 857 persons, injured 2,058 and caused nearly £1,500,000 worth of damage–a great deal of money in 1918–for the expenditure of 2,772 bombs weighing a total of 196 tons. The public were aware that Handley Page had responded to Murray Sueter's request for a 'bloody paralyser' by producing a twin-engined bomber known as the 'O-100' which was even better than the Gotha. They could not yet know that the still more mighty, four-engined Handley Page V-1500 was under development to attack Berlin and German industrial targets from bases in Britain. If they had, they would certainly have approved.

Public and Parliamentary disquiet led to a reorganization of Britain's air forces and aircraft supply system that was to be a model for others to follow. An Air Ministry was established, and on 1 April 1918 the R.F.C. and R.N.A.S. were merged into the Royal Air Force, the world's first major air service that was independent of and co-equal with the Army and Navy. The Royal Aircraft Factory was renamed the Royal Aircraft Establishment to avoid confusion of initials with the new service. Henceforth, its task was to provide a centre for advanced research on behalf of the private firms who would be responsible for both aeroplane design and manufacture.

To satisfy the general wish for reprisals against Germany, and to test the claim that bombing might have a major influence on the outcome of the war, an Independent Force was formed within the R.A.F., on 6 June, with the sole task of mounting a sustained strategic attack. The officer chosen to lead this Force was General Hugh (later Marshal of the Royal Air Force, Viscount) Trenchard, who had earlier commanded the entire R.F.C. on active service in France.

The nucleus of the Independent Force was the squadrons of the former 41st Wing, VIII Brigade, which had carried out a non-stop series of 142 attacks on German military centres between 24 and 25 October 1917 and on 5 June 1918. In doing so, it had inherited the earlier ideas of the R.N.A.S., and it was no coincidence that its 'heavy' element comprised No. 16 Naval Squadron, equipped with Handley Page O-100s. The capability of these big bombers had been evident since 25 April 1917, when four of them had spotted a similar number of German destroyers at sea off Ostend and had promptly sunk one of the ships. One of the O-100s was itself lost to enemy fighters, resulting in a decision to use the 'heavies' thereafter only at night.

Trenchard had four squadrons of O-100s and improved O-400s in the Independent Force, with one squadron of F.E.2b pusher night bombers, one of D.H.4 day bombers, two of D.H.9 day bombers, and one of D.H.9As, plus a squadron of Camels to escort and protect the D.H.9s. This was necessary because the D.H.9, intended as a replacement for the superb D.H.4, proved vastly inferior to its predecessor.

If anyone doubted this fact, an unescorted mission by twelve D.H.9s of No. 99 Squadron on 31 July should have convinced him. The intention was to bomb Mainz; after three aircraft had turned back with the all-too-familiar engine

right
This replica of the blood-red Fokker Dr.I triplane which had been von Richthofen's favourite mount was exhibited in Berlin in 1936. He was flying the original Dr.I when killed on 21 April 1918, after claiming eighty victories in air combat.

below
Remembered chiefly as Adolf Hitler's Air Minister, Hermann Goering was a successor to von Richthofen as leader of Jagdgeschwader No. 1 in 1918, and was credited with twenty-two victories. He is shown here in his all-white Fokker D.VII.
Chaz Bowyer

trouble, the others were pounced upon by forty enemy fighters and it was decided to try to battle through to the alternative target at Saarbrücken. Four D.H.9s were destroyed before they could drop their bombs; three more were lost on the return journey. The remaining two survived only through the intervention of two formations of D.H.9s from No. 104 Squadron.

Even the big Handley Pages, operating at night, did not have an easy time. Up to the end of August 1918, there were never enough of them to permit the use of more than ten on any night. At last, following the formation of additional squadrons, the Independent Force was able to dispatch forty, from Nos. 97, 100, 215 and 216

Squadrons, to hammer six targets on the night of 14–15 September. Nine turned back with engine trouble; one forced-landed in the British front lines; three were lost. In the last five months of the war eighteen were recorded as missing and fifty-one were wrecked. Those that got through to their targets were dropping bombs weighing 1,650 lb – the heaviest bombs of the First World War.

With such crippling losses experienced by the pick of the R.A.F.'s bomber crews, who were well trained in the art of mutual protection by cross-fire in formation, it is easy to imagine what a rough time the British reconnaissance and artillery-spotting pilots had, even after the early defenceless types like the B.E.2c had given way to the sturdy R.E.8 with front and rear guns. In *British Aeroplanes 1914–18*, J M Bruce comments: 'Those who flew in France during the years 1917 and 1918 are not likely to forget the seemingly ever-present R.E.8, flying its stolid, elliptical course, and trailing a wake of anti-aircraft shell-bursts behind it.' When the shell-bursts stopped was time to worry, as this usually indicated the arrival of enemy fighters.

Air superiority had been gained and lost repeatedly by both sides since the Fokker *Eindecker* days. For the Allies, April 1917 had been the grimmest month of the war, and was well named 'Bloody April'. To carry out a planned major air offensive five days before the infantry began the battle of Arras, twenty-five R.F.C. squadrons, with 365 serviceable aircraft, a third of them single-seater fighters, were concentrated along the front held by the First and Third Armies. The opposing German Sixth Army could count on only 195 aeroplanes, but nearly half of

Such is the aura of excitement and adventure surrounding the fighters of the First World War that they are favourite subjects for modern enthusiasts who build and fly their own aircraft. The replicas illustrated on this page are faithful reproductions of a Fokker Triplane (*top*), as flown by Germany's 'Red Baron', Manfred von Richthofen, and a Sopwith Pup (*bottom*), often claimed to be the finest flying machine ever produced. *James Gilbert*

these were equipped for fighting and their pilots included Germany's leading aces.

In the first five days of the air offensive, the R.F.C. lost seventy-five aircraft and 105 aircrew, with a further fifty-six aircraft written off in flying accidents. Inadequate training of the pilots was one explanation. Too many squadrons were flying outdated aircraft, and the new ones fared no better until the pilots who survived learned to use them properly. A typical example is provided by the offensive patrol carried out on 5 April by No. 48 Squadron in the first six Bristol Fighters to reach France. When they encountered five Albatros D.III fighters led by Manfred von Richthofen, the 'Red Baron' himself, their crews tried to fight in the usual two-seater fashion, which involved trying to put the observer in the best position to use his gun. Only two of the Bristols returned to their airfield. Eight more had been lost by 16 April. It was not until pilots began flying the aircraft like a single-seater, using its great strength, manoeuvrability and speed of 123 mph to outfly the enemy and to bring their front gun to bear on him, that the 'Brisfit' became one of the war's great aeroplanes.

Since the days of the Fokker *Eindeckers*, the Germans had been organizing their fighters into ever-larger groups. The Fokkers had been allocated to just three single-seater fighter units (*Kampfeinsitzerkommando*) which sometimes worked together. At the suggestion of Oswald Boelcke, one of their outstanding early aces,

above
Pilots and other personnel of No. 1 Squadron R.A.F., with their S.E.5a fighters, at Clairmarais airfield, near St Omer, France, on 3 July 1918.

left
The crews of observation balloons were the only people provided with parachutes as standard equipment during the First World War, although a few German combat pilots followed their lead. These R.F.C. officers in a Cacqot kite balloon have parachutes of the static-line type (which were pulled open automatically as they jumped) suspended from the sides of the basket.
Imperial War Museum

opposite, top
Carefully restored at the Royal Aircraft Establishment, Farnborough, where it was designed, this S.E.5a still flies regularly at air shows. S.E.5as were flown by many of the great R.F.C. and R.A.F. fighter aces of 1917–18.
Keystone

opposite, bottom
On 2 August 1917 Flight Commander Dunning proves that a Sopwith Pup can be landed on the forward flying-off deck of H.M.S. *Furious*. By Kenneth McDonough.

Manfred von Richthofen (*centre*) with pilots of his *Jagdstaffel.*

they began the creation of thirty-seven special fighter squadrons (*Jagdstaffeln*), each with fourteen aircraft, in the summer of 1916. Each squadron was put under the command of a highly experienced pilot and was equipped with the latest available aircraft. It was these 'Jastas' that created 'Bloody April'. Afterwards, the Germans went to the ultimate stage of concentrating these experienced units into fighter wings (*Jagdgeschwaden*), each consisting of four 'Jastas'. Jagdgeschwader 1 was led by von Richthofen, whose pilots painted their Albatros D.IIIs in such garish colours that it was soon known to the Allies as 'Richthofen's Flying Circus'. Its tremendous offensive power swamped the Allies for a time, enabling its leader to become the war's top-scoring pilot, with eighty victories to his credit.

When the Allied air forces re-equipped with Bristol Fighters, Camels, S.E.5s and French SPAD XIIIs, the Circuses met their match. This was the era of the great dogfights, and when the first combat squadrons of the U.S. Air Service began to fly into action, side-by-side with the weary French and British air forces, in April 1918, it gave a tremendous boost to the spirit of the Allies. The aircraft flown by the Americans were mostly French Nieuport 28 and SPAD XIII fighters and Breguet 14B2 and D.H.4 bombers, as the Americans had no aircraft of their own design for combat service; but the pilots were fresh and eager to get into action.

The Chief of the U.S. Air Service, General Mason M Patrick, organized all American units on the Western Front into the Air Service, First Army in August 1918, and placed them under the command of General William Mitchell. To-

gether with certain French units, they were divided into pursuit, bombardment and observation wings. Before long, Mitchell found himself with forty-nine squadrons, half of them American, with a French aerial division of more than forty squadrons also under his control, and nine bombing squadrons of the R.A.F. Independent Force ready to cooperate with him.

Never before had nearly 1,500 combat aircraft been available for a single operation. Mitchell flung them against the Germans during the battle for the Saint-Mihiel salient, which had been a thorn in the side of the French Army for years. Two thirds of the force was used for offensive operations, often far behind the enemy lines. The remaining one third was committed to direct support of the Army on the ground, shooting down the enemy observation balloons and strafing (machine-gunning) and bombing everything that moved in the enemy lines. This form of low-level attack on the trenches was exciting and hazardous—just right for the brash new boys from 'over there'. They became old with experience in days, and learned why Sopwith had taken the trouble to experiment with downward-firing guns on Camels, and had put into production the spritely Salamander with solid slabs of armour-plate round and beneath the cockpit.

Such tactics overwhelmed the German Air Service, although it still fought well in aircraft like the Fokker D VII, its best fighter of the war. Von Richthofen was dead. So, to be honest, were most of the great aces of both sides. It was not the kind of war in which fighting man survived for long. Yet neither side won a final, clear-cut victory in the air over the Western Front.

Sand and Sea

Aircraft operated virtually everywhere that ground forces engaged in battle in the First World War. When conditions and circumstances called for machines able to operate from water, or where places were so situated that the best approach was from the sea, naval air units often provided the necessary support. In doing so, they evolved concepts of aircraft-carrier warfare that were to have immense future significance.

One of the main overseas theatres of war was in the Middle East, where the entry of Turkey into the war as an ally of Germany, in November 1914, posed a threat to the vital lifeline of the Suez Canal, half-way between Britain and India and on the shortest route to Australia and New Zealand. In southern Europe, Italy engaged the forces of Austria-Hungary from May 1915 and, as noted earlier, became a pioneer of strategic bombing with multi-engined aircraft in the process. Other campaigns took the air services of the combatants as far afield as South West and East Africa, and the wild North West Frontier of India.

Aircrews learned to battle with turbulent air over Palestine and monsoons in East Africa. Ground crews learned to cope with dust and sand which choked aircraft engines, caused radiators to boil over, warped wooden spars and split propellers. When the heat became so great that tyres burst, grounding every aeroplane, they learned to adapt the inner tubes of Ford motor-car tyres to get their charges back into action.

The superiority of metal construction in hot climates was quickly appreciated, then conveniently forgotten, as wood was easier to fashion and good enough for use in most hot areas. Lessons learned and not forgotten included the value of air power for keeping recalcitrant tribesmen under control in Middle Eastern trouble spots; the potential of air-dropped supplies to sustain a besieged garrison; and the occasional benefit to be derived from the use of decoys, feints, and what would now be termed electronic counter-measures.

Such advanced ideas were far from the minds of most personnel posted to backwaters of the war in 1915. A proportion of them came from other parts of the British Empire, such as Australia and South Africa, and represented the nuclei of what were to grow eventually into large and well-equipped independent air forces in those countries.

Thus the air component which arrived at Walvis Bay on 30 April 1915, to support the Union Expeditionary Force in its campaign against German South West Africa, was based on a South African Aviation Unit manned by officers formerly attached to the R.F.C. in France. To ensure equipment serviceability in a hot climate, twelve all-steel Henry Farman biplanes had been ordered from Paris; but only three had been delivered by the time the Unit sailed from the United Kingdom; so the Admiralty supplemented them with two B.E.2cs.

Backed up by an armoured-car detachment of the R.N.A.S., the aircraft played an important part in the brief campaign, covering as much as 270 miles on individual reconnaissance sorties in terrain offering no emergency landing grounds, and making occasional attacks on enemy encampments with 20-lb and 112-lb bombs. By 9 July the Germans had suffered enough and capitulated. The men of the Aviation Unit returned to Britain to form No. 26 (South African) Squadron of the R.F.C.

Meanwhile, on the other side of that continent, it had been decided to see if air power could flush out or destroy the German cruiser *Königsberg*, which had sought refuge in the maze of channels in the Rufiji Delta, German East Africa, after sinking the British light cruiser *Pegasus* off Zanzibar.

Initial reconnaissance sorties to locate the enemy vessel were made in November–December 1914 by a 90-hp Curtiss flying-boat, used previously by a Mr H D Cutler for exhibition flights at Durban. Cutler himself was given a commission in the R.N.A.S., and obtained the information wanted by the Royal Navy before an engine failure led to his being taken prisoner by the Germans.

Pending the arrival of two shallow-draught monitors, with which to sink the *Königsberg*, the R.N.A.S. sent out a pair of Sopwith seaplanes with 100-hp Gnome engines to keep track of the ship should it change its hiding-place. When they

One of the Sopwith Type 807 seaplanes sent to Niororo Island in January 1915 to bomb the German cruiser *Königsberg*. Even after the cowling over its 100-hp Gnome engine had been removed, to improve cooling, it was incapable of leaving the water with any part of its normal load of two 50-lb and four 16-lb bombs. As the airframes were also damaged by the heat, the Sopwiths were replaced by two ancient Shorts which could at least lift cameras to photograph the *Königsberg*.

proved entirely useless for operations in the tropics, they were followed by two ancient Shorts. One of these took photographs of the *Königsberg* on 25 April 1915 but, being incapable of climbing above 600 feet, fell victim to rifle-fire on the return journey, force-landed and had to be towed back to its base on Niororo Island.

By the time the monitors *Severn* and *Mersey* arrived, two Henry Farmans and two 80-hp Caudron biplanes had been hauled through the jungle to an airstrip on Mafia Island, so that they could spot for the naval guns. One aircraft of each type was wrecked during practice. The others were airborne for over fifteen hours on 6 July, when the monitors began their battle with the enemy cruiser over a range of 10,000 yards. German gunnery was as good then as in the Second World War, and the *Mersey* was soon forced to withdraw to lick its wounds. By the end of the day, the *Königsberg*, too, had suffered repeated hits, but still struck back.

Battle was rejoined at 12.30 p.m. on the 11th. As one of the aircraft corrected the *Severn*'s fire, it gradually lost height through engine trouble. Suddenly, it was hit by anti-aircraft shrapnel and the pilot decided to glide down as near as possible to the monitors. As the river drew closer, the observer asked by radio for a rescue boat to be launched, and reported that the *Severn*'s fire was now hitting the cruiser forward. The gunners on the monitor made a slight change of deflection. Almost immediately there was a tremendous explosion, followed by fire and a column of smoke rising above their target. The second spotter-plane had little to do after that, as further direct hits and explosions turned the *Königsberg* into a burning wreck. By 2.20 p.m. it was all over.

Two months later, reinforced by two new Caudrons, one flight of the R.N.A.S. squadron that had supported the *Königsberg* action was sent to assist the British forces preparing to invade German East Africa. It was soon joined by No. 26 (South African) Squadron from the United Kingdom, whose personnel found themselves reunited with one of the R.N.A.S. armoured-car sections beside which they had fought in South West Africa. No. 26 retained a few of the all-steel Henry Farmans bought for that campaign, supplemented by B.E.2cs. It provided reconnaissance and close support for the ground forces throughout the campaign, which continued until the German surrender in the autumn of 1917, which brought to an end the Kaiser's dream of gaining a vast empire in Africa.

By this time the R.F.C. and the R.N.A.S. had become efficient in many forms of close support, the brightest new ideas in Army cooperation coming from the long Middle Eastern campaign to the north. Far more mobile than the trench warfare in France, it tested the ingenuity of air and ground crews and logistics staff under harsh conditions, and created what would now be called tactical air forces working closely with their local Army command. Results were impressive, even with the primitive aircraft and aero-engines of the time. These successes foreshadowed the German *Blitzkrieg* tactics of 1940.

The defence of the Suez Canal had been entrusted originally to troops provided by the Indian Government. For air support, they were sent an R.A.F. detachment formed from personnel of the newly established Indian Central Flying School who had been in England in the autumn of 1914. The detachment consisted of four officers and thirty-seven other ranks, and was equipped with three Maurice Farmans and two Henry Farmans. In reserve were two more Maurice Farmans and a B.E.2a, without engines, received from India.

Headquarters of the detachment was at Ismailia, which meant that the slow pusher biplanes had to fly fifty miles before beginning reconnaissance sorties east of Port Said or Suez. They were, however, supplemented by seven French 80-hp Nieuport seaplanes based on the captured cargo steamer *Aenne Rickmers* (now a seaplane-carrier) and placed at the disposal of the British Commander-in-Chief, Egypt.

The anticipated Turkish attack on the Canal, across the desert from Beersheba, began on 3 February 1915. It was beaten off, and was not repeated as both Turkish and British ground forces were soon needed for the desperate fighting at Gallipoli on the other side of the Mediterranean. Sufficient Turks remained in Sinai to require constant surveillance by the air detachment, but combat activity was restricted largely to a bombing raid on a suspected enemy airfield in April. The air detachment was reconstituted as No. 30 Squadron, R.F.C. in August and was eventually transferred to Mesopotamia, its place being taken by Nos. 14 and 17 Squadrons.

To facilitate reconnaissance over Sinai, several advanced landing grounds were cleared, as well as more permanent facilities at Qantara in the

left
Already the hero of pre-war pioneering flights and armoured car exploits in Belgium in the early months of the war, C R Samson found himself on the Aegean island of Tenedos in the spring of 1915. As commander of No. 3 (R.N.A.S.) Squadron, formerly Eastchurch Squadron, he had eighteen aircraft of six types, most of which were unsuitable for the task of supporting operations in the Dardanelles. Only later did more efficient types arrive, like these Nieuport XI scouts, each with a Lewis gun arranged to fire upward through the centre-section of the top wing.
Imperial War Museum

below
First hint of mounting German air superiority in Sinai came in March 1916, when the 300th Squadron of the German Army Air Service arrived at an airfield near Beersheba with fourteen Rumpler CI armed two-seaters.
Imperial War Museum

north and Suez to the south. But the Turks were not the only enemies, and the R.F.C. had to prepare to deal with threats from powerful local rulers in the west and south.

Old quarrels with the Italians in Cyrenaica, which had been exacerbated by Turkey's proclamation of a Holy War against its enemies, had incited the Grand Senussi to attack British positions in the Western Desert and on the coast. Supply dumps laid down in the desert allowed No. 14 Squadron to provide support for the ground forces as they pushed westward to capture Sollum on 14 March; further reconnaissance was carried out by R.N.A.S. seaplanes from the carrier *Ben-my-Chree* sailing off the coast. Detailed knowledge of every move made by the Senussi kept down casualties in the ground fighting, and the campaign virtually ended when armoured cars under the command of Major the Duke of Westminster routed the main body of

D.H.2s, powered by a 100-hp Gnome engine, were the R.F.C.'s first single-seat fighters. Lack of interrupter gear for their forward-firing Vickers gun necessitated a pusher-engine configuration. None the less, their top speed of 93 mph and their manœuvrability enabled them to end the supremacy in France of the Fokker *Eindecker*. Some D.H.2s later took part in the Palestine operations.
Imperial War Museum

the enemy at Bir Azziza, where they had been found by air reconnaissance.

At the same time as these incursions by the Senussi, the Sultan of Darfur had decided to attack the British in the Sudan. General Sir Reginald Wingate, Sirdar of the Egyptian Army and Governor-General of the Sudan, thought it would be advantageous if aircraft could accompany the troops dispatched to deal with this situation, as the enemy could hardly fail to be impressed by a sudden descent from the sky of 'flying chariots' such as they had never seen before. The problem was to keep the 'chariots' flying in temperatures which reached 120 degrees in the shade in May and June, with frequent unpredictable sandstorms rising to 2,000 feet and the knowledge that at least 50 per cent of all petrol would be lost by evaporation.

Wingate was partially correct. Whatever people in Europe thought of the unfortunate B.E.2c at the time of the 'Fokker Scourge', in the Sudan it had a tonic effect on the Sudanese, Egyptians and Arabs who were about to engage the Darfur force. The arrival of the first one was described by Major A J Pott in *People of the Book.* *For the first time the astonished troops saw the beautiful sight of an aeroplane gleaming against a golden sunset as it turned in a downward circle to land on the prepared stretch of ground. The ship of the air brought down the house. 'By God! our General is very clever,' murmured the marvelling soldiery. . . .*

Ali Dinar, Sultan of Darfur, was less impressed. After the B.E.s had dropped small green leaflets (the green of the Prophet) over his followers, explaining that there was no intention of forcing Christianity on them and warning them of the imminent danger of bombing raids, he succeeded in getting a message to Wingate saying that he did not care what the 'iron horses that flew in the air' might do.

It was not easy for them to do anything. The tents in which they were kept at Jebel el Hilla, just inside the Darfur border, had been transported there on the backs of fifty-six camels. The only way the pilots could navigate in the featureless terrain was with the aid of large cloth arrows, laid out on the ground at thirty-mile intervals. They were directed to these arrows by fires lit by local sheikhs, who were informed whenever an aeroplane might be expected in their vicinity.

The British attack began on 15–16 May 1916, the first objective being Bir Melit, sixty-eight miles from the starting-point, where water was said to be available. This was confirmed indirectly when a reconnaissance by Captain Bannatyne was greeted with rifle-fire. His propeller was hit, but this did not prevent his driving the enemy from Melit with machine-gun fire and 20-lb Hales bombs.

On 22 May, a major battle at Beringiya resulted in defeat for Ali Dinar's army. The end came next day, when Second Lieutenant J C (later Marshal of the Royal Air Force Sir John) Slessor first found and then machine-gunned the enemy rearguard of Baggara horsemen, and then bombed the 3,000 men who represented the remnants of the Dervish Army. Ali Dinar himself had a narrow escape, one of the bombs killing a camel he was preparing to mount and two of his servants. The enemy split into small parties, and many perished of thirst in the desert. The Sultan fled, only to die when his pursuers caught up with him on 6 November.

Meanwhile the British defeat and evacuation at Gallipoli had led to a renewed threat to the Suez Canal. In April 1916 the Turks recaptured Qatiya, only twenty-five miles to the east, where the British had established a railhead. They were driven out later the same month; but there had been an ominous new development by then.

Back in March, the pilots of two reconnaissance seaplanes from the *Ben-my-Chree* had been startled to discover the 300th Squadron of the German Army Air Service installed in six hangars on an aerodrome near Beersheba. Its fourteen 160-hp Rumpler CI biplanes had a better all-round performance than the B.E.2c. Even worse, it was not long before they were joined by Fokker single-seater fighters. This heralded the beginning of an eighteen-month period during which the R.F.C. in the Middle East was always outclassed by German tactical superiority, although it outnumbered the enemy, who had to contend with the problems of extended lines of supply. Not until the R.F.C. felt able to spare Bristol Fighters for service in this area, in the autumn of 1917, was it to regain a measure of superiority.

Nevertheless, the second half of 1916 saw a reversal of fortunes on the ground in Sinai. In June, in response to enemy bombing raids on Port Said, eleven B.E.2cs had made an attack on the enemy forward airfield at El Arish, surprising the occupants by flying well out to sea at a height of 7,000 feet and then circling past the air base in order to approach from the south-east at only 600 feet. Three of the attackers were brought down by ground fire, and the raid did not prevent the German aircrew from playing their part in the big battle at Romani at the beginning of August. Six R.F.C. officers were wounded, one fatally, in the air fighting at Romani, which cost the enemy only one aircraft destroyed. However, the achievements of the German airmen were of no help to the Turks. By 9 August they were soundly defeated, and the threat to the Canal was finally removed.

Only seventeen British aircraft had been available for duty at Romani, but they included B.E.2cs from a significant new unit–No. 1 Squadron, Australian Flying Corps–which had replaced No. 17 Squadron, R.F.C. Soon renumbered No. 67 (Australian) Squadron, R.F.C., this unit was the first result of an Army Council suggestion that the Dominions might like to raise complete squadrons for service with the R.F.C., thereby laying the foundations for their own future air forces.

By this time, all R.F.C. detachments in Egypt, Mesopotamia, East Africa and, later, Salonika had been combined in the Middle East Brigade, under Brigadier-General W G H (later Air Chief Marshal Sir Geoffrey) Salmond. As one component of the Brigade, No. 14 Squadron and No. 1 Australian Squadron became the operational units of the Fifth Wing, under Lieutenant-Colonel P B Joubert de la Ferté.

While both sides kept up periodic bombing raids, the British ground forces began moving forward in a long and hard-fought campaign that was to end in Jerusalem. By November 1916 they were more than half-way from the Suez Canal to the Palestine frontier. On 23 December the first ship unloaded supplies at El Arish, which had been occupied without a fight. During the previous day, 13 B.E.2cs had dropped six 100-lb and 120 16- and 20-lb bombs on Turkish encampments at Magdhaba, and this last remaining enemy stronghold in Sinai was taken on the 23rd.

Just over the border in Palestine, the Turks were strongly entrenched at Rafah. When the British Desert Column closed on this position, on 9 January 1917, its commander had an accurate trench map, based on aerial photographs, with the Turkish redoubts clearly numbered to facilitate artillery cooperation. New aircraft had reached Fifth Wing to replace some of the veteran B.E.2cs. While three Martinsydes, escorted by three Bristol Scouts, bombed the aerodrome at Beersheba, to keep the enemy grounded, a constant patrol of two artillery-spotting aircraft was maintained over Rafah.

Of the handful of 80-hp Martinsyde S.1 scouts delivered to operational squadrons, four served in Mesopotamia with No. 30 Squadron, R.F.C. Although their Gnome engines proved quite unsuitable for use in such a hot and dusty environment, one of the scouts distinguished itself on 16 September 1915. Its pilot, Major H L Reilly, brought back such thorough and valuable data from a reconnaissance of the Turkish positions at Es Sinn that General Townshend was able to capture both that place and Kut.

Four of the five ground stations with which they kept in contact by wireless were mounted on sand sleighs, the operators riding on horseback.

By late afternoon Rafah had fallen, but the next step was to prove more difficult and costly. The Turks had turned the coastal town of Gaza into a strongly held outpost and were well supported by German air units, based at Beersheba and Ramleh and re-equipped with Halberstadts and Fokkers. With the Palestine Railway behind their lines as an efficient supply route, they would clearly be difficult to shift.

Fifth Wing was now commanded by Lieutenant-Colonel A E Borton. His two squadrons had a nominal strength of 21 B.E.2cs and B.E.2es, 14 Martinsydes and 7 Bristol Scouts. In fact, only 12 B.E.s and 9 Martinsydes were serviceable on 22 March, a few days before the attack on Gaza was mounted, plus a B.E. flight in Arabia. With this small force, the R.F.C. was expected to provide 1 aeroplane for permanent contact patrol with the Desert Column, 5 for general reconnaissance with the main Eastern Force, 6 for artillery cooperation and 6 for patrol duties. At any sign of the enemy's sending in reinforcements, all aircraft were to switch to offensive action against these troops.

Unhindered reconnaissance by the superior German aircraft, both before the battle began and during the fighting, gave the Turks adequate warning and enabled them to resist all attacks. With only two of the new Halberstadt fighters available at any one time, the enemy air units killed one British pilot and wounded three other aircrew; three more pilots were posted as missing. Two German aircraft were forced down.

'Bloody April' was about to begin for the R.F.C. in France; so Fifth Wing would clearly receive no equipment fit to challenge its opponents. On the ground, the Turks rapidly improved their position, until Gaza had become a strongpoint on a line extending inland twelve miles towards Beersheba.

The second battle of Gaza, on 19–20 April, proved no more successful for the British than had the first. It might have been even more disastrous had not a reconnaissance pilot spotted 2,000 enemy infantry and 800 cavalry massing for a counterattack on the British flank. Four aircraft, each armed with twelve 20-lb bombs, scattered this force before it could do any harm. Another ingenious enemy move which had little effect was an attempt to cut off the British water supply. Landing their aircraft ninety miles behind the British lines, two airmen laid an explosive charge which blew a gap several feet long in the pipe. Taking some of the pieces as souvenirs, they then returned home safely. The damage was repaired within a few hours.

Before the third assault on Gaza was made, there was an important new development in Arabia. The Grand Sherif of Mecca, Hussein Ibu Ali, ruler of Hedjaz and guardian of the Islamic holy cities of Mecca and Medina, had long been a friend of Britain and refused to acknowledge the Turkish Holy War. On 5 June 1916, under his leadership, the Arabs began a revolt that was to end only when the Turks were finally expelled from all their lands. This was the thrilling period of guerrilla warfare in which Colonel T E Lawrence took such a prominent part and which he described later in his masterpiece, *The Seven Pillars of Wisdom*.

Air power played an outstanding role in the initial stages of the revolt. On 7 June the little carrier *Ben-my-Chree* had arrived off Aden, from where her seaplanes were dispatched to bomb Turkish positions in the Lakej Delta. Within a week she had reached Jidda, from where the seaplanes took off to reconnoitre, machine-gun and bomb the local enemy. It had been intended to use the aircraft next day to direct the fire of naval guns that had been pounding the Turks since the 9th; but this proved unnecessary. The enemy surrendered, and it was generally agreed that the air attack had been the clinching factor. Having opened the port to supplies for the rebels in the interior, *Ben-my-Chree* returned to Port Said.

Later, six of the aircraft of No. 14 Squadron were put ashore for reconnaissance duties near Mecca. Unsure of the reaction of local Arabs to the thought of infidels gazing down on their holy city, the R.F.C. felt it prudent to advise the ground crews to work with rifles stacked ready for use. They need not have worried; the Arabs were deeply appreciative of the powerful war-machines that had been sent to their aid.

As autumn approached, most of the Hedjaz was in Arab hands; but the Turks retained control of the railway to Medina and it was feared that this might enable them to mass forces for a drive on Mecca. On 24 November two R.F.C. pilots took off from Sinai on a five-hour, 350-mile round trip in an effort to cut the railway. Captain H R Freeman of No. 14 Squadron dived his B.E.2e towards the railway bridge near Qalat el Hasa, and released his two 100-lb delayed-action bombs from a height of only twenty feet. One bounced off the bridge and exploded beneath it; the other damaged the track. Freeman's colleague, Lieutenant S K Muir of No. 67 Squadron, dropped one 100-lb and four 20-lb bombs near enough to Jurfed Derawish Railway Station to damage it.

Cooperation with the Arabs continued through the winter and on into the spring and summer of the following year. In December 1916 seaplanes from the carrier *Raven II* helped to turn back a strong Turkish foray towards Rabigh and Yenbo. When this ship was relieved by the *Anne* (formerly the *Aenne Rickmers*), seaplane reconnaissance supported a combined Arab-naval force which occupied the port of Wejh on 24 January 1917. The R.N.A.S. then withdrew; but the R.F.C. detachment kept up its reconnaissance activities and attacks on the Hedjaz Railway until its aircraft were wrecked by strong winds

on 16 July. By then, in any case, it had more urgent commitments at Gaza.

Since the second battle, the situation there had been horribly reminiscent of the trench warfare in France. Fifth Wing had been in continuous action and had even received some new aircraft in the shape of B.E.12s and Bristol Monoplanes; but the Germans still dominated the air.

General Sir Edmund Allenby had assumed over-all command in Egypt in June 1917, and at once demanded more air support. When it arrived he established the Palestine Brigade under Salmond, who was to be succeeded by Major-General W S Brancker during the coming battle.

The Brigade had two major components. Fifth (Corps) Wing comprised No. 14 Squadron, operating 16 B.E.2es from the coastal town of Deir el Balah for tactical reconnaissance and artillery spotting, in support of XXI Corps before Gaza; and No. 113 Squadron, providing similar service for XX Corps and the Desert Mounted Corps before Beersheba, with 8 B.E.2es and 5 R.E.8s based inland at Weli Sheikh Nuran. Fortieth (Army) Wing was to devote its energies to strategic reconnaissance and photography, protection of Fifth Wing aircraft from enemy fighters, and disruption of enemy aerial reconnaissance. To do this, No. 111 Squadron at Deir el Balah had a mixed bag of 6 Bristol Fighters, 5 Vickers 'Bullets', 3 D.H.2s, 2 Bristol Monoplanes and 1 Bristol Scout. No. 67 Squadron, at Weli Sheikh Nuran, had 7 B.E.2cs and B.E.2es, 5 R.E.8s, 5 B.E.12as and 1 Martinsyde. Of these types only the Bristol Fighters could match the best enemy machines.

Palestine Brigade also included two sections of No. 21 Balloon Company, with kite balloons, 'X' Aircraft Park at Cairo and an Advanced Aircraft Park at Qantara. Allenby's request for a squadron of D.H.4 bombers and a squadron of S.E.5s and Bristol Fighters was turned down by the War Office, as these modern types were needed on the Italian Front. He was told, none the less, that the Government desired Turkey to be eliminated from the war with a single blow!

The air units did their best to make this possible. By October twenty sheets of a map, based almost entirely on air photographs, showed more than 500 miles of enemy-held territory at a scale of 1:20,000. To update them, new photographs were being taken at the rate of nearly 900 a month, and 21,126 prints were made from negatives during October. For artillery-spotting duty there were fifty-three wireless stations in the field.

Attempts were made to deceive the Turks into believing that the main blow would be directed against Gaza. A staff officer, pretending to be wounded during a contrived brush with enemy cavalry, dropped a bloodstained haversack containing faked notes of a meeting at G.H.Q. concerning such an assault. This worked, but the truth was nearly revealed when a German reconnaissance aircraft eluded British patrols and photographed large troop dispositions opposite Beersheba. Hastening home, the crew had the misfortune to encounter a Bristol Fighter and were soon prisoners.

Any lingering doubts as to where the attack would be made were dispelled on 27 October, when a heavy bombardment of Gaza began, supplemented on the 29th by naval gunfire directed by seaplanes from three carriers. The genuine assault, on Beersheba on the 31st, achieved the hoped-for surprise and was soon over; 2,000 prisoners had been taken. Gaza's turn came on the night of 1–2 November, when the moonlight was so intense that No. 14 Squadron flew through the night, bombing and machine-gunning Turkish batteries.

Day after day the pressure was kept up. Even

Armstrong Whitworth F.K.8 'Big Acks' served with the Palestine Brigade but are better remembered for their exploits in France and Macedonia. On 21 September 1918 the F.K.8s and D.H.9s of No. 47 Squadron, R.A.F. caught the retreating Bulgarian Army in the Kosturino Pass, exacting heavy toll with 5,000 lb of bombs and 1,200 rounds of ammunition. By coincidence this was the day on which the Bristol Fighters of No. 1 Australian Squadron massacred the retreating Turks in the Wadi el Far'a, a valley in Palestine. *Imperial War Museum*

the balloon units played their part, directing artillery fire against sixty-one targets between the 1st and 7th. By the following day the Turks were in full and confused retreat, harried by the entire strength of the R.F.C., which was switched to ground attack with guns and bombs. In their haste to escape, the Germans burned five good aeroplanes on the aerodrome at Iraq el Menshiye, where others had already been destroyed and damaged by bombing.

Inevitably, there were occasional mistakes in which British troops in close contact with the enemy were attacked mistakenly by the R.F.C. But such incidents were thankfully rare; moreover, the Turkish Eighth Army hardly existed any longer. When the Germans fell back with them to an airfield at El Tine, an attack by twenty-two R.F.C. aircraft caused not only widespread destruction but also a temporary panic. Not until Allenby's armies were sweeping on towards Jerusalem did the Turkish Seventh and Eighth Armies recover sufficiently to mount a small counterattack. German aircraft also began to reappear from about 24 November. But it was too late, and on 11 December General Allenby entered Jerusalem by the Jaffa Gate to take possession of a city that had changed hands thirty-four times in a lifetime of 3,000 years.

Mecca and Jerusalem had fallen; Jaffa and Lydda had been occupied; Damascus remained in Turkish hands, and this was no time to call a halt. Re-equipment of No. 111 Squadron with Nieuport Scouts and S.E.5as was soon under way; and these aircraft, together with the Bristol Fighters of No. 67 Squadron (to become No. 1 Squadron, Australian Flying Corps on 6 February 1918), maintained an air superiority that would

not be lost again in Palestine. Ten enemy aircraft were destroyed in twenty-four combats in January 1918, and heavy attacks were made on their airfields.

By this time, Fortieth Wing had been reinforced with the nucleus of No. 142 Squadron, newly formed with B.E.12as (single-seater fighters evolved from the B.E.2c); and a new technique to improve the efficiency of contact flying was evolved. This entailed dropping messages in canvas bags in the usual way, but then picking up replies from a cord stretched between two poles, by means of a weighted hook trailed at the end of aerial wire.

Jericho was occupied on 21 February and on 23 March Allenby's forces crossed the Jordan. His anxiety to do so resulted from a wish to assist Lawrence's Arabs, who had faced increasingly tough resistance since capturing Aqaba in July 1917. Their advance northward up the Hedjaz Railway, with support from the two B.E.2es and one D.H.2 of the independent 'X' Flight, R.F.C., would obviously be made easier if the British could destroy the railway at Amman and so cut off the Turkish forces that had been diverted southward to stop the Arab advance.

Repeated attempts to capture Amman and Es Salt had failed, and on 2 April Allenby recalled his exhausted troops across the Jordan. It was the only setback they had suffered since the second battle of Gaza, and it came at the worst possible moment. The news from France was grim, as the final German offensive was going well at this stage. The Turks could also gain confidence from the fact that their newly appointed Commander-in-Chief, the German General der Kavallerie Limon von Sanders, had

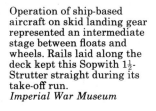

Operation of ship-based aircraft on skid landing gear represented an intermediate stage between floats and wheels. Rails laid along the deck kept this Sopwith 1½-Strutter straight during its take-off run.
Imperial War Museum

started so successfully. Allenby's gloom was heightened when many of his best and most experienced troops were transferred to France and replaced with Indian units. Nor was the situation improved by a further abortive move against Es Salt, with strong air support, on 30 April.

A combination of bad weather and the demands for increasing numbers of men to pour into the insatiable war machine in France produced a few months of relative inactivity. An enemy attack, mainly by German troops, was repelled in the Jordan Valley on 14 July. Next month Allenby sent two companies of the Camel Brigade to capture Mudanwara Station, which was too strongly defended for the Arabs to deal with. All the time, he was planning the big blow that would end forever the Turkish hold on Palestine.

In France, the Germans' great offensive had failed, and they were stubbornly installed behind the 'granite wall' of the Hindenburg Line, hoping to break the tide of Allied attack. Aircraft could now be spared in small numbers for Allenby, and when he struck with all his might on a narrow front, on 19 September, Palestine Brigade comprised seven aeroplane squadrons and three sections of balloons. Two of the Corps squadrons had R.E.8s, supported by Nieuport fighters which, in the absence of enemy aircraft, operated as 'runners' with urgent reconnaissance data during the battle. The third had Armstrong Whitworth F.K.8s and one flight of R.E.8s. The Army Wing was strong enough to cope with anything the enemy could put into the air, with two squadrons of S.E.5as, one of D.H.9s and one of Bristol Fighters, supplemented by a single Handley Page 0-400 that had made a surprise but welcome appearance at the end of July.

Lawrence told later in *The Seven Pillars of Wisdom* of the effect that the first sight of this aircraft had on Sherif Feisal's Arabs:

At Um el Surab, the Handley stood majestic on the grass, with Bristols and 9A like fledglings beneath its spread of wings. Round it admired the Arabs, saying: 'Indeed, and at last, they have sent us THE aeroplane, of which these things were foals.' Before night, rumours of Feisal's resource went over Jabal Druse and the hollow of Hauran, telling people that the balance was weighed on our side.

Once more, and not for the last time, the effect of clearly evident air power on morale was as important as the military results it achieved – not that the results themselves were insignificant. Throughout the time of preparation for the offensive, the Bristol Fighters of the Australian Squadron, in particular, denied the skies to the enemy. In a single week in June, the Germans had crossed the British lines one hundred times. During the last week of August, they broke through the fighter screen only eighteen times. A total of four flights reached their objectives in the next three weeks. General von Sanders noted, despondently:

Two consignments of aeroplanes sent out as replacements proved, almost without exception, to be useless. Owing to the urgent needs of the German Western Front further replacements were out of the question. Between the spring and the autumn the excellent air service lost 59 pilots and observers. In September air reconnaissances of the British positions had almost ceased. Immediately a German aeroplane put in an appearance it would be attacked by such superior

By placing wheeled trolleys under their floats, it was possible to fly seaplanes from the decks of early carriers. Previously it had been necessary to lower such aircraft into the water for take-off, leading to wrecked floats when the sea was rough. This Fairey IIID was still using the technique to fly from H.M.S. *Argus* as late as August 1922.
Ministry of Defence

British formations that air reconnaissance was impossible.

In the face of such air supremacy, what followed was predictable, even though an Indian deserter warned the enemy that the main attack would be made against the Turkish Eighth Army in the coastal area. General von Sanders preferred to believe Intelligence reports that had been generated by British deception and decoys.

On 19 September the bombers of Palestine Brigade concentrated their attacks against enemy communications and headquarters, beginning with sixteen 112-lb bombs dropped by the Handley Page on the central telephone exchange of the Army Group. The pilot of the Handley Page on this sortie was Captain Ross Smith, who was to make the first flight between the United Kingdom and Australia, with his brother, in a Vickers Vimy in November–December 1919. Not until noon did von Sanders learn that the Eighth Army front was already broken, and that the Seventh Army in the centre was being hard pressed.

No German pilot took off that day from the main aerodrome at Jenin. Nos. 111 and 145 Squadrons kept standing patrols of two S.E.5as over the field from dawn to dusk, and the slightest sign of movement provoked an attack with 20-lb bombs. Worse was to come.

Before the offensive was launched, every possible line of retreat available to the enemy had been photographed in detail. Maps now showed the best points at which to drop bombs in defiles, in order to block them with damaged guns and vehicles, thus bottling up the Turkish troops so that they could be strafed without hope of escape. Bristol Fighters of No. 1 Australian Squadron circled over these points, ready to call in an attack by radio as soon as the targets presented themselves.

What eventually transpired made some of the pilots sick, as a rout turned to a massacre. Many of the Turks had been involved in the earlier panic after the Gaza battle. This was far worse, with no escape from the bombs and machine-gun fire; every way was blocked with smashed equipment and dead and dying men. Lorry drivers leaped frantically from their cabs, leaving the vehicles to carry their helpless passengers over the edge into the ravine below. The Turkish Seventh and Eighth Armies were eliminated. Never had the weapon of air power been wielded with more terrible results.

It was now the turn of the relatively unscathed Fourth Army on the eastern side of the Jordan. Ordered to withdraw, it was harried by a British force under Major-General Chaytor, and by the Arabs, whose long campaign up the Hedjaz Railway was about to reap its reward.

A dawn reconnaissance by No. 1 Squadron, R.F.C. on 23 September brought the Bristol Fighters, D.H.9s and S.E.5as homing in like wasps round a honey-pot. This time there were no defiles to trap the enemy; but neither was there much cover. In one day 6¼ tons of bombs were dropped and more than 33,000 rounds of ammunition were fired. Amman fell, and when a message was dropped to the Turks in Ziza, explaining that they were cut off from all water, they surrendered, bringing Chaytor's haul of prisoners to 10,322. By one of those strange quirks of war, the night after the surrender saw fully armed Turks and Britons shoulder-to-shoulder, ready to ward off the hordes of Bedouin horsemen who stood against the skyline, waiting to pounce upon the supposedly disarmed enemy for loot,

The remains of a Turkish Army column trapped in the Wadi el Far'a by massed squadrons of the Palestine Brigade, spearheaded by No. 1 Australian Squadron, on 21 September 1918.
Imperial War Museum

Sopwith Camel fighter tied down on a flying-off platform mounted over the forward gun turret of a light cruiser. By the end of the First World War more than 100 aircraft had been allotted for operation from ships of the Grand Fleet. Every battleship and battle-cruiser was entitled to one single-fighter and one two-seater. *Imperial War Museum*

especially guns and ammunition.

Damascus was entered by the Desert Mounted Corps and the Arabs on 1 October. The Indian 7th Division reached Beirut on the 8th. Aleppo fell to the Arabs on the 25th. An armistice on the 31st marked the completion of Allenby's task.

So much of what the air forces had done since the first battles for the Suez Canal, in 1915, was new to air warfare, and of the greatest significance for the future, that the progress of the campaign had to be traced in detail in this book. The experience gained was put to good effect on other fronts; but every theatre posed its own particular problems, demanding ingenuity and courage from the aircrews and ground crews.

Although it could not be appreciated at the time, operations in Mesopotamia were to have a special significance. Four years after the war ended, when the very name 'Mespot' was forgotten in favour of 'Iraq', this was to be the place in which air power would prove its ability to keep the peace as well as to win wars.

Peace was still so far away as to be unimaginable when in May 1915 two Maurice Farmans from Egypt arrived at Basra. They were the first equipment of a detachment manned by personnel from Australia, England, India and New Zealand. Workshops and stores were housed on board one river steamer and two barges.

The basic purpose of operations by the original Indian Expeditionary Force in Mesopotamia was to keep the Turks away from the installations of the Anglo-Persian Oil Company at Abadan in Persia, to the south. The best way of ensuring this was to drive them as far north as possible, from Basra to Baghdad and even Mosul. The only route lay along the River Tigris, by which Baghdad was some 500 miles from Basra via Qurna (legendary site of the Garden of Eden) and Kut al Imara.

Basra had been occupied on 22 November 1914. The small flying detachment completed its first reconnaissance during the battle of Qurna on 31 May, informing the Army Commander, by means of a message dropped into the river in a tin can with a streamer attached, that the Turks were retreating north. After locating the enemy at Kut al Imara, well over half-way to Baghdad, the unit was recalled to Basra and supplemented with two Caudrons.

The 80-hp Gnome rotary engines of these aircraft were unreliable in the extreme heat and dusty atmosphere of Mesopotamia. Both Caudrons made forced landings on their way back to base after the battle of Nasinya, on 24–25 July. One got home; the other was attacked by Arabs. The two officers, armed only with revolvers, kept the marauders at bay as long as possible, killing and wounding several before they were overwhelmed. A few days later, a search party found the Caudron hacked to pieces, but no sign of the crew. After this incident, long flights were forbidden until more reliable aircraft arrived.

When No. 30 Squadron, R.F.C. was formed in Egypt in August, the Mesopotamian detachment was designated one of its Flights. Reinforced with four 80-hp Martinsyde Scouts, it worked in partnership with three Short seaplanes of the R.N.A.S. (converted to landplanes), spotting for artillery, and supporting the ground forces as they battled against both sickness and the Turks, driving the latter first from Es Sinn and then from Kut.

Soon No. 30's other Flights arrived from Egypt; but at this stage its fortune slumped even more. One of the strange tasks that the slow go-anywhere aeroplanes of 1915 could perform was that of setting down their crew near telephone lines, so that they could cut the wires. While cutting wires near Baghdad, the crew of a Maurice Farman were taken prisoner. The other Farman had already been wrecked, and the surviving Caudron was shot down by rifle-fire on 16 September. Four B.E.2cs arrived to restore No. 30's strength, but both Martinsydes were lost soon afterwards.

Had the pilot of one of the Martinsydes escaped

capture, his report would have warned Major-General Townshend, commanding the ground forces, that large enemy reinforcements were moving up. The officer who did get back from the same mission was insufficiently trained to realize the significance of what he had seen; so Townshend soon found himself besieged in Kut, with 13,840 British and Indian troops and followers, members of No. 30 Squadron, and three unserviceable aircraft.

The defenders beat off several fierce attacks, after which the Turks decided to starve them into submission. The column sent to relieve Kut failed to get through, and it was decided finally that the only possible way of helping the besieged troops to survive was by organizing the first airlift of supplies in history.

Since the start of the siege, various small packages of medical supplies, wireless parts, spares for the engines of launches, mail, newspapers and money had been dropped into the town by aircraft making reconnaissance flights. At the request of General Townshend, a 70-lb millstone had been parachuted to him on 27 March 1916; but the repeated delivery of sufficient food and supplies to keep such a large force alive and fit was another matter. Nor was it made easier by the fact that the enemy now had the support of three Fokker Monoplanes and an Aviatik biplane.

The R.F.C. and R.N.A.S. units had between them the eight B.E.2cs of No. 30 Squadron, one Voisin biplane, one all-steel Henry Farman and four Short seaplanes. Of these it was decided to allocate four B.E.s, the naval Voisin and Farman, and three of the Shorts to the airlift.

From the airfield at Ora to Kut was 23½ miles. By removing bomb gear from the aircraft, it was

Lieutenant S D Culley's Camel, here taking off from its lighter, is today a treasured exhibit in the Imperial War Museum in London. When it destroyed Zeppelin L53, Rear-Admiral Tyrwhitt made the signal: 'Flag–general: your attention is called to Hymn No. 224, verse 7.' Reference to *Hymns Ancient and Modern* decoded the signal to mean:

*O happy band of pilgrims,
Look upward to the skies,
Where such a light affliction
Shall win so great a prize.*

reckoned that each landplane could carry 150–200 lb of food, and each of the seaplanes 200–250 lb, provided they were flown as single-seaters. Despite the threat from the Fokkers, there was no possibility of carrying armament, except for the pilot's personal revolver.

The Voisin and Farman hauled their loads beneath their fuselage, with the food tightly packed in one sack inside a larger one, which retained the contents when the inner sack burst on reaching the ground.

The B.E.2c, because of its inherent stability, was more of a problem. Eventually, it was found to be flyable with a 50-lb sack laid on each lower wing, against the fuselage, and with two 25-lb bags slung over a long bar between its under-carriage struts. This bar was held by release gear at one end, and was pivoted to permit dumping of the load at the opportune moment. The drag of the sacks alone made the B.E.s difficult to fly. With enemy *Eindeckers* based in the area, the operation was almost suicidal.

Townshend had asked originally for 5,000 lb of flour, sugar, chocolate, salt and *ghi* (clarified butter used in India for cooking) to be dropped into Kut every day–sufficient to provide a 6-ounce ration for each of his men and the 3,700 Arabs in the town. He had enough horse meat to last until 29 April. The airlift delivered a total of 19,000 lb between the 15th and 29th, the best day being the first, when 3,350 lb were delivered.

To make up the difference, an attempt was made on the evening of the 24th to take 270 tons of supplies into Kut on the *Julnar*, one of the fastest steamers on the Tigris. But the Turks had stretched a chain across the river, which fouled her propeller, and she was captured. On that day, too, the Fokkers intervened for the first time, necessitating an armed escort, which reduced the number of aircraft available for supply-carrying. Two days later a seaplane was shot down and the pilot of a B.E. was wounded. In an effort to strengthen the unit, three Maurice Farmans, newly arrived from Britain, were flown to Ora, only to be wrecked by strong winds on 2 May.

By then Townshend had surrendered. Of forty-four R.F.C. personnel who marched with his soldiers to captivity in Anatolia, 700 miles away, six are thought to have survived.

As in Palestine, the prime lesson taught by this campaign was the vital necessity for air superiority. When the offensive was renewed in greater strength, Baghdad was taken on 11 March 1917. By 2 April British troops had linked up with the Russians advancing through Persia. Even then, Mosul was not occupied until 3 November 1918, by which time it had been necessary to send S.E.5as, Camels, Bristol Mono-planes and R.E.8s to this outlandish area, in place of the tired old second-hand pushers once considered good enough.

Armament and equipment were also improved progressively throughout the war. By 1918 two

The need for folding wings on carrier-based aircraft was emphasized by the difficulty of moving even the tiny Sopwith Pup into and out of the below-deck hangar of H.M.S. *Furious* without them.
Imperial War Museum

synchronized machine-guns were standard on all single-seater fighters; many two-seaters had twin guns on a smoothly traversing ring in the rear cockpit. The Bristol Fighters which shot down two Gothas on the night of 19–20 May 1918 had illuminated gunsights; those of No. 22 Squadron, R.F.C. began using wireless experi-mentally for air-to-air communication in combat in mid-1918. Enthusiasm for the new device was lessened by the need for 45 lb of equipment in the already crowded cockpits, earphones which became painful above 15,000 feet, the required 120 feet of trailing aerial with a $2\frac{1}{2}$-lb weight on the end, and the knowledge that the Germans had offered a reward of two weeks' leave to any pilot who succeeded in shooting down a Bristol so equipped, enabling the 'secret weapon' to be studied.

In fact, it was not a particularly useful 'weapon'. The real requirement was for ground-to-air wireless, enabling fighters to be directed towards their targets, but this was still in the future. So was the general use of wireless, or radio as it soon became known, for deception and counter-measures–although one incident of this

kind was reported from Salonika.

While spotting for Allied artillery, an R.F.C. observer noticed ground strips laid out on the enemy side of the lines. Guessing their intention, he proceeded to transmit signals in German with his wireless. A well-concealed hostile battery at once opened fire, enabling the British observer to locate its position and direct his own artillery on to it.

More than half a century after these events, target location and designation are still primary duties of military aircraft, although the subsequent bombardment is more likely to be by heavily armed ground attack fighters than by artillery. One thing that has not changed since the First World War, as becomes evident throughout this book, is that there are few campaigns which cannot be conducted more effectively with the support of ship-based aircraft.

The story of how seaborne air power progressed from the pioneering of Eugene Ely and Glenn Curtiss to the entry into naval service of aircraft-carriers that were ranked as capital ships is traced largely through the history of the Royal Naval Air Service and the inter-war seagoing units of the Royal Air Force and Fleet Air Arm. For much of this time the stage was dominated by Charles Rumney Samson, who was concerned with the earliest take-offs from ships of the Royal Navy and with the first operations by strategic bombers and armoured cars in Belgium in 1914.

So far as the First World War at sea was concerned, the primary tasks of the R.N.A.S. were to provide reconnaissance and gunnery observation for the Fleet; to search for and attack enemy ships, especially submarines; and to protect the Fleet from surveillance and attack by enemy aircraft, especially Zeppelins. To carry out these commitments, it needed aircraft that could be carried on board ship and aircraft which could make long over-water patrols from coastal bases.

Profiting from the pre-war experiments by Samson, it made a start on meeting the first of those needs by taking over the cross-Channel steamers *Empress*, *Engadine* and *Riviera* as soon as war broke out, and adapting each of them to carry four seaplanes. The old cruiser H.M.S. *Hermes*, used in makeshift form for early seaplane-operating trials, was refitted to carry three seaplanes and recommissioned in October 1914, but did not last long. On her way back to Dover on the 31st of that month, after taking R.N.A.S. personnel to Dunkirk, she was torpedoed and sunk by a submarine.

Useful though the three small ships were, the Navy needed a larger ocean-going ship for service with the Grand Fleet. In September 1914 the Admiralty acquired the former Cunard liner *Campania*, of 20,000 tons. A 120-foot flight deck was fitted above the forecastle and she was commissioned in May 1915 as a carrier for ten or eleven seaplanes. The great advantage she offered over her predecessors was that the seaplanes no longer had to be put over the side for take-off. Instead, wheeled trolleys could be placed under their floats, enabling the seaplanes to fly from the wooden foredeck. As they became airborne, the trolleys dropped away. The chief problem still to be solved was that seaplanes still had to land on the water at the end of a flight for retrieval by crane.

Meanwhile, the small carriers had struck their first blow at the Zeppelin fleet, which was the main target of the R.N.A.S. in 1914. The raid by

Marix and Spenser Grey from Antwerp had been followed on 21 November by a daring attack on the Zeppelin works at Friedrichshafen by Squadron Commander E F Briggs, Flight Commander J T Babington and Flight Lieutenant S V Sippe of the R.N.A.S., flying Avro 504 biplanes. Each dropped four 20-lb bombs, damaging a Zeppelin under construction, destroying the gas-works and causing such a stir that countless people spent the remainder of the war maintaining military and civil precautions against a follow-up raid that never came.

The *Engadine*, *Empress* and *Riviera*, supported by two destroyers and ten submarines, had as their objectives the Zeppelin sheds at Cuxhaven on the other side of Germany. After attacking the sheds, it was hoped that the crews of their nine Short seaplanes (of three different types) would have time to note the numbers and classes of German warships in the harbour at Wilhelmshaven and anchored in the Schillig Roads and the mouth of the Elbe.

Seven of the Shorts took off safely at seven o'clock on Christmas morning 1914; the other two refused to 'unstick' from the water. Before the first three returned, the ships had to fight a spirited engagement with a Zeppelin and a seaplane which aimed four bombs at them. This attack caused no damage—a result which, it transpired, applied equally to the British attempts to destroy the airship sheds. The naval crews did not even see the sheds, which were blanketed in fog; but they did come down below the 300-foot cloud base to reconnoitre the German Fleet and drop bombs on it—a gallant effort which led to considerable damage to the seaplanes from enemy anti-aircraft fire.

Of the four pilots who had failed to return to

their carriers three landed near the submarine E.11, which picked them up and sank their aircraft, although under attack by a Zeppelin. The remaining pilot was rescued by a Dutch trawler.

Not until 1916 were the limitations of carrier-based seaplanes overcome. The aircraft which made this possible was the little 80-hp Sopwith Pup single-seater fighter, developed specifically for the R.N.A.S. and generally rated as the finest flying machine ever built. With an armament of one upward-firing Lewis gun and a top speed of 111 mph, it could take off easily from the short flight decks of the carriers *Manxman* and *Campania*, but still had to alight on the water after flight. It was then kept afloat by air-bags under the wings before being hoisted on board by crane.

At last the Navy could take to sea a fighter good enough to deal with the shadowing Zeppelins that had become so troublesome; but there were too few carriers. In an effort to remedy this shortage, it was decided to find out if a Pup could become airborne in 20 feet, from a platform erected above the forward gun-turret of the light cruiser *Yarmouth*, provided the ship sailed into wind at 20 knots. The Pup could, and did in June 1917, piloted by Flight Commander F J Rutland.

Two months later, on 21 August, the *Yarmouth* was escorting minelayers off the Danish coast when Zeppelin L23 arrived to make a careful note of what was happening. The Pup was still on board; so Flight Sub-Lieutenant B A Smart clambered into its cockpit, made his first take-off from a ship and began climbing towards the airship. Within a short time, L23 was falling in a mass of flames so fierce that little of it was left to hit the water.

Following the successes achieved by torpedo-dropping Short 184 seaplanes of the R.N.A.S. during the Dardanelles campaign, the Short 320 was produced as a long-range aircraft capable of carrying the Navy's new 18-inch Mk IX torpedo weighing 1,000 lb. The 320s had few opportunities to prove their capability; but at least one was sent to Japan after the war, to help in teaching the Japanese Navy to drop torpedoes from the air. The pupils learned their lessons well.

above
The R.N.A.S. used large numbers of non-rigid airships (blimps), including this S.S.Z. (Sea Scout Zero) craft, for coastal and North Sea patrol in the First World War. They were to have their counterparts in the highly effective Goodyear convoy-escort blimps of the U.S. Navy, a quarter of a century later.
Imperial War Museum

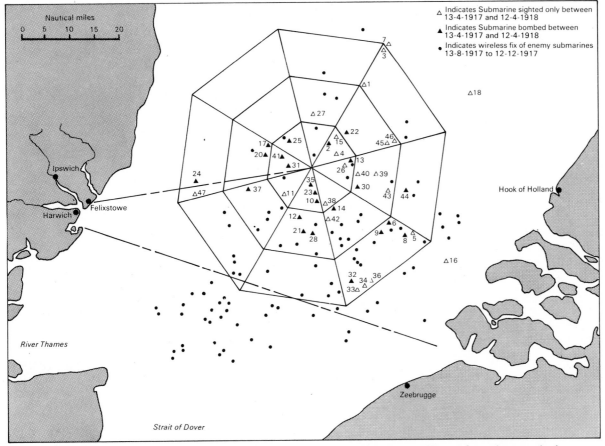

Indicates Submarine sighted only between 13-4-1917 and 12-4-1918
Indicates Submarine bombed between 13-4-1917 and 12-4-1918
Indicates wireless fix of enemy submarines 13-8-1917 to 12-12-1917

Flying-off platforms of this kind were fitted to many battleships and cruisers. A drawback initially was that a ship had to change course, into wind, to launch its aircraft. The answer to this was to mount the platform on a rotating turret that could be turned into wind while the ship maintained her existing course. First to prove this practicable was Flight Commander Rutland, who took off in a Pup from H.M.S. *Repulse* on 1 October 1917.

Pups were followed on such platforms by 1½-Strutters and then fast, formidable Sopwith Camels. Meanwhile, the Navy had put into service a considerable fleet of lighters, each carrying one large flying-boat, which could be towed behind destroyers in order to extend the aircraft's range. F.2A flying-boats carried in this fashion made reconnaissance flights over places like the Heligoland Bight, which would have been far beyond their reach from U.K. coastal bases.

C R Samson thought that it would be worth while trying to fly a Camel from one of these lighters, as it would offer a convenient way of taking a high-performance fighter on anti-Zeppelin patrols far from land bases. His first attempt, on 30 May 1918, nearly cost him his life. Instead of wheels the Camel had a skid undercarriage, which ran in troughs extending the length of the lighter. With the towing destroyer making 32 knots, Samson opened up to full throttle and began moving forward. Then everything went wrong. The skids left the troughs and the Camel disappeared over the bows of the lighter, which crashed over it. By a miracle, Samson survived. As he boarded the destroyer, after a whaler had picked him up, his first words

were: 'I think it well worth trying again.'

On 31 July it was tried again by Lieutenant S D Culley, in a Camel on wheels, operating from a wooden deck on the lighter. This time all went smoothly. Less than two weeks later, on 11 August, Culley took off for a second time, to shoot down Zeppelin L53 from a height of 19,000 feet. It was the last enemy airship to be destroyed in aerial combat.

Such techniques were valuable wartime experiences, but no real substitute for genuine, properly equipped aircraft-carriers. In 1916 the Royal Navy had commissioned H.M.S. *Furious*, a 22,000-ton vessel with a lengthy flying-off deck forward. Its aircraft still had to alight on the sea, until Flight Commander E H Dunning decided to prove that a Pup could be put down safely on the foredeck. On 2 August 1917 he flew alongside *Furious*, dodged round the midships structures, edged over sideways and cut his throttle. As he settled on the deck, friends grabbed loops attached to the little aircraft to hold it down.

Five days later, while repeating the experiment, the Pup went over the side of the ship and Dunning was drowned. But he had proved his point. H.M.S. *Furious* was rebuilt as the first carrier with a landing deck aft as well as a flying-off deck. Earlier, in the Mediterranean, Flight Commander C H K Edmonds had been the first to sink a ship with an air-launched torpedo, when he dispatched a 5,000-ton Turkish steamer while flying one of *Ben-my-Chree*'s Short 184 seaplanes on 12 August 1915. The combination of carrier and torpedo-bomber was destined to produce in due course some of the most terrible moments in the history of aerial warfare.

The photograph (*opposite, bottom*) shows Felixstowe F.5 flying-boats of the R.A.F. on the slipway at Calshot Air Station in the early twenties. The F.5 was the last of a line of twin-engined, wooden-hulled craft evolved from original Curtiss designs. Its predecessors, the Curtiss H-12 'Large America' and Felixstowe F.2A, had operated the famous wartime 'Spider Web' patrol system (*left*).

The 'Spider Web' was devised in the spring of 1917, when intercepted wireless messages proved that large numbers of German U-boats were passing through the area of the North Sea around the North Hinder Light Vessel, en route to hunting grounds around the British coast. Most of them made the passage on the surface, to conserve the batteries for the electric motors which drove them when submerged. Under these conditions they offered excellent targets for the bombs of R.N.A.S. flying-boats from Felixstowe Naval Air Station, if only they could be found. The 'Spider Web' was so designed that 4,000 square miles of sea could be searched thoroughly by a team of four flying-boats in less than five hours.

Centred on the North Hinder Light Vessel, the web was an octagonal figure, 60 miles across, with eight radiating arms 30 miles in length, and three sets of circumferential lines joining the arms 10, 20 and 30 miles out from the centre. Eight sectors were thus provided for patrol, right across the path of the U-boats, which were also in danger of being spotted 10 miles outside the web in any direction. It took a U-boat ten hours to cross the area at cruising speed.

The 'Spider Web' patrols were inaugurated on 13 April 1917. With only five flying-boats available, twenty-seven patrols were completed in the first eighteen days. Eight U-boats were sighted and three of them were bombed. On 20 May the first positive results came with the sinking of the U.C.36 10 miles east of the North Hinder, by a Large America flown by Flight Sub-Lieutenant C R Morrish. This was the first confirmed sinking of a submarine by aircraft. By the end of September, large Americas had played their part in disposing of U.B.20, U.C.72 and U.C.6.

The flying-boats were also great Zeppelin hunters. Large Americas shot down L22 on 14 May 1917 and L43 on 14 June. An F.2A destroyed L62 on 10 May 1918. When fourteen enemy seaplanes pounced on three F.2As on 4 June 1918, the big 'boats shot down six of the German aircraft in the ensuing dog-fight without loss to themselves.

Between the Wars

All statistics concerning the First World War seem astronomical when quoted today. The end-of-the-month inventory for October 1918, less than a fortnight before the fighting ended, shows that the Royal Air Force had 22,171 aeroplanes in service and in store, with 37,702 engines. Altogether, 55,093 airframes and 41,034 aero-engines had been manufactured in the United Kingdom during the war years. A total of 347,112 men, women and boys were employed by the aircraft industry, which at that time was delivering new aeroplanes at an average rate of 2,668 each month. The R.F.C. had 2,630 aircraft in service on all fronts, and 291,175 personnel. Total casualties in the British air services throughout the war were 16,623 killed, wounded and missing.

Of the casualties, 12,787 were officers, emphasizing that–unlike other military services –it is normally the officers who fight in the air and the other ranks who remain in the relative security of the airfields from which aircraft fly. This fact no doubt contributed to the suggestion that aircrew were modern 'knights in shining armour', until the long, wearisome battle of attrition between Allied bomber forces and Luftwaffe fighters was fought in the Second World War.

French official figures for August 1918 revealed a total of 15,342 serviceable aircraft; the German air services had about 20,000 at the time of the Armistice. On that date the French and German first-line strengths were 4,511 and 2,390 aircraft respectively. During the war years, production had totalled 67,982 airframes and 85,317 engines in France; 20,000 airframes and 38,000 engines in Italy; and 47,637 airframes and 40,449 engines in Germany.

In the twenty-one months after its entry into the war, the United States had displayed immense ingenuity and industrial capability by producing for its own use 15,000 aeroplanes and 41,000 engines, almost from scratch. Many of the aircraft were of European design; in fact, no American-designed combat aircraft was used operationally, except for the Curtiss flying-boat, which was developed and re-engined by the

R.N.A.S. But the significant point was that, at last, Europe faced competition from an aircraft industry of vast potential.

However, competition could not have come at a worse time. With thousands of new aeroplanes in store, economic problems already beginning to loom, and the 'war to end wars' over, it would clearly be a long time before the Governments of the victorious Allies in Europe would need to buy new military aeroplanes. Companies like Sopwith, which had built some of the war's great aircraft, went into liquidation; others survived by making anything and everything from motor cycles to milk-churns.

What the politicians failed to appreciate was that the war had never really ended. In the case of the R.A.F. alone, there was never a time between the two world wars when it was not fighting somebody somewhere. In those years there were civil wars in Russia and Spain, wars of conquest everywhere from China to Ethiopia, dissidence and insurrections throughout the Middle East, and so many revolutions and border quarrels in South America that they became music-hall jokes, except for those caught up in them.

Two of the initial crises had their beginnings during or before the First World War. The more serious of them stemmed from the Communist Revolution in Russia in 1917 and the subsequent signing of a separate peace treaty with Germany in March 1918, leaving the Germans free of their major involvement in the east as they prepared to launch their final offensive in France.

The Allies were in a desperate position. While staving off defeat on the Western Front, they had to do their utmost to ensure that the U-boats would not be presented with secure bases in the Russian Arctic ports of Archangel and Murmansk. Efforts had to be made to extricate, via Vladivostock, the 92,000 newly independent Czechoslovakian troops who had been fighting in the east, so that they could be transferred to the Western Front; and it was important to deny Germany the resources of western Siberia.

It was for these reasons that General Poole was sent to Murmansk in May 1918 to organize a

North Russian Expeditionary Force. Before long, R.A.F. units were supporting land forces in both the north and south, flying D.H.4 and D.H.9 day bombers, one Camel fighter, and an assortment of Fairey, Short and Sopwith seaplanes that had arrived on the carrier *Nairana*. Archangel was occupied in August, and for a time the anti-Communist forces achieved further successes with British and French assistance. The carrier *Vindictive* brought seaplanes to support the naval forces which were trying to keep the Russian Fleet bottled up in harbour at Kronstadt, so that it could not be used against Finland, Esthonia and other States unsympathetic to the Revolution.

Before the end of 1919, the decision was taken to evacuate the northern forces and to concentrate all effort in the south. In October, a division of the enemy was seen advancing over the Steppes towards Tsaritsin and suffered heavy casualties under a combined onslaught by cavalry and the Camels of No. 47 Squadron, R.A.F., which made repeated low-level attacks on the unfortunate troops. But successes of this kind were rare. By June 1920, victory had to be conceded to the Communists, and the Royal Air Force withdrew from Russia.

Meanwhile, on the other side of the globe, U.S. aviation had been engaged in a succession of skirmishes along the border with Mexico.

The Army's first, and only, tactical unit prior to American involvement in the First World War was the 1st Aero Squadron, based at San Diego and comprising sixteen officers, seventy-seven enlisted men, and eight Curtiss 'Jennies'. These were the U.S. equivalents to the British Avro 504 and, like this type, they were used operationally before becoming the trainers which eventually produced a great air force.

When sent in support of the U.S. expedition against Vera Cruz in 1914, the 1st Aero Squadron arrived too late and had to return to San Diego without unpacking its aircraft. In April of the following year, two officers and one 'Jenny' were

Typical of the assembly lines that produced aircraft by the thousand in the First World War was this one in the Sopwith works at Kingston-upon-Thames. Dolphin four-gun fighters are shown under construction in November 1917.
Sopwith Aviation Co.

right
One of the first inter-war campaigns in which the R.A.F. took part was that in support of anti-Communist forces in Russia. These Fairey IIICs and a flight of Short seaplanes were part of the North Russian Expeditionary Force at Murmansk in June 1919.
Imperial War Museum

below
Curtiss 'Jennies'. Known more correctly as JNs, these sturdy two-seaters were the aircraft on which U.S. military pilots did their training for a decade from 1914. These particular models are JN-4Ds, powered by a 90-hp Curtiss OX-5 engine and with a top speed of 75 mph. Jennies were not armed, although some were used operationally on the Mexican border.
U.S. Air Force

dispatched to Brownsville, Texas to patrol the border area after Pancho Villa had emerged as a Mexican revolutionary leader. They had the distinction of being the first representatives of U.S. air power to come under enemy fire. Their discovery that liaison between American aircraft and artillery was non-existent led to a period of training in this work for the entire Squadron.

What happened next is best told in the words of the U.S.A.F. Historical Division:
On March 9, 1916, Pancho Villa raided

Columbus, New Mexico, and killed seventeen Americans. Provoked to retaliatory action, the United States government ordered Brigadier-General John J Pershing to organize a force of 15,000 troops to pursue Villa into Mexico and take him dead or alive. The 1st Aero Squadron was ordered to Columbus almost immediately, and arrived there on March 15. Foulois had ten pilots, eighty-four enlisted men, and eight planes. Eventually, in May, the unit reached a strength of sixteen officers and 122 men.

above
Mitchell, Assistant-Chief of the U.S. Air Service believed that strategic bombing had made other forms of warfare obsolete. Early vehicles for his ideas were the 130 twin-engined Martin MB-2 and NBS-1 (Night Bomber, Short-range) aircraft which equipped four squadrons of the 2nd Bomb Group in the United States and other units in the Panama Canal Zone, Hawaii and the Philippines in the early twenties.
U.S. Air Force

left
America's fiery prophet of air power, Brigadier-General William (Billy) Mitchell, with a Lewis & Vought VE-7 advanced trainer in May 1920. Only fourteen VE-7s were built for the Army as it was cheaper to fit 150-hp Hispano engines to Jennies.
U.S. Air Force

above
The unfortunate Lieutenant H A Dargue at Chihuahua City. This photograph was taken just after the pilot and his JN-4 had been stoned by the locals. Being alone at the time, Dargue kept the photographer busy posing him as long as possible, so as to avoid further violence, feeling confident that the Mexicans would want to look their best in any pictures that resulted.
U.S. Air Force

right
In spectacular tests to demonstrate the validity of his ideas, Mitchell used MB-2–NBS-1 bombers to sink several old battleships at sea in 1921–23. This photograph illustrates a direct hit on the crow's-nest of one vessel with a 100-lb phosphorus bomb. The aircraft's maximum load of 3,000 lb could include a single 1,650-pounder.
U.S. Air Force

Operating in the high winds of the mountains of northern Mexico, the squadron's handful of battered aeroplanes never had a real chance. On the very first squadron flight on March 19, from Columbus to the advanced base at Casas Grandes, Mexico, one plane had to turn back, one cracked up in a forced night landing, and the other six were forced down by darkness, four of them managing to stay together. This experience established the pattern of future operations. The planes could not get across the 10,000- to 12,000-foot mountains of the area on reconnaissance flights; they could not battle the terrific air currents and whirlwinds; and they could not fly in the high winds, dust storms and snow storms. Short flights in good weather, with mail and dispatches, appeared to be about as much as could be expected.

Some of the flyers had experiences that bordered on comic opera. Two planes landed at Chihuahua City in Mexico to deliver duplicate dispatches to the American consul there. One was fired on by mounted rurales, and Foulois was arrested and jailed. Meanwhile, a crowd surrounded the machines, burned holes in the wings with cigarettes, slashed the fabric with knives, and removed nuts and bolts. Both planes took off, but one was forced down almost immediately when the top section of the fuselage blew off, damaging the stabilizer. The pilot, Lieutenant Dargue, had to stand off the threatening crowd until Mexican soldiers arrived to guard the plane. It was repaired, and Dargue took off at 5.30 next morning, to avoid the mob.

By April 20, only two planes were still operational. These were taken to Columbus, where they were condemned and destroyed.

Such events would have seemed part of a different world if they had been known to the pilots in France, where the Fokker *Eindeckers* were then at the height of their murderous success. Nevertheless, this incident provides an amusing curtain-raiser to the growth of American air power, which was to play so important a part in two world wars.

Both Britain and America had built prototypes to study the possibility of using pilotless aircraft for bombing during the First World War. This 600-lb 'aerial torpedo' biplane, built by the Sperry and Delco companies and powered by a 40-hp Ford engine, flew successfully before U.S. Navy observers in 1915.

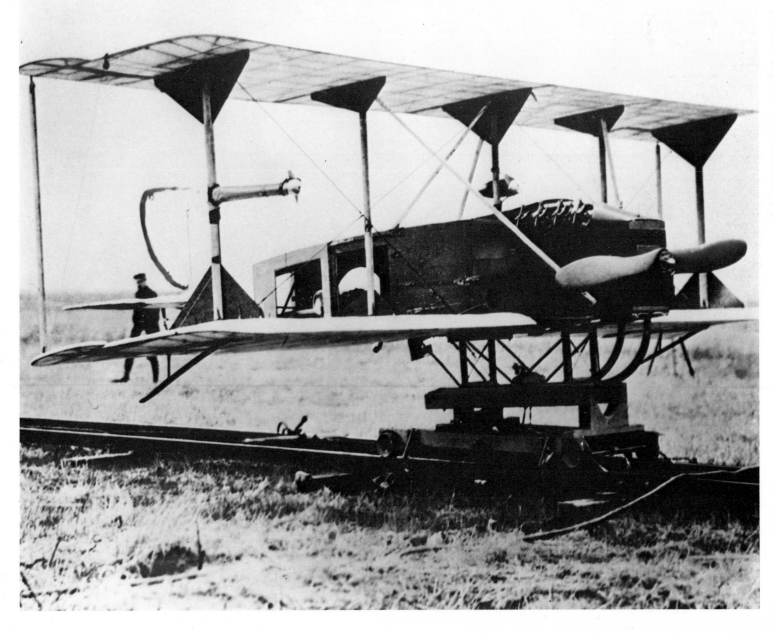

The lessons of the First World War had sunk home in the United States. This was demonstrated when Brigadier-General Mitchell was called on for assistance in policing the border with Mexico. In 1919 he instituted a border patrol between Brownsville, Texas and San Diego, California. Flying twice daily in each direction, the pilots spotted illegal border crossings and discouraged marauding bands by a show of military strength.

Unfortunately, in his fierce crusade to have the potential of air power fully recognized by Government and Defence Department, Mitchell provoked enmity in the older services. While his immediate superior, Major-General Mason M Patrick, Chief of the Air Service from 1921 to 1927, battled with words for 'a properly balanced Air Service, with twenty per cent of the total strength made up of observation units and the remaining eighty per cent devoted to combat aviation', Mitchell set out to influence public opinion with demonstrations of the great new capabilities of air power.

Directing his scorn primarily at the Navy, he organized a series of bombing trials against old warships. In July 1921, his Martin MB-2 heavy bombers sank three former German ships, including the 'unsinkable' battleship *Ostfriesland*, off the mouth of Chesapeake Bay. The obsolete U.S. battleships *Virginia* and *New Jersey* were sent to the bottom in a similar manner off Cape Hatteras in September 1923. The Navy pointed out that results might have been different had the ships been mobile, manned and able to hit back. Mitchell simply became more bitter, and used every means of emphasizing the head-in-the-sand attitude of the older services in the face of irresistible air power.

The opportunity for which his enemies had waited came in September 1925. The Navy had continued experiments with giant airships on the Zeppelin pattern long after the war had proved such aircraft defenceless, difficult to handle in bad weather, and a waste of money that would be better spent on aeroplanes. When the Navy airship *Shenandoah* broke up in a storm, at the cost of fourteen lives, Mitchell issued a statement in which he declared the high command of the Army and Navy guilty of 'incompetency, criminal negligence, and almost treasonable administration of the National Defense'.

There could be only one outcome after such insubordination. Mitchell was court-martialled, found guilty and suspended from duty for five years. He resigned in 1926, to continue his crusade as a civilian for the last ten years of his life. Had he lived, he would have seen many of his beliefs confirmed by his country's enemies at Pearl Harbor in 1941 and then, finally, adopted with great success by the U.S. Navy. In the event, he was restored to service posthumously, with the rank of Major-General, and given the highest award his nation could bestow upon a long-dead officer.

Mitchell was not alone as a prophet and martyr of air power in that era. In Italy, Giulio Douhet had served from 1912 to 1915 as commander of his country's first aviation unit, only to be court-martialled and later imprisoned for criticizing the conduct of the war. Italy's defeat at Caporetto in 1917 so clearly justified his views that he was restored to command of the Italian aviation service, reaching the rank of Major-General by 1921. In that year he published a book entitled *Command of the Air*. This contended that an independent air force, devoted primarily to strategic bombing, would so disorganize the

projected war effort of an enemy that armies and navies could be reduced considerably in size and all three services eventually be unified.

The extent to which Britain's Chief of Air Staff, Major-General Sir Hugh (later Marshal of the Royal Air Force Viscount) Trenchard, shared such views is a matter of endless debate. What cannot be denied is that he was the brilliant conceiver of a Government document published on 11 December 1919 under the title of *Permanent Organization of the Royal Air Force – Note by the Secretary of State for Air on a Scheme Outlined by the Chief of the Air Staff*. The price of the document was just one penny. The Secretary of State who presented it was Winston Churchill. Perhaps more than anything else it persuaded the British Government to allow the Royal Air Force to remain an independent service.

The great wartime force of 188 combat squadrons and 15 flights had been allowed to collapse in a matter of months to a mere 33 squadrons, which the Army and Navy hoped to divide among themselves. In what is now known as 'Trenchard's White Paper', its author noted first that the R.A.F. should consist primarily of an independent force, with 'a small part of it

Military rigid airships enjoyed one last fling in the twenties and early thirties. The U.S. Navy's *Macon* even demonstrated successfully the possibility of a large airship carrying aircraft to extend its search range during reconnaissance operations. Like the U.S. Navy's other two American-built rigids, *Shenandoah* and *Akron*, it was destroyed in an accident. Eighty-nine men died in the three disasters, and no more military rigid airships were built.
U.S. Navy

specially trained for work with the Navy, and a small part specially trained for work with the Army, these two small portions probably becoming, in the future, arms of the older services'. This came about with creation of the Fleet Air Arm and the Army Air Corps.

Under the heading of 'Government Principles', the document stated:

We now come to that on which the whole future of the Royal Air Force depends, namely, the training of its officers and men. The present need is not, under existing conditions, the creation of the full number of squadrons we may eventually require to meet strategical needs, but it is first and foremost the making of a sound framework on which to build a service, which while giving us now the few essential service squadrons, adequately trained and equipped, will be capable of producing whatever time may show to be necessary in the future.

What Trenchard proposed as the basis for future air power was the creation of a Cadet College for officers, an apprenticeship scheme for young technicians, an Air Force Staff College, a scheme for short-service commissions, and a school for flying instructors evolved from the old

Central Flying School. He added privately: 'I have laid the foundations for a castle: if nobody builds anything bigger than a cottage on them, it will at least be a very good cottage.'

Trenchard was to live long enough to see his cottage-turned-castle survive an unprecedented siege in the summer of 1940 and then offer the base from which liberating forces swept through Europe. More than this, his pattern for air power based on sound training and the independence of the older services was to become the pattern for the world to follow.

His 'few essential service squadrons' achieved miracles in the twenties. The groundwork for their operations had been laid during the First World War in India, where tribesmen on the wild North West Frontier with Afghanistan had been restless ever since Turkey entered the war.

The part played by Indian forces in the Middle Eastern campaign has already been mentioned. Cooperation in the reverse direction dated from November 1915, when a request for air support by the Viceroy of India was answered by sending five B.E.2cs and a nucleus of personnel from Farnborough, as 'A' Flight of No. 31 Squadron. Two more flights followed, provided by No. 22

above
One of the *Macon*'s Curtiss
F9C Sparrowhawks about to
hook on to the trapeze
lowered from the belly of
the airship to retrieve it.
Pilots experienced no great
difficulty once they had
become accustomed to this
system of being launched
and recovered. Both the
Macon and its sister-ship
Akron had an internal
hangar large enough to
house four Sparrowhawks.
U.S. Navy

right
When a small R.A.F.
striking force, known as
'Z Force', operated against
the 'Mad Mullah',
Mohammed bin Abdullah
Hassan, in Somaliland in
1920, a D.H.9 was modified
to carry a stretcher under a
hinged cover built on to its
rear fuselage.
Ministry of Defence

above
Most of the aircraft used in the early years of 'air control' were of First World War vintage. The Bristol Fighter proved itself so well suited to such duties that the 3,100 built before the Armistice were followed by 1,369 more, the last being delivered in December 1926. This F.2B Mk II Fighter of No. 5 Squadron is shown over Quetta, in India.
Ministry of Defence

left
The first aircraft to operate over the troublesome North-West Frontier area between India and Afghanistan were veteran B.E.2cs. This one is shown leaving the camp at Tank on 11 March 1917 during operations against the Mahsuds.
Imperial War Museum

right
Air control in action: the fort at Darwa under attack by Bristol Fighters of Aden Flight during operations against raiding Zeidi tribesmen in 1925.
Air Marshal Sir Robert Saundby

below
After Samson's Eastchurch Squadron proved the value of armoured cars working in conjunction with aircraft, during operations in Belgium in 1914, vehicles of this kind became an integral part of Britain's air services. Cars like this one played a particularly important role in Middle Eastern air control operations between the wars.
Ministry of Defence

Squadron and the Home Defence Brigade. The complete Squadron was able to begin operations from Risalpur, within striking distance of the infamous Khyber Pass between Afghanistan and what is now Pakistan.

The tribesmen on the frontier had their first experience of air attack on 15 November, when about 6,000 of them arrived to threaten Shabkadar in India. While Major-General Campbell's ground forces engaged the invaders, twelve aeroplanes from Risalpur – operating from an advanced air base – used their air-to-ground radio to direct artillery on to the enemy concentrations. When the tribesmen fled, the aircraft switched to ground attack with machine-gun fire. By the 17th all was again quiet.

Rumours concerning flying chariots began to circulate in the region, but they convinced few tribesmen. Then, in February 1917, a Mahsud force was reported to be heading for Sarwekai, a post manned by South Waziristan Militia. Three aeroplanes were sent to find out what was happening. But all was quiet, as the tribesmen slipped away at the sight of such obviously superior weapons.

Soon, however, the tale was told in Mahsud encampments that the flying chariots were harmless, merely casting a shadow on the ground as they passed overhead. Reconnaissances revealed an encampment of 1,000 Mahsuds spoiling for action. A few bombs from the B.E.s caused the camp to disperse. Maps were then prepared on the basis of fresh air photographs, and in the second half of June combined ground and air operations brought the danger of more prolonged fighting to an end. A message received by No. 31 Squadron said: 'G.O.C. Forces congratulates Royal Flying Corps on successful bombing raids in Mahsud territory. These raids have had great effect and this morning a messenger arrived from Koniguran asking that they might be stopped while peace terms were being considered. He says one bomb killed 12 men, wounded a number and destroyed some cattle. If Mahsuds now come to terms a full share of the credit will be due to Royal Flying Corps.'

Peace was declared on 12 August, and the authorities were so impressed by what No. 31 had achieved that a second squadron, No. 114, was formed at Lahore.

It would be difficult to find a better photograph than this to illustrate a typical aircraft employed on inter-war air control duties in the Middle East. A spare wheel could be a real lifesaver when operating in rough country among thoroughly hostile tribesmen. By the time racks for bombs and containers, water-carriers, flare-holders and a dozen other necessities had been added, the result was a 'Christmas tree' like this D.H.9A of No. 30 Squadron. *Ministry of Defence*

above
The Curtiss NC-4 flying-boat of the U.S. Navy which made the first flight across the North Atlantic, from Newfoundland to Lisbon and Plymouth via the Azores, between 16 and 31 May 1919.

right
Profiting from experience gained during the 1923 airlift of troops into Kirkuk, the R.A.F. organized the first major airlift in history during the rebellion in Afghanistan in the winter of 1928–29. Flying from bases in India, R.A.F. aircraft rescued 586 people, including the Afghan royal family, from Kabul as well as carrying more than 24,000 lb of luggage.
Ministry of Defence

The period of quiet could not last long in such an area, and in March 1918 it was the turn of the Marri tribes in Baluchistan to be troublesome. Their neighbours, the Khetran tribes, burned and looted Government buildings in Barkhan, and nine aeroplanes were sent to deal with the incursions. Kahan, capital of the Marri district, was bombed repeatedly and was finally occupied on 19 April, after which there was another brief spell of comparative peace.

What must be appreciated is that raiding and fighting were second nature to these tough tribes from the hills. To get at them, the British squadrons had to fly in mountainous country, where every rock might conceal a sniper and every narrow valley might hide a hundred fierce riflemen. In the heat and dust of the North West Frontier, engine failure was more to be feared than bullets. Notes promising the captors of any

airman a reward if he were returned safely seldom prolonged the lives of those who forced-landed; frequently they were handed over to the women of the tribe for torture.

It was this primitive, excessively cruel and sporadic warfare, regarded almost as sport by many of the tribesmen, that the R.A.F. set out to eliminate with a few handfuls of war-weary biplanes. Until the R.A.F. entered the arena, every uprising called for the dispatch of a punitive expedition of troops, who usually had to fight their way through to where the enemy were concentrated, carry out a pitched battle in a place and at a time chosen by a tribal leader skilled in guerrilla warfare, and then fight their way back, contending with intense heat and thirst as well as guns.

The policy of air control was conceived as a more effective alternative to such expeditions,

This photograph shows the arrangement of the NC-4's four 400-hp Liberty engines, with the centre pair mounted in tandem, driving tractor and pusher propellers respectively. Lieutenant-Commander A C Read, commander of the six-man crew, is standing between the side-by-side cockpits for the two pilots.

right
Sopwith Snipe single-seater fighters of No. 1 Squadron, R.A.F. flying near Baghdad in 1926. Part of the original air control force in Iraq, No. 1 was the last squadron to use Snipes operationally. The R.A.F. was so short of funds after the First World War that other Snipes, equipping No. 25 Squadron at Hawkinge, Kent, had represented the sole fighter defence of the United Kingdom from April 1920 to September 1922.
Ministry of Defence

below
Personnel of No. 216 Squadron snatch a quick meal near their Vickers Vimy bomber while surveying possible landing grounds in the desert. This was one of the squadrons which operated the pioneer air mail service between Cairo and Baghdad in 1921–27.
Ministry of Defence

opposite, top
The D.H.4 of Smith and Richter was refuelled in flight fifteen times during its 3,293 miles of flying over a measured 50-kilometre (31-mile) course at San Diego, California on 27–28 August 1923.
U.S. Air Force

opposite, bottom
Lieutenants Frank Seifert (holding hose) and Virgil Hines in the American-built D.H.4 which served as a flight refuelling tanker during the record-breaking 37¼-hour endurance flight by Captain Lowell Smith and Lieutenant John Richter in August 1923.
U.S. Air Force

which were costly in lives on both sides. Firstly, a message was delivered or air-dropped to a recalcitrant tribal leader, instructing him to submit himself for trial in a court of law on a charge of insurrection, raiding, murder, or some other offence. If he refused, the warning was given, by every possible means, including air-dropped leaflets, that his village would be bombed on a certain date. This gave the inhabitants time to leave for a safe spot and, if it was considered necessary, the village was then bombed.

It was seldom desirable to cause much damage to the houses. The primary objective was to deny shelter and comfort to the people, and to disrupt their daily lives. Only occasionally was it considered essential to destroy the home or fortress of a particularly troublesome leader, and this demanded a high degree of bombing accuracy.

Few among even the toughest men were willing to endure such tactics for long. Once they gave in, troops or police, and medical staff, were flown in to restore order, deal with casualties, distribute food, and get life back to a peaceful order as quickly as possible.

Unfortunately, the Army insisted on retaining control of the North West Frontier of India, and

the R.A.F. was never allowed to practise the techniques of air control there, although conditions for it were perfect. Elsewhere, when air control was applied properly it never failed. Protests from the well-intentioned but ignorant greeted every report of 'poor, defenceless natives' being attacked by air power. In fact, it is easy to show, statistically, that this policy saved countless lives in the Middle East between the wars.

The campaigns extended far beyond the North West Frontier. As early as 1920, in Somaliland, twelve D.H.9s were dispatched from the United Kingdom on the carrier *Ark Royal* to support a small force of the Camel Corps in a final effort to end the career of the 'Mad Mullah', who had defied authority for twenty years. The task was concluded in three weeks. Other operations subdued the Garjak Nuers in the Sudan in 1920, a rebellious sheikh in Transjordan in 1922, and the Zeidis in Aden in 1925; but it was in Iraq, formerly Mesopotamia, that air control achieved its most striking success.

There was no more unsettled place in all the world in 1920. It was, therefore, with very mixed feelings that Britain accepted a League of Nations mandate making her responsible for the

A Vickers Vernon troop-carrier engaged on the desert air mail service. Like many military transports, the Vernon consisted basically of the wings and tail of a bomber (the Vimy) attached to a new and roomy fuselage for passengers. It could carry eleven troops.

security and orderly development of the new States of Iraq, Palestine and Transjordan, and to guide them towards full independence. Turkey refused to recognize the three States in what had long been its sphere of influence. To the south, Ibn Saud, Sheikh of Nejd and most powerful of all the Arab rulers (later King of Saudi Arabia), also considered the terms unacceptable. As a result border clashes, subversion and infiltration threatened to throw the area into chaos.

Iraq itself was not inclined to take steps to restore order, taking the view that the responsibility lay with Britain. This attitude was echoed in the United Kingdom, where the people were tired of wars, big or little, and felt that any tribes who still wanted to fight should be left alone to do so. This put the Government in a difficult position. If it discarded its responsibilities, the whole area would clearly sink into chaos, with dire

results for the growing Jewish colony in Palestine, which Britain had fostered.

At the Cairo Conference of 1922, Trenchard suggested that most of the ground forces could be withdrawn if the Royal Air Force was made responsible for peace-keeping in Iraq. Even he admitted that such a project was untried and risky; but the British Government was only too happy to hand over an unwanted duty, and the R.A.F. was given the job.

Except for a mixed brigade of British and Indian infantry, some native levies, and four squadrons of R.A.F. armoured cars, all ground forces were removed from Iraq. Their place was taken by a total of eight R.A.F. squadrons, comprising Nos. 45 and 70, which were equipped with twin-engined eleven-passenger Vickers Vernon troop transports, Nos. 8 and 30 with D.H.9a general-purpose day bombers, and No. 1 with

Sopwith Snipe single-seater fighters, all based at Hinaidi, near Baghdad; No. 84 with D.H.9as at Shaibah, near Basra; No. 55 with D.H.9as at Mosul; and No. 6 with Bristol Fighters at Kirkuk, in the north-east, on the Kurdish border. The troops were garrisoned mainly near Hinaidi.

If the potential troublemakers viewed gleefully the replacement of 33 battalions of infantry, 6 of cavalry and 16 batteries of artillery with such a force, they were soon disillusioned. Air Officer Commanding Iraq was Air Vice-Marshal Sir John Salmond, a future Chief of Air Staff. The unit commanders included Squadron Leader A T (Bert) Harris of No. 45 Squadron, whose leadership of Bomber Command in the Second World War was foreshadowed in Iraq by the fitting of bomb-racks to his Vernons, so that they could be operated more aggressively.

The D.H.9a which equipped half the squad-rons was very different from the old, unreliable D.H.9. The latter's 240-hp BHP engine had given way to a massive 400-hp Liberty – by far the finest wartime product of America's aircraft industry. On this much power, the 'Nine-ack' could fly at up to 114 mph, carry 450 lb of bombs in addition to fore and aft machine-guns, and accommodate externally all the accoutrements of an inter-war 'colonial' aircraft, from a spare wheel to a goatskin of water, survival rations and anything else required by the situation in hand.

Dealing with the Wahabis who made periodical raids over Ibn Saud's border was a fairly routine affair, using familiar air-control and ground-attack techniques. The real pioneering took place in the north-east, where Turkish infiltrators offered the Kurds their independence if they would help to regain the Mosul area for Turkey.

Two of the Douglas World Cruisers built for the U.S. Army Air Service's 1924 round-the-world flight preparing to leave Santa Monica, California where they were manufactured. *Douglas Aircraft Co.*

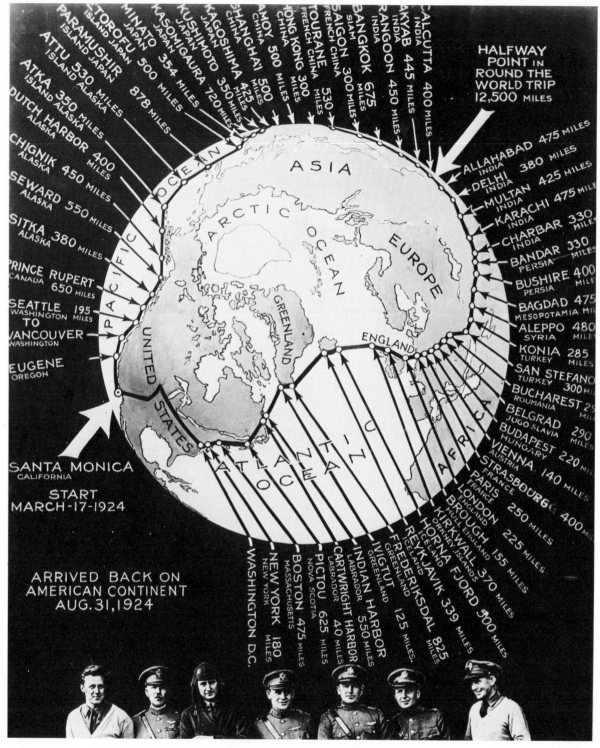

right
Pilots and mechanics who took part in the 1924 round-the-world flight, and the route followed by the two aircraft which completed the journey.
U.S. Air Force

opposite page
This painting, showing R.A.F. Bristol Fighters in action followed by dissident tribesmen on India's North West Frontier in the late twenties, conveys something of the difficulties and dangers involved in air control operations. The policy was highly successful and saved many lives on both sides. By Kenneth McDonough.

Leader of the Kurds was Sheikh Mahmud, who had been reinstated as the only practicable governor of Southern Kurdistan by the British, despite an earlier rebellion against them.

In February 1923 a large force of Mahmud's Kurds, reinforced by hill Arabs, descended on Kirkuk, where the greatly outnumbered garrison called for R.A.F. assistance. Having already mounted the first airlift of supplies, to Kut, in that same country seven years earlier, the R.A.F. now followed with the first airlift of troops. Using its squadrons of Vernons, it flew about 480 officers and men of the 14th Sikhs into the town so speedily that the invaders were taken completely by surprise.

Knowing that heavy rains had made the roads round Kirkuk impassable, the Kurds and their friends had already begun looting the bazaar and terrorizing the townsfolk. The unexpected appearance of the tall, highly disciplined Sikhs sent them scurrying away, and Kirkuk was soon peaceful again. There was an unexpected bonus shortly afterwards, when an important local sheikh, known for his pro-Turk leanings, told the District Political Officer that he wished to be regarded in future as pro-British. He explained: 'With my own eyes I saw what happened. Hundreds of soldiers marching through the town, having come by air straight from London, where it is well known there is an inexhaustible supply. Allah is great, but who can stand against that?' Nobody bothered to explain that the Sikhs had actually embarked at Kingerban, a railhead seventy-five miles from Kirkuk.

132

Vickers Victoria troop transports of the Royal Air Force engaged on the evacuation of civilians from Kabul during the rebellion of 1928–29. By Kenneth McDonough.

Designed in 1922 to replace the Vimy, the Vickers Virginia remained in service from 1924 until 1937. Despite its antique appearance and maximum speed of 108 mph, it equipped first-line bomber squadrons for several years after the R.A.F. had raised the world speed record to more than 400 mph with the highly streamlined Supermarine S.6B monoplane racing seaplane. *Charles E Brown*

Mahmud was made of sterner stuff. He kept up his opposition to the British, through alternate periods of peace and 'holy war', until the 1930s.

In those inter-war years, air power developed and enhanced its capabilities in ways which were not always related directly to armed combat. Its pilots were well trained, often combining experience with a keen sense of adventure that found few outlets in peacetime. Perhaps, therefore, it was not surprising that the first transatlantic flight, via the Azores, was made by the Curtiss flying-boat NC-4 of the U.S. Navy – the only one of three similar craft which left Newfoundland to complete the crossing. Soon afterwards, the first non-stop crossing of the Atlantic, and the first flights from England to Australia and South Africa, were made by former R.A.F. pilots in Rolls-Royce-engined Vickers Vimy aircraft built originally for the R.A.F. as bombers.

It would be more true to say that Wing Commander H A Van Ryneveld and Flight Lieutenant C J Q Brand *set out* in a Vimy, bound for Cape Town. They wrecked it while making an emergency landing at Wadi Halfa in the Sudan, went on from there in a replacement Vimy which they crashed at Bulawayo in Rhodesia, and eventually completed their odyssey in a D.H.9.

The large size of R.A.F. flying-boats of the thirties made it practicable to fit equally large guns. Thus the Blackburn Perth was unique in mounting on its bows a 37-mm Coventry Ordnance Works automatic gun, which could fire 1½-lb shells at the rate of 100 rounds a minute.
Flight International

opposite, top
Seventy Douglas Havoc night fighters, acquired from America for the R.A.F. in 1940–41, were fitted with Turbinlites. These were high-powered searchlights used to illuminate enemy bombers tracked down by the Havocs' radar. Hurricane fighters accompanied the Turbinlite aircraft, to attack any bomber caught in the spotlight. By Kenneth McDonough.

opposite, bottom
Rocket-firing Typhoon fighter-bombers of the Royal Air Force attacking a German V-1 flying-bomb missile launch-site in France in the summer of 1944. By Kenneth McDonough.

Two metal-hulled
Supermarine Southampton
Mk II flying-boats of the
kind used by the R.A.F. Far
East Flight for its 27,000-
mile cruise in 1927–28. Two
502-hp Napier Lion engines
gave the aircraft a maximum
speed of 108 mph.
Charles E Brown

Ignoring the accidents, such flights pointed the way to future airline routes. So did the airmail service which R.A.F. transport squadrons operated across the desert route between Cairo and Baghdad from 1921, reducing from twenty-eight to five days the time taken for letters to travel from London to troops stationed in Iraq. After six years the service was taken over by Imperial Airways, for whom this far-away route was to become the first link in an eventual network of airline services to every part of the British Empire.

In the Western Hemisphere, too, military pilots led the way. Lieutenants Oakley G Kelly

and John A Macready made the first non-stop transcontinental flights, 2,520 miles from New York to San Diego, in a Fokker T-2 monoplane in May 1923. Next month the Army Air Service made its first successful attempt to refuel one aeroplane from another in the air, pioneering a technique which enabled Lieutenants Lowell H Smith and John P Richter to keep their D.H.4 airborne for a record 37 hours 15 minutes over San Diego in August.

In 1924 came the 'big one', when four Douglas World Cruisers of the U.S. Army left Seattle in an attempt to be first to fly round the world. Two of them arrived back in Seattle 175 days and

Squadrons vied with each other to provide aerobatic teams, and to take part in set-piece 'attacks' on dummy forts, ships and other targets built on the airfield.

It was all good fun, with a serious purpose. Visiting foreign air attachés always found something of interest in the 'new types' park, and did not fail to note major technical advances like that in 1925, when H.M. King George V directed by ground-to-air radio the formation aerobatics of No. 25 Squadron's Grebe fighters.

Long-distance flights, too, had both training and public relations value. During the First World War, the R.N.A.S. had developed the twin-engined flying-boats of Glenn Curtiss into the sturdy F.2A and F.3, which operated the Spider Web anti-submarine patrols over the North Sea (see p 111) and even dared to exchange blows with enemy seaplanes and Zeppelins. Post-war technological refinement was continued, reaching an early milestone in the metal-hulled Supermarine Southampton Mk II designed by a young man named R J Mitchell.

Powered by two 502-hp Napier Lion engines and carrying a crew of five, the Southamptons were ideal aircraft for showing the flag. The greatest of their cruises began on 14 October 1927, when a Far East Flight of four Southamptons, commanded by Group Captain H M Cave-Brown-Cave, left Felixstowe. They flew majestically to Singapore via the Mediterranean and India, flew round Australia and back to Singapore, and then continued up to Hong Kong before returning once more to their operational base at Singapore. The total distance flown was 27,000 miles; it was the finest example of organized formation flying ever seen at that time.

Such cruises helped to persuade Imperial Airways to switch gradually from landplanes to flying-boats on its long Empire routes, leading

In 1931 the Italian Air Minister, General Italo Balbo, led a mass flight of twelve Savoia-Marchetti flying-boats across the South Atlantic from Rome to Brazil. Two years later he led an even more impressive armada of twenty-four flying-boats across the North Atlantic. Neither flight was achieved without loss of life, but they gave proof of the growing reliability and potential of aviation.

more than 26,000 miles later, having changed their undercarriage from wheels to floats and vice versa several times en route.

Such exploits were worth while as methods of 'showing the flag' overseas, and of building up public interest in the air services at home, as well as being important technical achievements. In Britain the Royal Air Force also staged an elaborate air display at Hendon Aerodrome each year from 1920. As well as interesting the public –60,000 of whom turned up for the first R.A.F. Display–the event earned money for service charities and contributed to the high standards of efficiency and flying skill in the air force.

View from the rear gun-
turret of a Virginia
approaching the airfield at
Weybridge where it was
built. The encircling
Brooklands racing circuit
was still the Mecca for fast
cars.
Charles E Brown

to the introduction of the celebrated fleet of
Empire flying-boats in 1936. From the Empire
flying-boat was evolved, in turn, the Short
Sunderland—designed to be the last and greatest
R.A.F. maritime patrol flying-boat.

Nor was the Southampton alone in the mid-
twenties in progressing from a wooden hull to
metal. In doing so, its structure weight was
reduced by 540 lb, giving increases in performance
and payload, quite apart from the better durabi-
lity of metal in a variety of climates. There was a
similar progressive change from wooden to metal
structures in almost all combat aircraft in the
late twenties. Initially, the fabric covering of

wings and fuselage was retained; but from the
mid-thirties this gave way gradually to metal,
as monoplanes with semi-monocoque fuselages
(consisting of a load-bearing metal skin riveted
to frames and stiffened with longitudinal string-
ers) replaced the old built-up girder structures.
Simultaneously, undercarriages began to be
made retractable, wing flaps were fitted to
reduce take-off and landing speeds, and cockpits
were enclosed by transparent canopies.

The man whose achievements will always be
associated with this design revolution was
R J Mitchell of Supermarine. He had designed
seaplanes which, piloted by men of the R.A.F.

High Speed Flight, had won the important Schneider Trophy outright for Britain, with successive victories in 1927, 1929 and 1931. The S.6B of 1931, powered by a 2,600-hp Rolls-Royce engine, had also put the world speed record above 400 mph, with Flight Lieutenant G H Stainforth at the controls. Using experience gained with their Schneider engines, Rolls-Royce developed a new 1,000-hp twelve-cylinder engine, named the Merlin, for military aircraft. Using *his* experience, Mitchell designed round the Merlin a beautiful little elliptical-winged monoplane fighter known as the Spitfire. Seeing it for the first time, the German Air Attaché in England poured scorn on the R.A.F.'s pretty little toy aeroplane. Many of his countrymen would wish one day that its eight machine-guns were toys.

There was some excuse for such arrogance from the Attaché. Under the new National Socialist régime of their Führer, Adolf Hitler, the Germans had built up a secret air force in defiance of the Versailles Peace Treaty of 1920. The training of this force, the Luftwaffe, had been under way in Russia, at an airfield named Lipezk, for a full eight years before its build-up was announced by Hermann Goering, the distinguished fighter ace of the First World War

who was now German Air Minister. By the time the lone Spitfire prototype was flying, Germany already had large production lines of her own new fighter, the Bf 109, designed by Willy Messerschmitt, as well as modern monoplane bombers.

Having established a sound training scheme, and having built up a force of 1,888 aircraft and 20,000 men by March 1935, Germany inaugurated a development and manufacturing programme that would eventually give her the most formidable force of thoroughly modern warplanes in the world. Special attention was devoted to long-range radio navigation and bombing aids, evolved through the Lorenz blind-landing system with which German engineers had already set the pace in the electronic field. Early-warning radar systems were also developed and put into service in the second half of the decade; in some

respects they were better than those being set up secretly in Britain. But, inevitably, mistakes were made.

It had been assumed that any imminent war would involve countries on Germany's borders, but not Britain. To meet anticipated commitments, the Luftwaffe was intended to reach its peak strength and efficiency in 1942, whereas the Führer precipitated the Second World War three years earlier than this, and involved Britain. In the technical and operational spheres, far too much emphasis was placed on Army cooperation rather than independent air power; and the Luftwaffe's technical staff were mesmerized by the attractions of the dive-bomber as opposed to the conventional long-range strategic bomber.

The U.S. Navy had been the first to demonstrate the full potential of dive-bombing in tactical situations, on 22 October 1926. That day, as the Pacific Fleet left San Pedro, its operational crews were at full alert in anticipation of a simulated attack by the Curtiss F6C-2 fighters of Navy Squadron VF-2. The assault came at the precise moment of which warning had been given, but from a direction that caught the Fleet with its defences down. Entering in almost vertical dive at 12,000 feet, the fighters achieved complete surprise. The Navy was so impressed that dive-bombing was adopted as a standard anti-ship tactic. Unknown to Washington, the military leaders in Tokyo and Berlin took equal note, for future action.

In the mid-thirties, the Luftwaffe not only ordered into massive production the gull-winged Junkers Ju 87, specifically designed for dive-bombing, but insisted that even the big, four-engined Heinkel He 177, then at an early design stage, must be strong enough to deliver its attacks in a 60-degree dive. This misguided requirement, added to an untried coupled power plant and other problems, was to deny the war-time Luftwaffe the availability of a reliable strategic bomber when it was most needed.

Initially, however, the quality of the new Luftwaffe was so impressive that Britain and France launched huge rearmament programmes, in a desperate attempt to avert war. The French programme, entrusted to a newly nationalized and completely disorganized aircraft industry, was doomed to failure. Britain's plan was to prove adequate–by a hair's breadth–mainly because Sydney Camm of Hawkers had designed a fighter named the Hurricane. This had the same Merlin engine and eight-gun armament as the Spitfire, but retained the simpler (non-monocoque) structure of the earlier Hawker biplanes, making it quicker to get into production and service.

The R.A.F. also initiated development, in 1936, of a new generation of heavy strategic bombers that was to result in the wartime Stirlings, Halifaxes and Lancasters–the most destructive aircraft used in the European war.

left
During the twenties, the international races for the Schneider Trophy attracted such advanced aircraft that only Governments could afford to pay for them, and they were usually flown by highly experienced military pilots. This Supermarine S.6, piloted by Flying Officer H R D Waghorn of the R.A.F. High Speed Flight, won the 1929 contest at a speed of 328·63 mph. The improved S.6B gained the trophy outright for Britain in 1931. More important, it pointed the way to Supermarine's Spitfire fighter.

Italy's brief campaign in Ethiopia, in continuance of its colonial expansion in Africa, provided but a scanty trial of the power of the Regia Aeronautica. The poorly armed soldiers and horsemen of Emperor Haile Selassie were easy targets for bombs and machine-guns, leaving people in many nations merely sickened by the pilots' stories of groups that opened out 'like beautiful flowers' as bombs burst among them.

The civil war in Spain was different, with Russia supporting the Socialist Government against General Franco's insurgents and his German and Italian friends.

The Luftwaffe flung itself into the fray with tremendous enthusiasm. Franco's request for aid in carrying troops from North Africa to Spain was answered by the immediate dispatch of twenty Ju 52 transports. By ferrying twenty-five men and their equipment on each 130-mile hop from Tetuan to Seville, up to four times a day, they brought in some 15,000 Moorish troops, whose presence meant the difference between possible defeat or survival for Franco at that initial stage of the war.

Soon the Luftwaffe contingent was large enough to be graced by the title of the Condor Legion. Its Chief of Staff, Lieutenant-Colonel Freiherr von Richthofen, was a cousin of the revered ace of aces. Its aircraft comprised about 30 Ju 52 bomber-transports, 27 He 51 single-seater biplane fighters, 12 He 70 reconnaissance-bombers, 6 He 45 biplane reconnaissance-bombers, 9 He 59s and 1 He 60 for coastal patrols.

Against the Condor Legion, plus the many squadrons of superb Fiat C.R.32 fighter biplanes, Savoia-Marchetti S.M.81 bomber-transports and other types operated by Italy's Aviazione Legionaria and Franco's own air units, the Government

top
The Treaty of Versailles forbade the manufacture of military aeroplanes in Germany. Leading German designers and industrialists, like Hugo Junkers and Claude Dornier, formed companies in neighbouring Sweden and Switzerland, where they could develop and produce their military types while the parent firms in Germany concentrated on more or less peaceful designs. A typical product of AB Flygindustri in Sweden in the late twenties was the K 39 reconnaissance monoplane.

above
The Caproni Ca 101, which served in Ethiopia in 1935–36, was a typical 'colonial' bomber-transport of the era.
Italian Air Ministry

right
Mainstay of the fighter forces supporting General Franco in the Spanish Civil War, Fiat's C.R.32 had a 600-hp Fiat A.30 engine and was fitted with either two or four machine-guns.
Italian Air Ministry

put up a motley collection of aircraft. Its service-ability and spares problems were not helped by the clandestine supply of every 'rare bird' on which its sympathizers could lay hands, including two of the only four Fairey Féroce fighters built, which arrived via Russia. The Russians also sent, more usefully, large numbers of Tupolev SB-2 twin-engined bombers, and Poli-karpov I-15 biplane and I-16 monoplane fighters. The latter outfought the Condor Legion's He 51s and even provided stiff opposition for the early Bf 109Bs sent to replace them; but this only showed the Germans how to make important improvements on the later Bf 109E.

By December 1938, the Condor Legion had re-equipped itself almost entirely with modern types—40 He 111 and 5 Do 17 monoplane bombers, an experimental flight of 3 Ju 87 dive-bombers, 45 Bf 109s (soon to be re-designated Me 109s), 5 He 45s and 8 He 59s. Franco had 146 operational aircraft, the Italians 134. Against its own losses of 96 aircraft in Spain, 40 of them by enemy action, the Luftwaffe claimed the destruction of 335 aircraft—277 in combat and 58 by its supporting anti-aircraft guns. More important, it had learned anew the value of fighters for ground attack. This was to stand the Luftwaffe in good stead on the outbreak of war.

The Luftwaffe rejected as inconclusive the poor results achieved by the three Ju 87 dive-bombers at this early stage of their development. Its evaluation staff noted that: 'It did not prove possible to inflict lasting damage on, or to put out of action completely, any enemy air installations on the ground. It also proved impossible to knock out enemy air forces on the ground. The reason for this was the high degree of flexibility of the enemy formations and the effective use of

top
First standard single-seater fighter of the newly created Luftwaffe in the mid-thirties was the Heinkel He 51 biplane. This one bears the markings carried by aircraft of the Condor Legion during the Spanish Civil War.
Hans Obert

above
The standard Soviet heavy bomber up to 1941, the TB-3 was an obvious choice for carrying and dropping parachute troops—a military technique in which the Russians were early pace-setters. Its maximum speed was 179 mph at 10,000 feet. As a bomber, its maximum weapon load was 12,800 lb over short ranges.

left
Two Italian high-speed bomber groups flew Savoia-Marchetti S.M.79-I bombers in Spain. Their success encouraged the Regia Aeronautica to acquire a total of around 1,200 S.M.79s over many years, and they became recognized among the best land-based bombers of the Second World War.

145

More than 500 Soviet-built Polikarpov I-15s fought on the Republican side in the Spanish Civil War. Contemporary with the monoplane I-16s, they were intended to fight as a team with these latter aircraft. The idea was for the faster but less manœuvrable I-16s to engage the enemy, giving time for the slower but more agile I-15s to catch up and polish him off. Lack of radio communication, and the fast-changing situations of air fighting, prevented the scheme from proving effective.

Second member of the Polikarpov team was the stubby little I-16, first seen in a fly-past over Moscow in May 1935. It was the first low-wing single-seater fighter monoplane with a retractable undercarriage to enter service with any air force, and many served in Spain. The final version, with a 1,000-hp M-63 engine, had a speed of 326 mph, and took the full shock of the initial German attack on Russia in 1941–42. *Imperial War Museum*

dummy installations and dummy aircraft on the ground.'

There were important lessons to be learned from this, particularly on the value of decoys. Conversely, a study of the dubious military value of what the *Encyclopaedia Britannica* still describes as 'the terroristic air bombardment' of Guernica by the Germans–weighed against the feeling of revulsion it aroused in many countries –might have prevented similar wanton attacks on places like Rotterdam and Belgrade in later years.

By the end of the civil war in Spain, time was fast running out for millions of people all over the world. Soon the Russians would regret bitterly the eight years in which they had provided a home for the clandestine Luftwaffe. On the other side of the globe, Britain and America were to be given a stern reminder of how well the Japanese Navy had learned the torpedo-bombing and other carrier tactics taught it by a British mission in 1921–3, and the subsequent possibilities of dive-bombing demonstrated by the U.S. Navy.

Through the twenties and thirties, Britain and America had developed the aircraft-carrier to a remarkable degree, but had failed to make equal progress in the design of carrier-based

aircraft. In Britain it was easy to blame the R.A.F. for this, by suggesting that, with defence budgets tightly restricted, it preferred to spend its money on land-based rather than ship-based combat aeroplanes. There was some truth in this, but Britain was not the only nation that believed that high-speed monoplanes were dangerous for operation from carriers. In addition, many naval pilots considered a second seat, for a navigator, to be absolutely essential, arguing that a pilot had enough on his mind, flying and fighting, without having to find his way back to a base that had moved many miles since he left it.

At least the old problems and dangers associated with deck flying had been largely overcome. After Dunning's death, the Pups and 1½-Strutters operated from H.M.S. *Furious* were fitted with skids instead of wheels. When they landed on the 284-foot-long after-deck, horns on the skids engaged in fore-and-aft cables strung along the deck a few inches above the surface—

at least, that was the idea. Unfortunately, if air currents round the midships superstructure caused the aircraft to touch down on one skid, there was a risk of tilting over and damaging a wing tip. Moreover, if the pilot failed to engage the cables for any reason, he was stopped abruptly by a 'crash barrier' of vertical ropes, which caused extensive damage to the aircraft. None the less, progress was being made.

To enable other ideas to be tried out, the carrier *Argus* was completed with an entirely unobstructed flush deck, which earned her the nickname of 'Flat Iron'. The deck was 550 feet long and 68 feet wide, and even the smoke from the funnels was exhausted from the stern. One series of 500 landings produced only 40 crashes and minor damage on 90 other occasions. Although considered good, these results were improved when the lift that carried aircraft down to the carrier's hangar was left 9 inches below deck-level. Aircraft then landed in the 'well',

After Dunning had proved that it was practicable to land a fighter on the deck of an aircraft-carrier, a landing-on deck was installed aft on H.M.S. *Furious*. In March 1918, Flight Commander F J Rutland made a first successful landing on this deck in a Pup with skid landing-gear.
Imperial War Museum

giving their skids a better chance of engaging the cables, before being braked by running up a slight slope with a narrowing gap between the cables and the deck.

When the new carrier *Eagle* was commissioned, this use of the lift was superseded by a pit extending right across the deck. After negotiating the pit, aircraft were slowed by knocking down a succession of hinged wooden flaps built into the deck. Sometimes, when undercarriages collapsed under the strain, the deceleration was more abrupt than intended. Eventually the pit and wires disappeared in favour of transverse 'spring-loaded' arrester wires, not so very different in principle from the sandbag-weighted ropes which halted Ely's Curtiss in 1911. After

As ship-based aircraft became faster, the First World War concept of flying aircraft from wooden platforms mounted over the gun-turrets of warships was superseded by the use of launching catapults. Many capital ships and cruisers carried an Osprey two-seat fighter-reconnaissance seaplane in this way in the thirties.
Flight International

wheels had replaced skids, and an arrester hook had superseded the old horns, there was little need for further change in basic technique.

However, the *Argus* had pointed the way to a feature found on every subsequent carrier but one. Tests with dummy superstructures, in various positions, showed that an 'island' on the starboard side of the deck gave the best compromise between operating efficiency for the ship's crew and safety for the aircraft. Pilots almost always tended to fly away to port if they had to make another circuit after a baulked landing; and only one carrier–used by the Japanese Navy in the Second World War–has ever had its island on the port side.

Six Years to Nagasaki

Nobody had any illusions concerning the major role that air power would play in the Second World War, although they could not foresee on 3 September 1939 how heart-rending the final act would be. Nagasaki was almost six years away when the air-raid warning sirens sounded in London, a few minutes after the 11 a.m. broadcast announcement by Prime Minister Neville Chamberlain that Britain was at war with Germany. Bombing was expected to start immediately, but at least the people who scurried towards shelter did not feel alone. Poland had been invaded by German forces two days earlier and was fighting courageously. France was again Britain's ally and, one by one, the overseas Dominions of the British Empire pledged their support for the home country.

It is doubtful whether a detailed knowledge of the numbers of aircraft available to each combatant would have helped in predicting the course of the air war, except in the initial stages. Germany's 3,609 modern combat aircraft, 552 transport aircraft and 500,000 Luftwaffe personnel formed an efficient force, not yet at full strength but confident that it could outfight any enemy. By the end of that September, events in Poland had strengthened such beliefs.

If bravery alone had been adequate, the Poles would have survived; but their small air force was hopelessly outdated. The twin-engined Los Bs of the Bomber Brigade were as good as anything in their class, with a speed of 273 mph and bomb-load of up to 5,685 lb; but there were only thirty-six of them in service. For as long as they lasted they attacked the tanks of the enemy Panzer divisions which, supported by Ju 87 dive-bombers, formed the spearhead weapons of *Blitzkrieg*, or 'lightning war'. Into action with the Los Bs flew twelve squadrons of Koras B single-engined reconnaissance-bombers; twelve of the fifteen Polish fighter squadrons operated PZL P.11c single-seater fighters, with open cockpit, braced wings, fixed undercarriage and a top speed of only 242 mph. The other squadrons had even older and slower P.7s.

The uneven battle raged for seventeen days, during which the Polish fighters shot down 126 Luftwaffe aircraft and lost 114 of their irreplaceable machines. After the fall of Poland many of the pilots set out on incredible journeys to Britain to continue the war in R.A.F. uniform.

With the war in the east over, Poland defeated, and Germany and Russia dividing the carcass, the Luftwaffe could concentrate its forces in the west. This time the opposition appeared more formidable. France alone had a nominal twenty fighter groups of Morane-Saulnier M.S.406s, which were not much inferior to the Hurricane in performance and armed with a cannon and two machine-guns. Dewoitine D.520s, which could fly nearly as fast as the Mk 1 Spitfire, were known to be in production. Not so well known was the fact that, as in the case of the Le0.451, the best French bomber, the D.520, would come into service too late to influence the outcome of the battle for France.

As for the Royal Air Force, it is easy to perceive, in retrospect, that if Britain and France had not gained an extra year of peace by signing the oft-maligned Munich Agreement of 1938, Czechoslovakia might still have been under the sign of the swastika today, together with the whole of western Europe and even the Soviet Union.

In September 1938 R.A.F. Fighter Command could have put up only 93 modern monoplane fighters and 573 obsolete biplanes to counter an assault by the Luftwaffe's 1,200 long-range bombers. It had no Spitfires in service, and its Hurricanes lacked the gun heating necessary to fight above 15,000 feet. Even in September 1939, Air Chief Marshal Sir Hugh Dowding, Commander-in-Chief of the Command, had at his disposal only 35 of the 53 squadrons considered essential for the defence of the United Kingdom; but 22 of them now had Hurricanes and Spitfires.

No less important, Britain was protected by a chain of early-warning radar stations and a network of visual reporting posts of the Observer Corps, extending over the whole country and feeding information continuously into control centres. Details of every aircraft approaching or flying over the United Kingdom could be assessed and passed by radio to fighter pilots

left
PZL P.11 interceptors
formed the backbone of the
Polish fighter force which
had to confront the full
might of the German
Blitzkrieg at the start of the
Second World War.
J B Cynk

below
From the start of the war,
Germany's intention of
cutting Britain's sea supply
routes by every conceivable
method was made clear.
Before the end of 1939, the
Luftwaffe began sowing
magnetic mines—Hitler's
much-publicized secret
weapon—in seaways and
estuaries around the United
Kingdom. Such mines were
detonated by the magnetic
field created by ships passing
above them. It was found
possible to explode them
harmlessly by flying over
them, at low altitude, a
Wellington DWI Mk I
aircraft fitted with a 48-foot-
diameter magnetic coil.
Vickers-Armstrongs Ltd.

waiting on airfields, or even in the cockpits of their aircraft, ready to go. This not only consumed less fuel than the old-fashioned standing patrols, but was less tiring for the pilots, who were 'scrambled' only when required to meet a specific threat. Once airborne, radar enabled them to be directed on an interception path towards the incoming raid, whose speed, height and approximate strength were given by the radar.

Although Germany had similar radar, it lacked an efficient system for making use of the data received. Reichsmarschall Goering did not consider such defensive measures necessary, having assured the German people that 'No enemy plane will fly over the Reich territory.'

Even without these supplements to early-warning radar in Germany, the daylight raids against German coastal and naval targets made by Hampdens and Wellingtons of R.A.F. Bomber Command in the autumn and winter of 1939–40 proved so costly that the decision had to be taken to use these aircraft only by night. Most of the fifteen Wellingtons that had been lost from a force of twenty-two on 18 December 1939 fell to beam attacks from above, by Me 109s and twin-engined Me 110s which punctured or set fire to their fuel-tanks. A programme was started immediately to fit beam machine-guns, self-sealing fuel-tanks and extra armour plate. Only by constant modification was it possible to continue using aircraft designed in the thirties throughout the Second World War, in steadily improved versions.

When the *Blitzkrieg* was directed to the Northern and Western Front, beginning on 3 April 1940, Denmark was occupied in only nine days. The occupation of Norway took rather longer,

In 1940 Britain was protected by the dual warning systems of radar and the personnel of the Observer Corps. By day and night the Observers, working in two-man teams, reported every aircraft that flew within their sight and hearing. One man operated the instrument which plotted the aircraft's position. His companion kept a watch with binoculars, and was in continuous telephone contact with a reporting centre which served clusters of Observer Corps posts over a large area.

although the ultimate success of the invasion was ensured at the outset by the availability of 500 Ju 52s to fly in paratroops, other troops and Luftwaffe ground crews. The main opposition in the air came from No. 263 Squadron of the R.A.F., flying its Gladiator biplanes first from the frozen surface of Lake Lesjaskog and then, side-by-side with Hurricanes of No. 46 Squadron, from Bardufoss in support of the British troops who captured and destroyed Narvik.

No. 263 Squadron claimed fifty enemy aircraft destroyed. At Lesjaskog, not one of its own Gladiators was lost in the air, but all were wrecked by German bombing. From Bardufoss, all the surviving Gladiators and Hurricanes

were flown safely out to the cruiser *Glorious*, although none of the forty-six Squadron pilots had ever before landed on a ship and it had always been considered out of the question to do so in such high-performance aircraft as Hurricanes–particularly without an arrester hook. All but two of the pilots died when *Glorious*, on its way back to the United Kingdom, was sunk by the battle-cruisers *Scharnhorst* and *Gneisenau*. In July 1941 Sea Hurricanes became the first single-seater monoplanes to operate from a British carrier. They were followed in July 1941 by the even faster Seafire counterparts of the Spitfire.

In June 1940, Belgium, Holland and France were overrun. Benito Mussolini brought Italy

left
A CH (Chain Home) station
of the early RDF (Radio
Direction Finding) system
which played a major part
in the defeat of the
Luftwaffe over Britain in
the summer of 1940.
Officially, the technique
used was known as Radio
Detection and Ranging,
which became abbreviated
to radar.
Imperial War Museum

into the war as an ally of Germany in time to share the spoils. But the over-confident Italians were soon to receive a terrible mauling.

It would be wrong to suggest that Britain was alone at this stage. Australia, Canada, New Zealand, India, South Africa, Rhodesia and every other corner of its world-wide Empire had joined the struggle. By ship and aircraft, the men from the shattered armies, air forces and navies of its former allies in Europe also flooded into the United Kingdom, the pilots burning to get into the cockpits of Hurricanes, Spitfires and Wellingtons, to carry on the fight and liberate their homelands.

The main problem was to find sufficient aero-planes, quickly enough, for everyone to fly. The Germans were now on the Channel coast of France and Belgium, and the largest target in the world, London, was only an hour away from the largest air force in the world, which was poised to attack.

By this time, Winston Churchill had succeeded Neville Chamberlain as Prime Minister. New Hurricanes and Spitfires were desperately needed for the battle of Britain that was certain to come – as a prelude to full-scale German invasion. Churchill appointed Lord Beaverbrook, the dynamic 'Press baron' whose son led a Spitfire squadron, as Minister of Aircraft Production.

Beaverbrook faced a formidable task. The ten

above
The operations room at the
headquarters of R.A.F.
Fighter Command in 1940.
With the aid of reports fed in
from Observer Corps
centres and the radar chain,
it was possible for the
W.A.A.F. (Women's
Auxiliary Air Force) plotters
to move plaques over the
large map table, showing the
position and strength of
every enemy raid. Fighter
Command squadrons were
then 'scrambled', in what
seemed to be the most
economical and effective
manner, to meet the attack.
Imperial War Museum

above
These Gloster Gladiator fighters are not the R.A.F. machines which operated from the frozen Lake Lesjaskog during the Norwegian campaign in 1940. Similar aircraft in service with the Belgian Air Force were held at the alert in the bitter first winter of the war, after documents retrieved from an Me 108 communications aircraft which crashed in Belgium revealed orders for the Ju 87 dive-dombers of the Luftwaffe's VIII Fliegerkorps to attack targets in that country. In fact, the attack was deferred until 10 May.

right
French equivalent of the American B-17 Flying Fortress, although older and slower, was the bulky Amiot 143. Its suitcase-like front fuselage was designed to dispose four defensive machine-guns so efficiently that they would protect the bomber against attack from every direction.
Imperial War Museum

opposite, top
The crank-winged Junkers Ju 87 *Stuka* was the shape most dreaded by troops subjected to its dive-bombing attacks when it paved the way for the Blitzkrieg armies in Poland and western Europe. Yet it was an easy target for any determined fighter pilot who followed it down when it dived.

opposite, bottom
With 'Mae West' lifejackets already donned, Spitfire pilots of No. 43 Squadron – the famous 'Fighting Cocks' – wait for the telephone ring that will send them racing to their aircraft and into action.
Imperial War Museum

squadrons of Fairey Battle day bombers of the R.A.F.'s Advanced Air Striking Force in France had been largely wiped out in gallant but hopeless attempts to halt the German Army by destroying bridges in its path. This is no criticism of the aircraft, which were simply outdated by 1940 and quite incapable of fending off Me 109s which were armed with cannon and had a speed advantage of more than 100 mph. However, such experience emphasized that only the best available aircraft would give Fighter Command a chance in the forthcoming battle.

The need was for Spitfires and Hurricanes by the hundred – initially to replace the 432 that had

been destroyed during May and June, when the R.A.F. had lost a total of 959 aircraft of all types. The sacrifice of their crews had enabled 340,000 British and French troops to be evacuated from Dunkirk. Furthermore, a high proportion of the 1,284 aircraft lost by the Luftwaffe in this period fell to the R.A.F. Air combat had normally taken place well inland, before the Germans had time to attack the armies exposed on the beaches. The result, understandably, was a frenzied cry of 'Where is the R.A.F.?' when the troops suffered under the bombs and bullets of those enemy aircraft that broke through to attack them.

Despite its losses, the Luftwaffe had at least 1,000 long-range bombers, 250 dive-bombers and 1,000 fighters in three huge *Luftflotten* (air fleets) to hurl against Britain in what Hitler had designated *Adlerangriff* (Eagle attack). Luftflotte 2, under General Kesselring, was based in the Netherlands, Belgium and north-eastern France. Luftflotte 3, under General Sperrle, was in northern and north-western France. Luftflotte 5, under General Stumpff, was based in Norway and Denmark.

By the same kind of miracle that had enabled tiny pleasure-boats to cross the Channel and pull

155

men off the beaches at Dunkirk, week after week
now passed without sign of the *Adlerangriff*. For
Beaverbrook and Dowding, every day was
precious. In early June, the Luftwaffe would
have had to contend with 331 Hurricanes and
Spitfires, plus 115 other fighters. By 11 August
there were 620 serviceable Hurricanes and Spitfires in a total force of 704 fighters; and reserves
had increased from 36 to 289 aircraft–nearly a
thousand aeroplanes, and a thousand pilots to
fly them.

'Softening-up' of the defences had been under
way since the night of 5–6 June, when about
thirty bombers crossed Britain's east coast to
attack airfields and other targets. Next came
daylight attacks on convoys of ships passing
through the no-man's-land of the English Channel. The contestants were weighing each other
up, and already there were important lessons to
be learned.

This dramatic photograph of a Heinkel He 111 over London was distributed in Germany to suggest how easy it was for the Luftwaffe to attack the capital of the British Empire. But by switching the attack to London, Hitler surrendered all chance of winning the Battle of Britain. *Imperial War Museum*

The Ju 87 Stukas (*Sturzkampfflugzeng*, or dive-bomber) that had punched a way through defending armies for the *Blitzkrieg* forces in Poland and France always had fear and confusion on their side. Sirens attached to their undercarriage legs screamed as they bore down at a steep angle on their victims, from skies that the Luftwaffe dominated. Now R.A.F. fighter pilots quickly discovered that a Stuka was a sitting target once it had entered its dive. Losses became so great that the Ju 87s were to play only a small part in the eventual Battle of Britain.

There is some doubt as to the actual date of *Adlerangriff* day. It appears to have been deferred from 10 to 12 August, although the Germans claim that the main assault began on the 13th. The 10th and 11th were devoted to further attacks on Channel convoys and the ports of Dover and Portland. The cost to the Luftwaffe was sixty-three aircraft, but the R.A.F. lost fifty-two–a ratio that would wipe out the defences if it continued.

The primary targets on the 12th were airfields and radar stations. The Germans acted on the assumption that the way would be clear for Operation *Seelöwe* (Sealion), the cross-Channel invasion of England by ship and barge, once Fighter Command had been eliminated. By the evening of that day the fighter airfield at Manston, in Kent, had been put out of action; and the airfields at Lympne and Hawkinge had taken such a pounding that pilots had to take off and land where they could find a narrow strip of grass between bomb craters. Five of the vital Chain Home line of radar warning stations had been hit with such determination that the Luftwaffe was justified in believing that they had been put out of action. These successes had cost the Germans thirty-six aircraft, against twenty-two defending fighters, mainly because, to the surprise of the Luftwaffe, all its raids had been intercepted. But tomorrow would be different . . .

The 13th *was* different from most days that summer in that it was cloudy, which should have

opposite page
As in the First World War, flying-boats performed nobly on maritime patrol, convoy escort, and other Coastal Command duties. Protected by up to ten machine-guns, Sunderlands of the kind shown here were known as 'flying porcupines' by Luftwaffe pilots.
Imperial War Museum

below
First of the R.A.F.'s four-engined 'heavies' of the Second World War, the Stirling symbolized Britain's intention of striking back after winning the Battle of Britain and surviving the subsequent 'night blitz'. The pilot delivering this one from factory to operational airfield was Joan Hughes, one of the women pilots of the Air Transport Auxiliary.

Finishing off a U-boat in the Bay of Biscay: coming in to drop its depth-charges, a Sunderland flies through the spray of those dropped earlier by another Sunderland.
Imperial War Museum

helped the attackers, especially with the radar defences weakened. No fewer than 485 bomber sorties and 1,000 fighter sorties were flown against Southampton, Portland and airfields in Kent and Hampshire. Far from seeming beaten, the R.A.F. improved its score, with forty-five kills against thirteen of its own fighters lost. Furthermore, it was already becoming apparent that the R.A.F. had one big advantage: fighting over England, it had a good chance of recovering those of its pilots who were able to escape by parachute from their crippled aircraft. Any Germans lucky enough to get out of their aircraft were invariably destined to spend the rest of the war in captivity.

For the Luftwaffe, the attacks became more and more frustrating. General Stapf had predicted that it would take between two and four weeks to smash the R.A.F. After five days, from 8 August, he reported that eight British air bases had been eliminated and that the R.A.F. was losing three aircraft for every Luftwaffe machine that failed to return. Two days after he made this report, the Luftwaffe mounted 1,786 sorties against Britain, hoping to crush the remaining R.A.F. airfields with 520 bomber sorties. On the first day it lost 76 aircraft; then 16 on the next day; and 71 on the 18th.

German plans were going badly awry. Only later, when all the facts could be made known in peacetime, did the reasons for this become clear.

The Luftwaffe had been designed to operate in conjunction with the German Army. It did so brilliantly in Poland and western Europe. In the face of determined and efficient defences in Britain, it had obvious deficiencies. Its Ju 87s were too vulnerable. Even its twin-engined Heinkel, Dornier and Junkers bombers required a fighter escort, for which the Messerschmitt Me 110 twin-engined 'destroyer' had been produced. But the Me 110 itself required fighter protection when opposed by Spitfires and Hurricanes.

There were plenty of Me 109s available to provide escort for the bomber formations, but they had never been designed for such work and had a combat radius of only 125 miles. This could get them as far as London from airfields in the Calais area, or somewhere north of Portsmouth from Cherbourg – provided they were not expected to spend time and fuel in fighting en route. If they ran short of fuel and had to desert the bombers, no amount of cross-fire from the German air-gunners in the Heinkels and Dorniers would deter the British fighter pilots.

This was made abundantly clear on the only occasion when Luftflotte 5 dispatched large bomber forces from its bases in Norway and Denmark, in support of its comrades farther south. There was no possibility of providing a fighter escort of anything but Me 110s over such

left
The three-engined Junkers
Ju 52 was the Luftwaffe's
wartime counterpart of the
Allies' C-47, or Dakota. It
carried the Wehrmacht into
Norway, dropped paratroops
and carried airborne troops
into Crete; it also tried to
relieve the surrounded
German armies at
Stalingrad.

below
For quick and comfortable
travel between units of the
Afrika Korps, General
Erwin Rommel used this
Fieseler Storch. Full-span
wing slots and flaps enabled
the Storch to take off in 213
feet, land in 61 feet and
virtually hover in a 25-mph
headwind. It pioneered what
we now call STOL (Short
Take-Off and Landing)
operations.
General Erwin Rommel

distances; but an attack from an unexpected direction could be expected to take the R.A.F. by surprise, especially when hundreds of aircraft from the other Luftflotten were keeping it busy over southern England.

The date chosen was 15 August. The first of the two Luftflotte 5 armadas, comprising a hundred He 111s and seventy Me 110s, was still 100 miles out to sea when they were detected by radar. A single Spitfire squadron (No. 72) from Acklington was enough to split the attacking force in two before it crossed the coast. Its colleagues of No. 79 Squadron mauled one of the resulting formations so thoroughly that the escorting Messerschmitts, running short of fuel, turned tail for home. The Spitfires and Hurricanes of Nos. 41, 605 and 607 Squadrons then fell upon the unescorted bombers to such good effect that no military objective suffered damage.

The fifty Ju 88s that made up Stumpff's second raiding force succeeded in blowing up an ammunition dump and destroying ten aircraft on the ground at Driffield, but had to battle past four squadrons while doing so. By the evening of that day Luftflotte 5 had lost one-eighth of its bombers and one-fifth of its long-range fighters. It took no further part in the battle of Britain, and 15 August went down in German history as *Schwarzer Donnestag* (Black Thursday). The R.A.F. had dealt the Luftwaffe a heavy blow.

A Dornier 17 lying in flames on a British beach. It was shot down by a Lewis gun while strafing a coastal town.
Fox Photos

Britain was greatly over-estimating the scale of success that its pilots were achieving in those blue summer skies. On the 15th, the B.B.C. news bulletins claimed 182 Luftwaffe aircraft destroyed and another 53 'probables'—more than three times the actual German losses. This provided a great boost for the morale of the British public, who still expected a cross-Channel invasion at any moment; but it might have been fatal.

By 18 August the R.A.F. had shot down a true total of 367 aircraft, against its own loss of 183 in combat and 30 on the ground. In comfortable retrospect, such figures look fine; but the production of Spitfires and Hurricanes was then only a little over 100 a week, and the reserves were down to 230 aircraft. Even worse, the training organization had supplied only 63 replacements for the 154 pilots already killed, missing or severely wounded.

Nor was the situation improved for Britain by a night bombing success achieved by the pilots of Kampfgruppe 100, whose He 111s were equipped with the Knickebein radio navigation aid. On 13 August, at the first attempt, they had hit the Spitfire factory at Castle Bromwich with seven bombs. This represented a new threat, as Luftwaffe night operations had attempted little but minelaying during the first eleven months of the war. Subsequent raids by Kampfgruppe 100 were less successful. Eight attacks on the Bristol works at Filton caused damage on only two occasions. When the targets were the Gloster, Rolls-Royce and Westland factories, few of the bombs fell within five miles of their objectives.

In the end, it was probably a combination of inadequate reconnaissance and Hitler's intuition that decided the result of the Battle of Britain. Better reconnaissance would have told the Luftwaffe commanders that only one of the five radar stations attacked on 12 August—that on the Isle of Wight—had been destroyed. The others were all operational next day. When the truth did become apparent, Goering decided not to repeat the attacks on radar sites, as they were more difficult to destroy than other targets.

Time after time during the Second World War, the Germans and the Allies were to fail to maintain air offensives that could have ended the war quickly in their favour. By leaving Britain's Chain Home radar stations free to report every move of their aircraft, the Luftwaffe command made one of their greatest mistakes. Hitler himself made the next one.

Realizing that the ability of No. 11 Group of Fighter Command to intercept raids depended on the seven sector stations of Biggin Hill, Debden, Hornchurch, Kenley, Northolt, North Weald and Tangmere, each of which controlled three fighter squadrons, the Germans decided to concentrate attacks on those stations. Kenley was hit hard on 18 August. Bad weather then caused a five-day lull; but North Weald suffered a heavy attack on the 24th; and Debden was hit on the 26th, with lesser damage at other stations.

By September the airfield at Manston was out of action, and the sector stations at Biggin Hill and Kenley were in a sorry state. The Luftwaffe made a determined effort to eliminate Biggin permanently, but failed—not least through the courage of members of the Women's Auxiliary Air Force (W.A.A.F.), who stayed at their posts even after the blocks in which they worked were hit by bombs.

During the two weeks from 24 August to 6 September, the sector stations bore the brunt of attacks by an average of nearly 1,000 aircraft

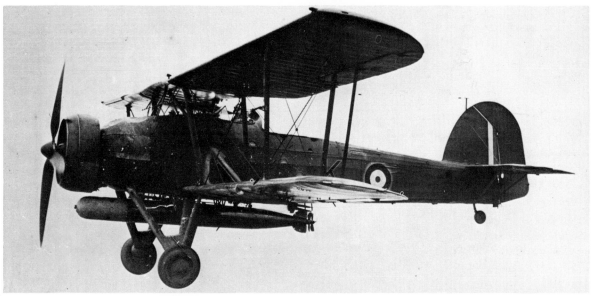

above
Members of the crew of a
Heinkel He 111 are marched
away after their aircraft has
been brought down by a
Hurricane. The remains of
the Heinkel burn away in
the background.
Fox Photos

centre
Another slow-flying aircraft
which achieved wartime
miracles was the Royal
Navy's Fairey Swordfish
torpedo-bomber. It disabled
a high proportion of Italy's
capital ships at Taranto in
November 1940, played a
major part in the sinking of
the German battleship
Bismarck, and sank many
submarines with rockets and
depth-charges during
operations from escort
carriers.
Royal Navy

left
This flight of Yak-9Ds of the
Red Air Force is made up of
just four of more than 37,000
single-seater fighters of
Yakovlev design produced
by 1945. The suffix 'D'
signified long-range, as this
version was evolved to
provide air cover for the
Russian tanks and mobile
units that broke through the
German defences when the
tide of battle turned against
the Wehrmacht.

a day, with a peak of 1,600 on 30 August and again on the 31st. By now bombers seldom made up more than 25 per cent of each formation; but reserves of Hurricanes and Spitfires were down to 125, and attacks on the Hawker and Vickers factories at Weybridge on 4 and 6 September suggested that fighter factories might follow the sector airfields as priority targets.

Throughout the battle, German bombers had been the main objectives of Fighter Command. Hurricanes, which were more numerous and at their best at 15,000 feet, were intended to deal with the Heinkels and Dorniers, leaving the faster, higher-flying Spitfires to drive off the escorting Messerschmitts. This gave the German fighters several advantages. If the Spitfires arrived late for any action, the Me 109s could often pick off Hurricanes by diving on them while their pilots were concentrating on the bombers. The German fighters could outfly even a Mk I Spitfire above the latter's rated altitude of 18,000 feet; and many combats took place above 20,000 feet. Also, if an Me 109 pilot got into trouble, he could put down his nose in a high-speed dive, knowing that his fuel-injected engine would not lose power momentarily, as would the carburettor-equipped Merlin of his pursuer. This explains why, in terms of pure fighter-to-fighter

combat, the Luftwaffe not only had a higher ratio of victories than the R.A.F. but also improved it as the battle neared its climax.

Paradoxically, it was Bomber Command which goaded Hitler into making his great blunder. Luftwaffe bombs dropped on London during the night of 24–25 August had been the first to hit the capital since 1918. Winston Churchill was unlikely to let such an incident go unanswered. Although it was obvious that there were more important strategic targets, eighty-one British aircraft made the long 600-mile haul to Berlin to show that the decision to attack London was not one that could be taken lightly. To underline the

point, they made further attacks on the German capital on succeeding nights.

Just how much Hitler was angered by this counterattack from a foe he had considered almost beaten, we shall never know. What is certain is that Fighter Command felt a tremendous sense of relief on 7 September, when the Luftwaffe suddenly switched its assault from R.A.F. airfields to London. The fighter squadrons had suffered in just two weeks, since 24 August, 103 pilots killed, another 128 seriously wounded, and 466 Spitfires and Hurricanes destroyed or heavily damaged. By diverting much of its bomber effort to ten successive night raids on

above
Wrecked Douglas B-18 bombers in a hangar at Hickham Field, Hawaii, after the Japanese attack on 7 December 1941.
U.S. Air Force

left
In 1942, after many years of fighting the Japanese invaders unaided, China received foreign help when a retired U.S. Army Air Corps officer named Claire Chennault brought a small band of volunteer pilots and P-40 Tomahawk fighters to defend the road to Burma and provide air support for the Chinese Army. The paint scheme adopted for the P-40s soon earned the unit the name 'Flying Tigers'. In July 1942 the American Volunteer Group became part of the U.S.A.A.F., and grew next year into the Fourteenth Air Force, still under Chennault.
U.S. Air Force

London, from 7 September, the Luftwaffe hit docks and railway centres, and killed many civilians; but Fighter Command was given a breathing space of which it had desperate need.

Meanwhile, the camera-carrying Spitfires and Hudsons of Coastal Command's Photographic Reconnaissance Unit (P.R.U.) had been keeping close watch on everything that moved along the German-held coastline from Texel to Cherbourg. There were 205 invasion barges at Ostend alone by 6 September. The number at Flushing grew by 120 in a week; a check on Dunkirk and Calais revealed an increase of 87 in three days. On the 7th, the authorities in London felt bound to issue

Alert No. 1–'Invasion imminent and probable within twelve hours.'

Even Tiger Moth biplane trainers had been fitted with racks for small bombs, and now stood by for what would almost certainly be suicidal missions against the invasion fleet. Bomber Command flung its entire strength against the German-held ports, the ships and barges they harboured, assembled troops and stores, roads and railways feeding into the ports, gun emplacements, anything and everything that might be useful to Operation *Seelöwe*. At the end of the twelve hours forewarned by Alert No. 1, no barges had left for England. The bombers kept up

their pounding, but the invasion fleet continued to grow. After twelve days there were more than 1,000 barges in the harbours, with 600 more up-river at Antwerp; but by then Hitler had decided to postpone *Seelöwe* indefinitely.

With 12 per cent of the barges wrecked before leaving port, the Royal Navy still in control of the seas round Britain, and Fighter Command holding firm, the odds on putting a large, well-organized army ashore in southern England were unacceptable. On 23 September, P.R.U. Spitfire pilots reported that at least one-third of the invasion fleet had already dispersed.

The daylight Battle of Britain had been lost by

the Luftwaffe. As September 1940 passed into history, it made a few final attempts to destroy aircraft factories and break through to London. It cost the Luftwaffe forty-seven aircraft on the 30th, against twenty defending fighters. Hoping to use their speed to escape interception, the Messerschmitts still came by day; but the bombers had to seek the cover of darkness to survive a little longer.

During August and September the Luftwaffe, according to its own reports, had lost 1,244 aircraft destroyed. Fighter Command had lost 721, but had gained the victory in one of history's great decisive battles. Honouring the R.A.F. pilots who had died, Winston Churchill commented that: 'Never in the field of human conflict was so much owed by so many to so few.' With them passed the heroic age of aerial warfare; from now on it was to be a war of attrition.

London's ordeal lasted non-stop, night after night, from 7 September until 13 November 1940. The Luftwaffe dropped more than 13,000 tons of high-explosive bombs on the capital's huge sprawling mass, killing one person for each ton that fell. Almost a million incendiary bombs also showered down, burning great holes amid the jagged wrecks of buildings. But London lived on, and Goering realized that this was no way to win the war. The 150 to 300 bombers dispatched each night would be far better used against smaller, military targets.

At last Goering got his way. On the night of 14–15 November the name of Coventry was written in blood and tears in the history books.

The engineers in Britain's Intelligence Research organization had already learned how to 'bend' the radio beams of the German Knickebein navigation system, so that they crossed over open country rather than the planned target for the night's bombing. When Coventry was bombed, Kampffgruppe 100, acting as pathfinders for the 449 other aircraft which converged on the city in three streams, used an improved system known as X-Gerät. This involved flying along a narrow radio beam, centred in a wider beam, until the distance-to-target was indicated by a succession of intersecting beams. Dr R V Jones, Head of Britain's Intelligence Research, had already learned enough about X-Gerät to work out the

Known officially as the Mitsubishi A6M Zero-Sen, this single-seat Japanese fighter will always be remembered as the 'Zero'. More than any other aircraft of 1941, it convinced the Allies of the competence of Japan's designers. *Smithsonian Institution*

identity of the target, and the time, route and height of the attack. He could not yet offer a method of jamming the system; nor were R.A.F. night fighters equipped to track down aircraft attacking at intervals of about four minutes over a period of ten hours. This is understandable. Relying on their eyesight in the darkness, and aided by searchlights, fighter pilots had to search for each bomber in an average 345 cubic miles of airspace.

Kampffgruppe 100 began marking the target areas in Coventry with incendiary bombs at about 8.15 p.m. The main force then aimed at these and later fires a total of 394 tons of high explosive, 56 tons of incendiary bombs and 127 parachute mines. Afterwards, British reports referred to the 380 people who had been killed and the historic buildings that had been destroyed, especially the Cathedral. Military security, and propaganda considerations, hid the fact that Coventry was a major centre of war production, and that the Luftwaffe crews had succeeded in hitting twelve aircraft factories and nine of the other industrial plants that had been their specific targets. For the loss of one bomber, they had reduced Britain's aircraft production temporarily by 20 per cent.

If we regard London's night 'blitz' in 1940 as the first phase of the German night offensive, statistics reveal that it involved a total of 12,000 sorties and that eighty-one aircraft were claimed as destroyed, eight of them by night fighters (postwar records showed that these last figures were underestimates). Phase two, beginning with the Coventry raid and consisting of thirty-one attacks on London, major ports and industrial centres up to mid-February 1941, again totalled 12,000 sorties but resulted in destruction of only seventy-five of the raiders. The sole consolation was that about one-third of the successes could be credited to fighters, reflecting a marked improvement in night combat techniques.

Contemporary colour
photographs of the great
combat aircraft of the
Second World War are rare—
none more so than this
sequence showing an R.A.F.
Lancaster squadron
preparing for and taking off
on a mission over enemy-
occupied Europe. The first
two photographs (*left*) show,
respectively, the aircraft
being loaded with incendiary
bomb containers and high-
explosive bombs of moderate
size. The Lancaster could be
adapted to carry a single
bomb of up to 22,000 lb in
weight—the heaviest carried
by any aircraft during the
war. The seven-man crew
of one of these aircraft,
made up of two pilots,
navigator, radio operator
and three gunners, is seen
in the bottom photograph,
wearing 'Mae West' life-
jackets and with their
parachute packs by their
feet. *Bottom right*, the
Lancasters are taxi-ing
towards the main runway
for take-off. The remaining
picture shows one of the
aircraft in flight.
Fox Photos

When the R.A.F. received Liberators from America, it was possible to close the mid-Atlantic 'gap' which had previously been beyond the range of shore-based aircraft. This Liberator GR Mk 5 had a range of 2,850 miles, a maximum speed of 303 mph and armament of ten 0·5-inch machine-guns. It could carry 8,800 lb of bombs, depth-charges or other weapons, and was fitted with radar to detect submarines and surface raiders.
Chaz Bowyer

When America entered the war, the U-boats found well-stocked killing-grounds in the western Atlantic. The U.S. Navy used its fleet of non-rigid airships for convoy escort up both coasts of the North American continent, in the Caribbean and South Atlantic and in the Mediterranean. No ship was ever lost to submarine attack from a convoy so escorted, and only one airship was lost, in a machine-gun duel with the U-134 off the coast of Florida.
U.S. Navy

opposite, top
Day-bomber version of the Havoc, the Boston III entered R.A.F. service in October 1941, replacing the Blenheim IV. It was used mainly for anti-shipping strikes and for attacking targets close to the coastline of occupied Europe.

opposite, bottom
Despite the successful operation of Sopwith Pup and Camel single-seater fighters from some of the Royal Navy's earliest aircraft carriers, it was believed in the inter-war years that naval fighters had to be two-seaters and would necessarily have a lower performance than their land-based counter-parts. These Seafires symbolize the changes brought about by the demands of the battle of the Atlantic in the Second World War. Generally similar to the R.A.F.'s Spitfires, they were preceded by similarly adapted Sea Hurricanes.
Fox Photos

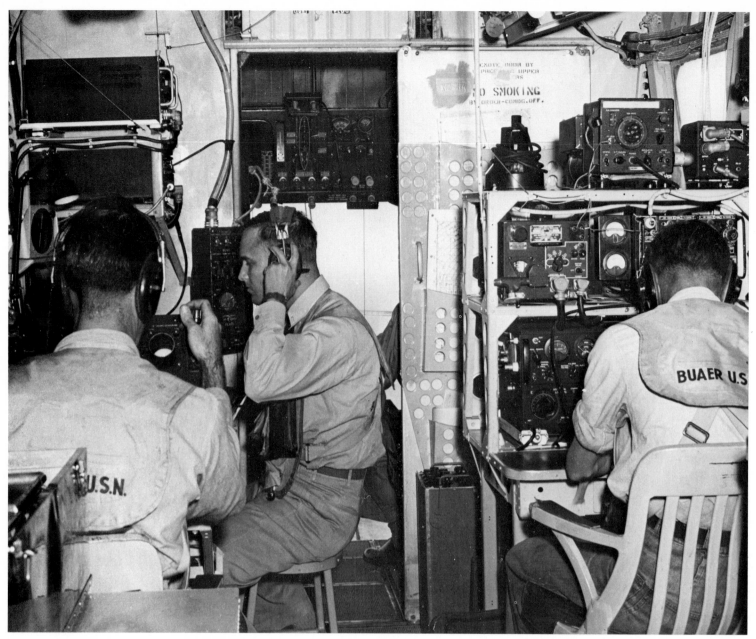

The improvement was even more apparent in
the third phase, which extended from 19 February
to 12 May. Fifteen heavy night attacks were made
on London, Birmingham, Coventry and Notting-
ham, but the main assault was directed against
eleven ports, which suffered a total of forty-six
raids. Off the coast, too, skip-bombing attacks on
British shipping, and minelaying by aircraft,
were stepped up considerably. Yet this phase
robbed the United Kingdom of only 70,000 tons
of food and one-half of one per cent of its oil
stocks. In contrast, R.A.F. fighter pilots claimed
twenty-two enemy aircraft shot down in March,
forty-eight in April and ninety-six in May –
totals which were found, after the war, to be
30 per cent lower than the actual German losses.

When Luftwaffe night raids on Britain ended
in mid-1941, it was because all the aircraft were
needed on the newly opened Russian Front
rather than because the $3\frac{1}{2}$ per cent loss rate was
causing concern. None the less, there had been
indications that Fighter Command might soon
make life very difficult for the bomber crews.

The R.A.F.'s new Beaufighters had a speed of

330 mph and an unprecedented firepower of four
20-millimetre cannon (soon to become standard
armament on British-built fighters) and six
machine-guns. Aerials bristling from the nose
and wings of these twin-engined two-seaters
showed that they were fitted with A.I.Mk IV
airborne interception radar – a miniaturization
of electronic equipment in which Britain was
establishing a clear lead over every other nation.
After take-off the Beaufighters were guided
towards a target bomber by ground control, as in
daytime, until they were close enough to the
enemy aircraft for the A.I.Mk IV to pick them up
and provide guidance for the actual interception.

Some anti-aircraft guns were also radar-
directed in early 1941, and were supplemented by
a variety of other weapons and 'devices', including rocket batteries. Most effective of the
devices were decoys and jammers. On 9 May, for
example, the German radio announced that heavy
damage had been inflicted on the Rolls-Royce
works and other targets at Derby and Notting-
ham during the previous night. In fact, the
combination of a jammer code-named 'Bromide'

above
'Scramble!' The pilots of a Hurricane squadron dash to their aircraft as an alarm reports the approach of enemy aircraft.
Imperial War Museum

left
During the Second World War, inter-service rivalries gradually gave way to inter-service co-operation, and even three-service joint operations under a single supreme commander. In Malta in 1942, army personnel were so conscious of what the R.A.F. was doing to defend the island against massive air attacks that airmen and soldiers worked side by side, refuelling and rearming the Spitfires inside sandbag revetments.

175

The blister under the rear fuselage of this Halifax of R.A.F. Bomber Command housed the rotating scanner of its radar, which did so much to improve the accuracy of night attacks.

and decoy fires known as 'Starfish' had limited the night's casualties to two cows and a pair of chickens.

'Bromide', which blotted out X-Gerät radio signals, protected every major target in southern England by the first weeks of 1941. All such counter-measures were the responsibility of the R.A.F.'s specially formed No. 80 Wing, which also looked after about sixty 'Starfish' and 'SF' sites. Produced with the assistance of film 'special effects' men and experts from the petroleum industry, these consisted of installations which could be set alight at points along the Knickebein and X-Gerät beams, to give the impression of, respectively, city areas or groups of small

buildings ablaze after bombing. Lit after the first aircraft in a bomber stream had passed overhead, they persuaded subsequent crews to drop their bombs where they would do little harm.

The first 'Starfish' was set up in Richmond Park, to protect London. The success achieved by the decoys can be gauged from the fact that 94 lightings drew bombs on 53 occasions between December 1940 and midsummer 1941. The very first 'Starfish' operation attracted 66 bombs intended for Bristol. The installation on Hayling Island collected 170 high-explosive bombs, 32 parachute mines and 5,000 incendiary bombs on the night of 17–18 April.

Equally impressive were the results achieved

placed around Berlin eventually included one that measured nine miles in diameter and simulated the whole city in cardboard and plywood, with even a dummy Tempelhof Airport. Russia, meanwhile, had increased the large number of British-supplied Hurricanes along its immense battlefront by supplementing the real thing with its own wooden replicas. (Such practices have continued to the present day, as was demonstrated by dummy SAM-2 and SAM-3 missiles and MiG-17 fighters found near the Suez Canal by Israeli forces after the October 1973 Yom Kippur War.)

The growing capability of radar-equipped night fighters, anti-aircraft rockets, radar-directed guns, decoys and dummies was hardly calculated to fill Bomber Command crews with the same delight as other Britons. In German service, they added to the already formidable difficulties and dangers of night operations.

There was no doubt of the vital importance of the air offensive from Britain, particularly at that point in the war. While the battle of Britain was still being fought, Winston Churchill had stated, in a minute put before the War Cabinet: 'The Navy can lose us the war, but only the Air Force can win it. Therefore our supreme effort must be made to gain overwhelming mastery in the air. The fighters are our salvation, but the bombers alone provide the means of victory. We must, therefore, develop the power to carry an ever-increasing volume of explosives to Germany, so as to pulverize the entire industry and scientific structure on which the war effort and economic life of the enemy depend, while holding him at arm's length from our island. In no other way at present visible can we hope to overcome the immense military power of Germany.'

At the time those words were written, R.A.F. Bomber Command lacked both the aircraft and equipment for such a task, but the 'heavies' conceived in 1936 were soon to put in an appearance. First of these was the four-engined Short Stirling, which had a maximum speed of 270 mph and a range of 590 miles with a 14,000-lb bombload or 2,010 miles with 3,500 lb. It could not fly above 17,000 feet, had a stalky undercarriage with a tendency to collapse, and a bomb-bay so designed that it would accommodate nothing larger than a 4,000-lb bomb. On the credit side, its armament of eight machine-guns in three turrets permitted its use over France in daylight from February 1941 onwards, and it compelled the Luftwaffe to come up and fight, as well as convincing the R.A.F. of the correctness of its decision in progressing to large aircraft, with a crew of seven or eight men. Furthermore, it continued to give good service as a glider tug and troop transport after better bombers had superseded it.

Avro's Manchester made its first night raid on 24–25 February 1941, only a fortnight after the Stirling. Its crews persisted with it for sixteen months, despite repeated engine failures and

by the 'K' and 'Q' sites, which protected fifty-three R.A.F. airfields by displaying dummy Hurricane, Spitfire, Defiant and Blenheim fighters, and Battle, Wellington and Whitley bombers. The 'Ks' were simply dummy airfields with about ten wooden aeroplanes apiece (the Hurricanes cost £50 each). The 'Qs' were more elaborate, and were complete with flare-path lighting for use at night.

Records covering German air raids up to June 1941 detail a total of 304 attacks on real R.A.F. airfields and 322 confirmed attacks on 'K' and 'Q' sites. Other nations took note. Bomber Command had to be wary of German versions of 'Starfish' in particular. The fifteen such sites

Sticks of bombs fall from B-17s of the U.S. Eighth Air Force as German flak (anti-aircraft fire) bursts at close quarters. At first, U.S.A.A.F. fighters lacked the range to escort the bombers on long-range missions and American losses were heavy. Many critics suggested that a switch should be made to night bombing, even if results might be less accurate. The U.S.A.A.F. persisted in daylight operations, introducing improved escort fighters.
U.S. Air Force

heavy losses. By then, Avro had begun delivery of the Lancaster, with four Merlin engines in place of the Manchester's two under-developed Vultures, and in so doing gave the R.A.F. the finest night bomber of the Second World War. By its side flew Handley Page Halifaxes, first used in action on the night of 11–12 March 1941, with a maximum bomb-load only 1,000 lb less at 13,000 lb.

With such aircraft leaving the factories in ever-increasing numbers (55 in December 1941, 81 in January 1942, 81 in February, 104 in March, 127 in April), Bomber Command might have expected German war production to begin showing signs of strain. Crews returning from

raids in the early part of the war had enthused about targets hit and destroyed; but in volume four of his history of the war, Winston Churchill recalled:

Late in 1940 Professor Lindemann had begun to raise doubts in my mind about the accuracy of our bombing, and in 1941 I authorized his Statistical Department to make an investigation at Bomber Headquarters. The results confirmed our fears. We learnt that although Bomber Command believed they had found the target, two-thirds of the crews actually failed to strike within five miles of it. The air photographs showed how little damage was being done.

It also appeared that the crews knew this, and

were discouraged by the poor results of so much hazard. Unless we could improve on this there did not seem much use in continuing night bombing.

Yet, as the Prime Minister had noted one year earlier, the bombers provided the only conceivable means of victory.

The lack of navigation aids to ensure accurate bombing was but one of many seemingly insoluble problems. The war was going badly and the situation seemed unlikely to improve, even if it got no worse. The mounting losses of merchant ships, upon which the survival of the nation depended, and the clear inability of the Royal Navy to end the U-boat menace, had

caused Churchill to allocate absolute priority to the battle of the Atlantic on 6 March 1941. The German submarines were being aided by Focke-Wulf Condor four-engined maritime patrol bombers, which could take off from bases in France, fly round the British west coast, far out into the North Atlantic and over the North Sea to Norway, refuel there and return next day. En route they bombed and machine-gunned ships, and reported the positions of convoys to the U-boats. As a result of such air-underwater teamwork, and events in the Mediterranean, British shipping losses averaged well over 500,000 tons every month in the spring of 1941.

Additional squadrons of long-range aircraft,

top
Waist gunners in a B-24 Liberator prepare for attack by enemy fighters. The men are wearing protective 'flak jackets'.
U.S. Air Force

above
A B-24 Liberator that did not return. Wreathed in flames, it was one of 22,948 U.S.A.A.F. aircraft lost in combat operations during the Second World War.
U.S. Air Force

right
No aircraft captured the imagination of the British more than the Mosquito. Built of wood, to save scarce metal, it could outfly any fighter sent to intercept it until the advent of jets. Towards the end of the war, from 20–21 February 1945, Mosquito bombers of the R.A.F.'s Light Night Striking Force raided Berlin on thirty-six consecutive nights. Flying between 30,000 and 40,000 feet, their loss rate was only one aircraft for every 2,000 sorties, a Bomber Command record.
Charles E Brown

below
The cutaway bomb-bay of this Lancaster identifies it as one of those used by No. 617 (Dambusters) Squadron to attack the Ruhr dams in May 1943. The story of the raid, which cost eight of the nineteen aircraft taking part, is one of the epics of military flying.

to supplement the Sunderland flying-boats of Coastal Command, could only come from Bomber Command, which transferred seventeen squadrons on a loan that was never repaid. Other bombers and crews were sent to North Africa, and, as a result of casualties, the bomber force was actually weaker at the end of 1941 than at the beginning.

It was difficult to suggest any aspect of the war that was going well as 1941 ended. In Africa and the Mediterranean, a see-saw battle had raged since Italy entered the war. In June 1940 there were a total of twenty-nine R.A.F. squadrons, with about 300 aircraft, in the entire Middle East Command under Air Chief Marshal Sir Arthur Longmore. This worked out at one aeroplane for each 15,000 square miles of territory for which he was responsible.

The best aircraft equipping the 13⅓ squadrons in Egypt were Blenheim I bombers and Gladiator biplane fighters. Others included Valentia bomber-transports which were not so very different from the Vernons used at Kirkuk in 1923. In the Western Desert of Egypt, face to face with the Italians, was No. 202 Group under Canadian Air Commodore Ray Collishaw. In the summer of 1917, as a young Flight Sub-Lieutenant in the R.N.A.S., he had led No. 10 Naval Squadron's famous Black Flight of Sopwith Triplanes (named *Black Maria*, *Black Death*, *Black Roger*, *Black Prince* and *Black Sheep*), which destroyed eighty-seven enemy aircraft in France in three months. Now he established a superiority over the Italian Fiat CR.42 biplane fighters and Savoia-Marchetti SM.79 bombers–which were every bit as good as his own aircraft–that was never to be reversed by the Regia Aeronautica and Luftwaffe during the three-year campaign.

The Italian Army, under Marshal Graziani, struck first on 10 September, marching into Egypt under a great triumphal arch through which it was intended that Benito Mussolini should ride at the head of his 'new Roman legions' when he took formal possession of Cairo.

With an American-built Rolls-Royce Merlin engine, the P-51 Mustang fighter was one of the outstanding aircraft of the war. These aircraft of the 1st Air Commando Force were photographed over the Chin Hills in Burma.
U.S. Air Force

181

right
Counter-measures in action.
Under 'Operation Corona',
fake messages were
broadcast to German night-
fighter pilots over a 'ghost
microphone'. At other times
the gramophone was used to
jam all radio signals
between the pilots and the
ground.
Imperial War Museum

below
With appropriate remarks
chalked on the side of their
Horsa glider, men of the
British Airborne Regiment
prepare to take off for
Normandy on the evening of
D-Day (6 June 1944), to
reinforce Allied troops
landed there earlier.
Imperial War Museum

After advancing sixty miles in two days, Graziani spent six weeks preparing for the next move. But within two months General O'Connor, commanding a much smaller force, pushed the Italians back 600 miles, occupying the whole coast of Cyrenaica as far as El Agheila, and taking 130,000 prisoners, 1,290 guns and 400 tanks.

While this was happening, British forces had been transferred to Greece, first to help repel Italian invaders and then in a vain bid to stem the German occupation of both that country and Yugoslavia. Hitler overwhelmed all opposition with twenty-seven divisions of the Wehrmacht and other troops from Italy, Hungary and Bulgaria, supported by the 1,200 combat aircraft of Luftflotte 4. The last act of this drama was played out in Crete, with the R.A.F. defenders reduced eventually to seven Hurricanes and Gladiators against Fliegerkorps VIII and XI, which had sent into the attack 430 bombers and 180 fighters, as well as 700 transport aircraft and 80 gliders to fly into the island 15,000 airborne troops.

The occupation of Crete cost Germany 220 aircraft, more than half of them transports. Some fell to Hurricanes flown over from Egypt. The

Royal Navy lost nine cruisers and destroyers sunk and seventeen other ships damaged in evacuating nearly 15,000 troops and members of the R.A.F. The Germans never again mounted a major airborne operation.

There were successes in this period for Britain. A combined land, sea and air assult cleared the whole of East Africa in three months, enabling Emperor Haile Selassie to re-enter his capital of Addis Ababa on 5 May 1941. In Iraq, an attempt to oust the British by a politician named Rashid Ali was quashed by what an official historian called 'makeshift crews in training aircraft'. As Rashid Ali's troops fled, the first He 111 bombers and Me 110 and CR.42 fighters arrived to assist them – just too late.

In North Africa the situation was less happy. General Erwin Rommel's Afrika Korps, with a full Panzer (armoured) division, and more than a hundred Ju 87 dive-bombers and Me 110 fighters, had arrived to bolster the Italians. The diversion of British forces to Greece left only one armoured brigade, one semi-trained infantry division and four squadrons of aircraft opposing them in Cyrenaica. A nine-day running battle saw the Germans and Italians back on the Egyptian border by March 1941.

The huge scale of the Anglo-American glider operation which supported the crossing of the Rhine, on 24 March 1945, is shown by this scene on the airfield of Tarrant Rushton, Dorset. On each side of the big Hamilcar gliders on the runway are their Halifax tugs. The complete armada used for the operation comprised 4,616 powered aircraft, including escorting fighters, and 1,326 gliders. *Imperial War Museum*

Over Malta, too, the Luftwaffe had joined the Italian Air Force, which was having difficulty in neutralizing this tiny island at Mussolini's back door. For most of the last three weeks in June 1940, Malta could put up only three Sea Gladiator biplanes to fend off more than 200 aircraft of the Regia Aeronautica based in Sicily. For the next month, these aircraft–known to the Maltese as *Faith*, *Hope* and *Charity*–were supplemented by four Hurricanes. The Italian bombers tried flying higher. When the fighters showed they could follow, a fighter escort was demanded. Finally, the attackers sought the cover of darkness.

Soon the defences were strengthened by Hurricanes flown in from the aircraft-carrier *Argus* and serviced by ground crews who had travelled to the island by submarine. Morale received a boost on 11 November 1940, when Swordfish torpedo-bombers of the Fleet Air Arm

(back under Admiralty control since 1937) from the new carrier *Illustrious* put three of Italy's six battleships out of action in an epic night attack on the harbour of Taranto. Soon afterwards, Malta itself received the first of a succession of Wellington bombers that were to prey constantly on Italian and German ships crossing to North Africa.

Here, too, success was to turn bitter before the end of 1941. Between 1 June and 31 October, nearly half of all the supplies dispatched to Rommel had been lost. R.A.F. and Fleet Air Arm aircraft from Malta had sunk well over one-third of the 220,000 tons of shipping sent to the bottom. As a counter-measure twenty-five U-boats were transferred from the Atlantic to the Mediterranean, and achieved a spectacular initial success by sinking the carrier *Ark Royal*. In Sicily the Italian Air Force was reinforced by Flieger-korps II of the Luftwaffe, under Generalfeld-

marschall Kesselring, flown in directly from its bases near Moscow.

Since invading Russia on 22 June, the Wehrmacht had made huge advances, inflicting terrible losses on both the Red Army and the civilian population. But the combination of Soviet courage and the same winter conditions that had defeated Napoleon in 1812, now halted the Germans before they reached their objectives of Moscow, Leningrad and the Lower Don.

The Red Air Force and those who built its aircraft were already giving a hint of their future strength. Aircraft factories, all their tools and all their workers had been transported hundreds of miles eastwards, to the safety of the Urals, as soon as the war on the Eastern Front began. Within one month of arrival at the new sites, deliveries of aircraft like the Yakovlev Yak-1 fighter were resumed. Some 37,000 single-seater Yaks of various types were to be produced by

1945, ranking in achievement with fighters like the British Hurricane and Spitfire, the American Mustang and the Japanese Zero.

Equally renowned was Sergei Ilyushin's Il-2 ground-attack aircraft, known in Russia as the *Sturmovik*. With a speed of about 250 mph, this tough two-seater was heavily armoured against ground fire, so that it could race in at low level to fire its two 20-millimetre or 37-millimetre guns and eight 82-millimetre rockets at German tanks, and drop its 220-lb high-explosive bombs or clusters of small anti-tank and anti-personnel bombs. Even the heavy German Tiger and Panther tanks could not withstand such attack, and many planned German offensives were crushed before they could be mounted.

As early as 24 December 1941, Stalin told aircraft workers that the Il-2 was 'as essential to the Red Army as air and bread'. Its successes, especially with rocket armament, were to have a major influence on fighter and attack aircraft design throughout the world.

In that closing month of 1941, it required a great deal of confidence to predict an eventual victory for Russia; or for the British against Rommel's Afrika Korps; or for R.A.F. Bomber Command; or for Malta, which mustered only 130 aircraft against 450 bombers and fighters in Sicily; or for the United States, which had suffered a shattering blow at Pearl Harbor on 7 December. Three hundred and sixty Japanese naval bombers, torpedo-bombers and escorting fighters had taken off before sunrise from a strike force of six carriers, with a supporting force of battleships and cruisers, 275 miles from the great U.S. Pacific base. By 10 a.m., the Japanese aircraft had completed their task, leaving behind them what Winston Churchill described as 'a shattered fleet hidden in a pall of fire and smoke, and the vengeance of the United States. . . . The mastery of the Pacific had passed into Japanese hands, and the strategic balance of the world was

Standard Allied glider tugs were C-47s (Dakotas), two of which are shown here towing Hadrian troop-carriers across the Normandy coastline. The success of the invasion would have been much less assured had it not been possible to land specially trained units at strategic points.
U.S. Air Force

for the time being fundamentally changed.'

The desperate situation for Britain and its new ally did not improve quickly; but Germany, Italy, Japan and those who aligned themselves with them had far overreached themselves. This was hardly apparent as the Japanese forces fanned out in the Pacific, occupying the Philippines, Thailand, Singapore, Malaya, and the Dutch East Indies. By early 1942 they were in New Guinea, a brief flight away from Australia, and had penetrated through Burma to the border of India.

A major shock to the Allied air forces at this period was the quality of Japanese aircraft, particularly the Mitsubishi Zero fighter. Yet British observers, and U.S. pilots flying as members of the American Volunteer Group (the famous Flying Tigers) in support of General Chiang Kai-Shek's forces in China, had reported

details of the Zero long before the Pacific War began. Like so many warnings from China, which had felt the weight of Japanese aggression since 1931, it was never passed on.

The long and bitterly contested struggle to drive the invaders back to their home islands began at sea, as had the action which opened the Pacific War. It was little more than a morale-booster for the American public when sixteen B-25B Mitchell bombers, led by Lieutenant-Colonel 'Jimmy' Doolittle, took off from the carrier *Hornet* on 18 April 1942 to attack targets 800 miles away in Tokyo, Kobe, Yokohama and Nagoya. They caused little damage, and all the aircraft were lost in attempting to find safety in China; but most of the crews survived.

A few weeks later the battle of the Coral Sea brought more tangible results. Anticipating a Japanese invasion of Port Moresby, in New

Guinea, Rear-Admiral Fletcher, U.S.N., placed part of his fleet of two carriers and other U.S. and Australian ships on the probable invasion course and used the remainder to hunt Japanese covering forces. For the first time in history, a major engagement was fought by ships which never made direct contact with each other, all attacks being carried out by aircraft. Each side lost one carrier and had another damaged.

The battle of Midway, in early June, ended in a far more convincing American victory, and marked the turning-point of the Pacific War. Again it was fought mainly by aircraft, with U.S. Army Air Force (U.S.A.A.F.) bombers supporting the naval squadrons, and submarines from both sides picking off ships damaged in the battle. Japan lost four carriers and a heavy cruiser, against one U.S. carrier and an escorting destroyer sunk. Losses in aircraft were about

250 Japanese and 151 American, a more damaging blow to Japan being the death of so many of its best aircrew.

In the Atlantic and northern waters, too, 1942 saw the tide of war turn in the Allies' favour. To offset a shortage of carriers, which offered the most effective protection for convoys, the Royal Navy had catapults fitted over the bows of merchant vessels (known as 'CAM-ships': Catapult Armed Merchantmen), and some naval craft, from which specially strengthened Hurricane fighters could be launched to intercept marauding Focke-Wulf Condors. The pilots were Fleet Air Arm and R.A.F. volunteers, who normally had to 'ditch' their aircraft after a sortie, in the hope of being picked up by a passing ship, unless they were close to a friendly shore.

The first victory by a Sea Hurricane 'catafighter' came on 3 August 1941, when Lieutenant R W H Everett was launched from H.M.S. *Maplin* and shot down a Condor. Meanwhile, the Royal Navy had achieved even more promising results with American-built Martlet naval fighters based on H.M.S. *Audacity*, a converted German merchant ship. In two voyages the Martlets shot down five Condors and forced a submarine to submerge hurriedly.

About twenty more MAC-ships (Merchant Aircraft Carriers) were quickly produced, by mounting a flight deck on an otherwise normal merchantman hull, which could be filled with grain or other cargo. In addition, about forty small escort carriers were built for the Royal Navy in the United States, each normally equipped with up to a dozen anti-submarine Swordfish and Hurricanes. Operations with these ships began on 2 September 1942, when convoy PQ 18 set sail from Scotland with supplies for Russia. Its predecessor, PQ 17, had suffered heavily from attacks by Luftwaffe aircraft based in Norway and Finland. This time Sea Hurricanes from H.M.S. *Avenger* destroyed five enemy raiders and damaged seventeen others.

In due course the U-boat menace, as well as the

A new era in warfare opened on 12 June 1944, when the Germans launched the first V-1 pilotless flying-bomb against London. Attacks on the launch sites by the Allied air forces, over a considerable period, restricted the attack to a fraction of what had been intended. None the less, more than 30,000 V-1s were built and the version illustrated was developed for a period as Germany's counterpart of the Japanese suicide aircraft. The main difference was that the pilot of the modified V-1 did at least have a chance of taking to his parachute in the moments before his aircraft rammed an enemy aircraft.
Harold Martin

anti-shipping aircraft of the Luftwaffe and Regia Aeronautica, had their depredations reduced considerably by carrier-borne and shore-based aircraft. New equipment and armament produced for these aircraft included ASV (air-to-surface-vessel) radar, which could locate surfaced submarines at night or in bad weather, making it hazardous for them to recharge the batteries on which underwater propulsion depended. Invention of the *Schnorkel* later reduced the need for surfacing, but radar became more efficient at picking up tiny 'echoes', and the use of improved depth-charges and air-to-surface rockets made air attacks more deadly. So did the powerful searchlights carried by aircraft like the Sunderland flying-boat and Liberator patrol bomber to illuminate any U-boat detected by radar.

The Liberator made an immense contribution to victory in the battle of the Atlantic by closing the mid-ocean 'gap', where previously U-boats had been able to operate beyond the range of shore-based aircraft. It was only one of many types bought by Britain from the United States since its rearmament programme began in the thirties. Indeed, U.S. industry initially built up

both its capacity and the fighting qualities of its aircraft by meeting large contracts for aircraft like the Hudson patrol bomber, Harvard trainer, Maryland reconnaissance-bomber, Fortress bomber and Mustang fighter (which was designed to an R.A.F. specification and fitted eventually with a Merlin engine).

American-built fighters and bombers played a major role in the final stages of the North African campaign. By January 1942 Rommel had been pushed back to El Agheila, but by mid-year he had returned to Egypt, after taking advantage of the plight of Malta, which was under heavy air attack, and the transfer of British troops to the Far East. It was to be the final fling for the Afrika Korps.

Blocking its path now, at a place named El Alamein, was the Eighth Army under its new commander, Lieutenant-General B L Montgomery. He had 165,000 men, 2,275 guns and 600 tanks. Rommel had 93,000 men, 1,450 guns and 470 tanks. The air commander, Air Vice-Marshal A W Tedder, had 1,500 aircraft in 60 R.A.F. and Fleet Air Arm squadrons. In addition, there were 13 U.S., 13 South African and a total of 10 more

left
The Berlin Airlift of 1948–49
showed how unarmed
transport aircraft could
prevent a third World War.
The successors of the C-54s
and Yorks of that era are
powerful turbine-engined
transports like this
American-built Lockheed
Hercules of the R.A.F. Their
duties include fighting
famine, and this Hercules
was photographed whilst
dropping food by parachute
to starving inhabitants of
remote areas in Nepal,
during Operation Khana
Cascade, in March 1973.
Ministry of Defence

below
Another of the big military
transports of the late fifties
and sixties, the Douglas
C-133 Cargomaster could
carry any of America's
intercontinental ballistic
missiles in its cavernous
hold.
Douglas Aircraft Co.

For many post-war years the strategic jet bombers of East and West were the vehicles of the nuclear deterrent policy. Most formidable of the R.A.F.'s series of three V-bomber types was the Avro Vulcan. Able to fly at just below the speed of sound, it could attack distant targets from high or low altitude with high-explosive or nuclear bombs and missiles. *Hawker Siddeley Aviation Ltd*

left
In the closing stages of the North African campaign, the Germans tried desperately to get supplies and reinforcements to the Afrika Korps. After twenty ships had been sunk in one month, the Luftwaffe tried to fill the gap with Ju 52 transports, and even with slow and cumbersome six-engined Me 323 glider-type aircraft. Between 5 and 22 April, 432 of the German transports were destroyed for the loss of 35 Allied fighters. The Me 323 shown here was weighted down with 10 tons of petrol, which turned it into an aerial bonfire when the fighters attacked

below
Another variation on the pilotless aircraft theme was the Mistel composite aircraft. The lower component, usually an old Ju 88, was packed with about 1½ tons of explosive. Above it was mounted a piloted Me 109 or Fw 190 fighter. The engines of both aircraft were run for take-off under the control of the pilot. The two aircraft then flew together to the target, where the pilot aimed and released the lower aircraft like a giant glider bomb.
Imperial War Museum

opposite, top
Air-to-air missiles, like this Firestreak carried on the side of a Lightning two-seater, form the basic armament of modern inter-ceptors. Wars in Vietnam and elsewhere have proved, however, that guns are often essential for close combat.
Charles E Brown

opposite, bottom
As naval aircraft became progressively larger, it was increasingly difficult to accommodate them in the restricted space on board carriers, and to transport them by lift between the flight deck and hangar deck. This A-3D Skywarrior attack aircraft of the U.S. Navy needed a folding fin as well as folding wings.

Australian, Greek, French, Rhodesian and Yugoslav squadrons. About 350 of Rommel's 689 aircraft were serviceable.

Among the R.A.F. aircraft were Mk IID versions of the Hurricane, carrying under each wing a 40-millimetre cannon as big as a Bofors anti-aircraft gun. Supplementing the immense hitting power of the wheel-to-wheel artillery barrage with which Montgomery began his offensive, the IIDs demoralized the German Panzer units. Hard fighting lay ahead, but there was no stopping the Eighth Army this time, as it swept along the whole North African coast, under its air umbrella, to link up finally with the Allied Expeditionary Force that had been put ashore in Algeria on 8 November, under General Dwight Eisenhower.

New concepts of three-service cooperation under a supreme Allied commander had been tried out in Operation Torch, the landing in Algeria. New efficiency in multi-nation tactical air power, in close accord with land forces, was born as the Eighth Army moved west. The German Army, nearly 250,000 strong, which surrendered on 12 May 1943 was but the tip of an iceberg. The North African campaign had cost Italy and Germany 950,000 men killed and captured, nearly 2,400,000 tons of shipping sunk, nearly 8,000 aircraft, 6,200 guns and 2,550 tanks.

In Russia the turning-point had come on 2 February, when the 90,000 survivors of 21 German divisions and one Romanian division followed their commander, Field-Marshal von Paulus, into Russian prison camps. Stalin now pressed for the opening of a second front. Churchill argued, instead, for the victorious armies to cross from North Africa, through Sicily, to Italy – and his views prevailed. Malta's siege was over, but the advance northward through Italy was to be long and hard.

The Italians had had enough. Mussolini was deposed. His successor, Marshal Badoglio, nego-tiated an armistice at the beginning of September 1943 but the Germans fought on.

Meanwhile, it could be claimed that the real second front demanded by Stalin had long been opened farther north in Europe by the bomber

above
As the end of the war in
Europe drew near, and the
Luftwaffe found itself
grounded increasingly by
lack of fuel, bombs were
exploded on board aircraft
that had to be left at
airfields in the path of the
Allied advance. This Me 110
was found on an airfield
near Brunswick.
U.S. Air Force

right
During operations in the
south-west Pacific, smoke-
screens were laid by B-25
Mitchells of the U.S. Far
Eastern Air Forces to hide
the movements of American
men and equipment from the
Japanese on shore, and to
enable other aircraft to
launch their attacks without
being detected.
U.S. Air Force

offensive, now waged by the R.A.F. at night and
the U.S.A.A.F. by day. In an effort to stay alive,
the Germans had to keep 2,000,000 people engaged
on anti-aircraft defence, 900,000 of them anti-
aircraft gunners in the homeland and occupied
territories in the west. Aircraft production had
to be concentrated on defensive fighters, ending
all hope of hitting back with long-range bombers.
This was bad for the morale of both the pilots and
the public in Germany. It provided direct help for
the Russians by reducing Luftwaffe units that
could be spared for the Eastern Front from
65 per cent of the air force's total strength in
June 1941 to only 32 per cent by late 1944.

The R.A.F.'s early bombing inaccuracy had
been ended by the introduction of electronic
navigation aids. First of them had been 'Gee',
giving a position fix within six miles anywhere
inside a 400-mile radius from its transmitters.
With its aid, Bomber Command had mounted the
first 'thousand-bomber raid' against Cologne, on
30-31 May 1942. Saturating the defences, 898 of
the 1,045 aircraft dispatched unloaded 1,455 tons
of bombs on the city, starting fires that could still
be seen 150 miles away on the journey home.
Losses, at 3·6 per cent, were lower than for the
average night raid. The 600 acres of Cologne
destroyed represented more than the damage
resulting from all previous Bomber Command
raids on Germany combined.

Before long, even better navigation aids were
available to the R.A.F. The best of them, H2S,
was a radar device, self-contained in the aircraft,
which produced a clear radar map of the terrain
beneath the bomber; large buildings were easily
identified.

Daylight raids by the U.S.A.A.F. had always
been more accurate in terms of target identification; but the huge formations of Eighth Air
Force B-17 Fortresses and B-24 Liberators
initially suffered terrible casualties as Luftwaffe
fighters tore into them. Only by persistent
wearing down of the opposition, perfection of
cross-fire from the massed guns of huge 'blocks'
of bombers, and the gradual extension of the
range of escorting fighters did the daylight
bombers survive. In doing so they sealed the fate
of Germany.

There were many great moments: the attack
on the Ruhr dams by No. 617 Squadron of the
R.A.F. on the night of 16–17 May 1943, dropping
Barnes Wallis's unique 'bouncing bombs' from
their specially adapted Lancasters; the continuous day and night onslaught on Hamburg by
Bomber Command and the U.S. Eighth Air
Force between 24 July and 3 August 1943 created
a fire-storm that swept through the city, killing
41,800 people and burning 6,000 acres of buildings. Having sown the wind, Germany was certainly reaping a whirlwind.

While the R.A.F. 'heavies' pounded city after
city, fast unarmed Mosquito bombers, made of
wood to save precious metal, dropped 4,000-
pounders on Berlin night after night and out-
paced all the fighters sent up to intercept them.
The Luftwaffe fighter pilots were themselves
directed to places far from the target areas by
'spoof' messages broadcast in German on their
special frequencies by radio stations in England.
Instead of producing signals to guide them
towards a bomber, their radar picture would
suddenly break up into a featureless pattern

because of jamming equipment fitted in British electronic counter-measures aircraft. Fake signals said that their home airfield was under attack and directed them to another, so that they ran out of fuel en route. If they were fortunate enough to arrive back at base safely, there could well be a Mosquito 'intruder' in the landing circuit, waiting to blast them out of the sky as soon as they were straight and level, with wheels and flaps down.

None of this made the invasion of Europe unnecessary. The team that led it was made up of the victors from North Africa, headed by Eisenhower, Tedder and Montgomery. The techniques learned there and in Italy were supplemented by new ones.

Preparatory raids all along the French Channel coastline kept the Germans guessing where the assault would fall. Agents dropped inside France, and even landed there by black-painted Lysanders from England, helped to organize and arm the local Resistance groups. On the day of the invasion, a carefully devised to-and-fro pattern of flying by aircraft of No. 100 Group, R.A.F., fitted with special electronic devices, gave the effect of a large naval force crossing the Channel at a point where the seas were devoid of traffic. Huge forces of transport aircraft then dropped parachute troops and towed gliders packed with men and equipment to supplement the forces landed from the sea.

Carpet bombing by large bomber forces, all dumping their loads simultaneously from tight formation, cleared whole areas ahead of the troops, but sometimes broke up the terrain so badly that a quick advance was thus rendered impossible. When the Germans did break, at Falaise, rocket-firing Typhoon fighters wrought an execution that was even more terrible than that inflicted on the Turks in Palestine in September 1918.

In vain the Germans rushed into service new 'wonder weapons' to snatch victory from disaster. Pulsejet-powered V-1 flying-bombs began their raucous, pilotless attacks on Britain on 12 June 1944, only six days after the Allied invasion began. In September they were followed by the first of 1,115 big V-2 rockets. Of 7,547 V-1s launched against Britain, 1,847 were destroyed by fighters, 1,866 by anti-aircraft guns, 232 by a balloon barrage and 12 by the Royal Navy. There was no defence against V-2 except, ultimately, to drive the enemy from the places used as launch-sites.

V-1 and V-2 were ingenious, representing the first, primitive weapons of the new Missile Age. They killed a total of 8,994 people in Britain, but were too few, too late, and too vulnerable to the Allied air forces which blasted their development centre, assembly sheds and V-1 launch-sites. The revolutionary rocket-powered aircraft flown by the Luftwaffe against U.S. bomber formations, and jet-propelled fighters flown by both sides were also too late to affect the outcome of the war. In the end, Germany was crushed between the vast armies of the United States, Britain and their Allies in the west and the Russians in the east. Their cities were laid waste and their aircraft and vehicles were grounded by a shortage of fuel, the result of the bomber offensive.

Benito Mussolini and his mistress were shot by Italian Communist partisans on 29 April,

right
During a B-29 raid on Tokyo, this aircraft was hit by a Japanese fighter, which shot away the transparent blister over Sergeant J R Krantz's gun-aiming station. The gunner was blown out of the aircraft, and remained hanging by one leg from a safety strap for nearly fifteen minutes, as shown in this photograph, until he could be hauled back on board by other crew members. Although unconscious when recovered, and suffering from frostbite through exposure at 25,000 feet, he was taken back safely to a base hospital for treatment.
U.S. Air Force

after which their bodies were exhibited, hanging head down, in a petrol station at Milan. On the same day, Adolf Hitler and his newly married wife, Eva Braun, committed suicide in Berlin after ordering that their bodies be burned. For Germany the war ended on 8 May 1945, with the Russians in Berlin.

Japan lasted a few more months. Her armies had been first harried in Burma by small units of tough jungle-fighters, known as 'Chindits', put down behind their lines by the Allied air forces. Twenty-three squadrons of transport aircraft–mostly Dakotas or C-47s–of the Combat Cargo Task Force and Air Cargo Headquarters of the U.S. Tenth Air Force then air-supplied every need of the 300,000 soldiers who drove the surviving Japanese from Burma.

In the Pacific the grim island-hopping campaign achieved its major objectives in July 1944, with the capture of Saipan and Tinian in the Mariana Islands. These were to become bases for the big B-29 Stratofortress bombers ordered by the U.S.A.F. for the pre-invasion offensive against Japan. Before long, these islands were to look like huge aircraft-carriers, packed with aeroplanes, as the assault developed.

Meanwhile, the Japanese adopted desperate measures to ward off the U.S. Marines and other forces coming ever closer to their home islands. None was more chilling to Western minds than the use of Kamikaze suicide aircraft against the U.S. naval forces, now reinforced with Royal Navy carriers and other warships. The first such attack had been made during the battle of the Philippine Sea in June 1944; but the main attacks date from 15 October, when Vice-Admiral Masebumi Arima tried to crash his aircraft deliberately into a U.S. aircraft-carrier. During the ten months that followed, the suicide pilots accounted for 48·1 per cent of all U.S. warships damaged and 21·3 per cent of ships sunk during the entire forty-four-month Pacific War.

The first Kamikazes were normal combat aircraft and dived into their targets with bombs in place. Later, the specially designed, rocket-powered Yokosuka Ohka (Cherry Blossom) was used. This was carried to the vicinity of U.S. naval forces under the belly of a Mitsubishi G4M2e 'mother-plane', released and dived at more than 600 mph into the selected ship, carrying 2,645 lb of explosive in its nose.

Pilots who gave their lives in this way became 'hero gods' among their kinsfolk; but such gods could not save Japan. On 9 March 1945, 334 B-29s attacked Tokyo with incendiary bombs, destroying one-quarter of all the buildings in the Japanese capital and taking the lives of 83,793 of its citizens. Neither of the atomic bombs, dropped on Hiroshima on 6 August and Nagasaki on 9 August, killed so many people; but they did end the war.

above
Maurauders of the U.S. Ninth Air Force Bombardment Group fly over the Allied fleet during the Normandy landings.

left
During the last nine months of the Pacific war, the Japanese launched a large-scale bombing offensive against the United States. The vehicles used were paper balloons, each 32 feet in diameter and carrying as payload a 33-lb anti-personnel bomb and two incendiary bombs. More than 9,000 were launched on the long journey across the Pacific. Of these, 1,000 are estimated to have reached their destination.
U.S. Army

opposite, bottom
Japanese cities were terribly vulnerable to incendiary raids. This photograph shows Oita (population 77,000) ablaze after a heavy fire-bomb attack on the night of 16 July 1945. As well as containing many industries, the city was an important distribution centre for both rail and waterborne traffic.
U.S. Air Force

right
While the Japanese were busy launching their paper balloons, American scientists were perfecting this strange bomb. Known as 'Little Boy', it was 10 feet long and 2 feet 4 inches in diameter, with a weight of about 9,000 lb. Dropped on Hiroshima from a B-29 Stratofortress on 6 August 1945, it produced results equivalent to 20,000 tons of high explosive and killed 66,000 people.
U.S. Air Force

below
Two B-29s of the 509th Composite Group, part of the 313th Wing of the U.S. Twentieth Air Force, flew over Nagasaki on 9 August 1945. One dropped a bomb and the other flew as escort. As they left, this huge mushroom-shape pillar of smoke billowed up to show where 39,000 people had suddenly ceased to exist. Five days later the war was over.
U.S. Air Force

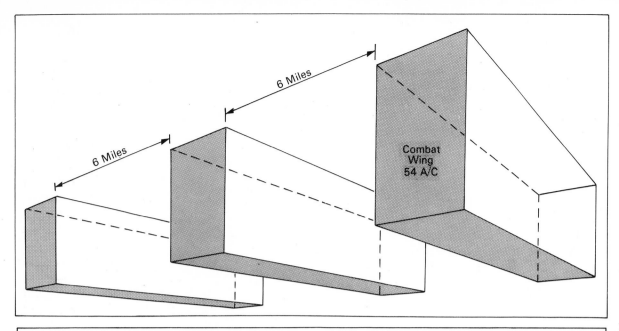

A combat wing formation, showing the 54-aircraft formation employed in March–April 1943 by American bombers during the early unescorted raids on Germany. Three group formations, as shown in (a), combined to form a combat wing formation, as shown in (b). The formation occupied a volume of sky about 600 yards long, over a mile wide and half a mile in depth. Prior to reaching their target, the groups split into line astern, to facilitate concentration of bombing.

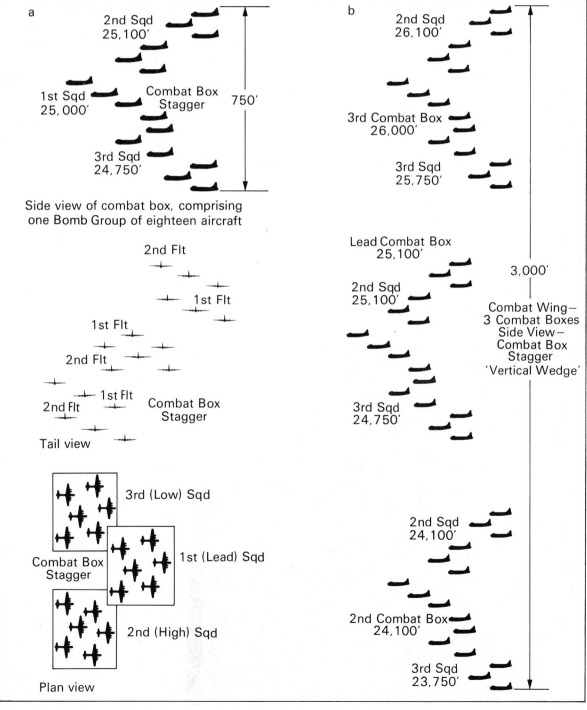

a

2nd Sqd
25,100'

1st Sqd
25,000'

Combat Box
Stagger

750'

3rd Sqd
24,750'

Side view of combat box, comprising
one Bomb Group of eighteen aircraft

2nd Flt

1st Flt

1st Flt

2nd Flt

1st Flt

2nd Flt

Combat Box
Stagger

Tail view

3rd (Low) Sqd

Combat Box
Stagger

1st (Lead) Sqd

2nd (High) Sqd

Plan view

b

2nd Sqd
26,100'

3rd Combat Box
26,000'

3rd Sqd
25,750'

Lead Combat Box
25,100'

2nd Sqd
25,100'

3,000'

Combat Wing—
3 Combat Boxes
Side View—
Combat Box
Stagger
'Vertical Wedge'

3rd Sqd
24,750'

2nd Sqd
24,100'

2nd Combat Box
24,100'

3rd Sqd
23,750'

The Big Stick

As memories of the Second World War recede, there is a growing tendency to belittle the contribution to victory made by air power. It would be wrong to suggest that bombing won the war against Germany; but the bomber offensive did cause the dearth of fuel that brought Hitler's war machine grinding to a halt. In the Pacific the clear ability of America's atomic bombs to erase Japan from the map made an invasion of the home islands unnecessary.

The cost of it all, in wasted time, machines and lives, was staggering. In terms of aircraft production alone, more than 750,000 aeroplanes were built between January 1935 and September 1945. Of these, 76,320 were manufactured in Japan, 111,787 in Germany (up to 1944), 131,549 in the United Kingdom, and 303,713 in the United States. According to Stalin, Soviet production was at a rate of 40,000 aircraft a year in 1944. German deliveries of combat aircraft continued to increase to the end, despite Allied bombing, but in 1944 65 per cent were single-engined fighters.

Statistics of this kind tend to become meaningless when one knows that the wasteland of Hiroshima, with its shadowed stonework providing the sole clue to where people were sitting at 8.15 a.m. on 6 August 1945, was the result of one aeroplane dropping one bomb.

To anyone possessing a spark of humanity, the thought of what occurred in Hiroshima and Nagasaki during that August must be heartbreaking. Those with minds as logical as a computer might ask if it is any worse to be atomized than to be burned by napalm 'sticky fire' bombs, first used by the U.S.A.A.F. against the Germans preparatory to the U.S. Army breakout from the Normandy beachhead on 25 July 1944. Others, wishing to emphasize that the harshest war is often tinged with humanity, will point to the fact that every day in late July and early August 1945 B-29s dropped on Japanese cities 1,500,000 leaflets warning of heavy raids to come.

Invasion of Japan by Allied armies would certainly have cost many more lives than the 71,379 lost at Hiroshima and 40,000 or so at Nagasaki; but was not Japan already virtually defeated? Even ignoring the U.S. air offensives, could there have been any future for a maritime nation which entered the war with 5,500,000 tons of shipping and, after adding captures and new construction, lost 8,500,000 tons in three and a half years?

For a nation like Britain, brought nearly to its knees by the U-boat campaign in two world wars, there is a lesson to be remembered in the fact that 5,000,000 tons of Japanese shipping were lost to submarine attack in 1941–45. The atomic bombs provided an even starker lesson for the whole world. True, the United States had a monopoly of such weapons in 1945, but it could not be long before other nations discovered how to build them. The fear which people felt after seeing films taken in Hiroshima was far more real than any produced by photographs of atomic bomb tests in a safe area of the New Mexican desert. Thus the present survival of all who read this book might be said to result from the 'peace through fear' bought with more than 110,000 Japanese lives. Its more formal name is the 'nuclear deterrent policy'.

To a high proportion of the world's population, rejoicing that another great war had ended, the sudden barrier of coldness, even hostility, that separated former Allies in the immediate postwar period was difficult to understand. Had the average Englishman been aware, before the war with Germany was over, that Winston Churchill believed 'Soviet Russia had become a mortal danger to the free world', he would have muttered something like: 'Old Winston's started his warmongering again.' Now, thirty years later, that same Englishman might agree that there was reason for Churchill's suggestions that the Anglo-American armies ought to occupy Berlin, liberate Czechoslovakia, and stay in being until a settlement had been reached on all major issues between East and West.

None of these things happened. The R.A.F., which had ended the war with 55,469 aircraft, 9,200 of them in first-line service, was allowed to shrink to a little over 1,000 aircraft in 100 under-strength squadrons by 1948.

opposite, top
First man to fly at supersonic speed, on 14 October 1947, was Captain Charles Yeager of the U.S.A.F. His rocket-powered Bell X-1, painted bright orange and named *Glamorous Glennis* after his wife, is shown here under the B-29 mother-plane from which it was launched at 30,000 feet. Yeager's speed of 670 mph at 42,000 feet was equivalent to Mach 1·015. *Bell Aircraft Corporation*

opposite, bottom
The 'big stick' which played a major role in keeping the peace for twelve troubled postwar years was the U.S.A.F's mighty Convair B-36 bomber. This RB-36D version was equipped as a reconnaissance bomber, carrying the most powerful cameras ever fitted to an aeroplane. *Consolidated Vultee Aircraft Corporation*

On 27 July 1944, it had been the first air force in the world to send a full squadron of jet aircraft into action, when the twin-engined Meteors of No. 616 Squadron began operations against German V-1 flying-bombs. The German Messerschmitt Me 262 might have been first if Hitler, obsessed by the success of Mosquitoes over Berlin, had not delayed its use by insisting on its conversion to carry bombs. In doing so he spared the U.S.A.A.F. daylight bomber force from an earlier and more serious mauling than it eventually received from the Me 262s.

Documents that fell into Allied hands after the war showed that far more advanced combat aircraft had been under design and development in Germany. Had the war continued, the Luftwaffe might ultimately have had a 620-mph Focke-Wulf helicopter fighter, with a jet-driven rotor that turned round rather than above its fuselage; and a tiny supersonic rocket-armed delta powered by a ram-jet engine which burned powdered coal. There were dozens of other equally exciting projects. Far more important in the short term were the results of wind-tunnel tests with swept-back wings. These showed, unmistakeably, the advantages of such wings by comparison with the unswept wings on the first generation of British, American and Russian jets.

With little money to spare for defence, as in the 1920s, Britain decided to set a new world speed record of 616 mph with the latest version of the Meteor in September 1946, and then soldier on with this fighter and the single-engined Vampire for a few more years. It was to be 1950 before the last R.A.F. day-fighter squadron progressed from piston-engines to jets. The last of the night-fighter units had to be patient until 1952; and no bomber squadron was to have jet aircraft until mid-1951, seven years after the Arado Ar 234 reconnaissance-bomber became operational with the wartime Luftwaffe.

America was more adventurous, and flew the prototype of its sweptwing F-86 Sabre on 1 October 1947. Later that month, a courageous U.S. Air Force officer, Captain Charles E Yeager, became the first person in the world to fly faster

than the speed of sound, after being air-launched from a B-29 bomber in a Bell X-1 rocket-plane. He had a rough ride; but on 26 April 1948, the F-86 also exceeded Mach 1 (the speed of sound, which varies from approximately 760 mph at sea level to 660 mph above 36,000 feet) much more comfortably. This was an important development, as the whole object of switching to jets had been to fly faster and higher than was practicable with a propeller-driving piston-engine. It had seemed for some years that the so-called 'sound barrier' of shock waves, built up as an object approaches the speed of sound, might prove impenetrable, and many pilots had lost their lives when aircraft were so badly buffeted by the shock-waves that they broke up. Now it was clear that careful design and plenty of power were the answers to breaking through the 'barrier' to the smooth air beyond the speed of sound.

What nobody knew until some years later was that the Soviet Union also had a workmanlike new sweptwing jet fighter known as the 'MiG-15', which had flown for the first time on 30 December 1947. Although not supersonic, it represented an enormous advance in Russian aviation technology. Its engine was a British Rolls-Royce Nene, one of a number of fine turbojets of this type released for export by the Labour Government which had ousted Churchill's administration even before the war with Japan was over.

During the war years, Russia had done very little strategic bombing, using its large air forces mainly in a tactical role, in support of the Red Army. This helps to explain why Americans tended to regard as little more than a political nuisance what Winston Churchill had called the 'iron curtain' dividing East and West in Europe. The United States alone possessed atomic bombs, and the means of delivering them. One of its former Presidents, Theodore Roosevelt, had advised that one should always 'Speak softly and

This queue of Yorks at Gatow gives a hint of the intensity at which the airlift operated. A pilot who made a faulty approach to land was not allowed to circuit again, but had to return to the airfield in West Germany from which he had taken off. *A V Roe & Co*

defensive armament of sixteen 20-millimetre cannon, housed in six remotely controlled fuse-lage turrets and nose and tail turrets. In its final form, as the B-36J, its six 3,800-hp piston-engines were supplemented by four jets in underwing pods, giving a maximum over-the-target speed of 411 mph at a height of 36,400 feet. Maximum bomb-load was an incredible 86,000 lb–far more than the take-off weight of a wartime Lancaster carrying a 22,000-pounder–and it had a range of 6,800 miles with 10,000 lb of bombs.

Perhaps the best tribute that can be paid to the B-36 is that it was never called upon to demonstrate its frightening capability in anger throughout its twelve years of service as America's primary peace-keeper. Instead, as at Kirkuk in 1923, it was the inspired use of trans-port aircraft that enabled the world to deal peaceably with the first crisis of the 'cold war'.

At every point at which East and West were in contact in Europe there was trouble, suggesting that the main aim of the Soviet Union was to tighten its hold on as much as possible of the territory once occupied by or allied to Germany, at the expense of its former Allies. America's High Commissioner in Austria, General Mark Clark, recalled later how he had said to his Soviet opposite number, Field-Marshal Konev: 'You've made ten demands at this council meeting that we can't meet. But suppose I should say "All right. We agree to all ten demands." Then what would you do?' "Tomorrow", he said, "I'd have ten new ones."'

above
Everyone knows that it is hazardous to land a helicopter too near to trees, because of the long, spinning rotor blades. But there are times when the chance of saving a life makes the risk worth while. This R.A.F. Whirlwind was in Malaya in 1966 during the 'Firedog' emergency.
Ministry of Defence

carry a big stick.' In place of earlier Super-fortress atom-bombers, the U.S.A.F. (now an independent service) had begun re-equipping in 1947 with a truly gigantic stick in the shape of the six-engined B-36 strategic bomber.

Still the largest combat aircraft ever to have served with any air force, the B-36 had a wing span of 230 feet and needed a crew of fifteen, including four reliefs, to fly it and man its

In the face of such intransigence, Berlin could not fail to be a trouble-spot. America's unwillingness to heed Churchill's advice concerning the importance of reaching Berlin ahead of the Red Army had produced a nightmare situation. The former German capital was under the four-Power control of the U.S.S.R., the United States, the United Kingdom and France. It was divided into zones of responsibility, with no freedom of movement between the eastern and western parts of the city so far as the inhabitants were concerned.

The 2,100,000 German civilians in West Berlin were, to all intents and purposes, confined on an island about 100 miles on the wrong side of the 'iron curtain' dividing the eastern and western zones of Germany itself. Their ability to scratch a living, even to stay alive, depended on the

13,500 tons of food, fuel, raw materials and other loads brought in daily by road, rail and water from the west.

When the Soviet authorities began finding pretexts for delaying, and finally halting, all traffic into and out of West Berlin, it seemed as if the only way out of the impasse would be for the Western Allies to leave and hand over to the Russians responsibility for the entire city. Nobody believed seriously at that stage that the United States would risk a Third World War by brandishing its nuclear 'big stick' as a threat to make the Russians reopen the roads and railways.

As so often happens in the game of power politics, the West had been left a virtually impossible course of action with which to prove their inadequacy to supply Berlin's needs before giving in without complete 'loss of face'.

Almost the only worthwhile agreement to come out of endless four-Power meetings had concerned the establishment of three twenty-mile-wide air corridors which converged on Berlin like an arrowhead from West Germany. They were used daily by a few passenger aircraft, which were permitted to climb above 10,000 feet. Even then there was no guarantee of safety, as had been shown on 5 April 1948, when a Soviet Yak fighter collided with a B.E.A. Viking inside one of the corridors, killing its own pilot and everyone on board the airliner.

Both the U.S.A.F. and R.A.F. had worked out emergency schemes for flying food and supplies down the air corridors for the benefit of their own people in Berlin, should the necessity arise. It was to be a small-scale enterprise, as is shown by the fact that the British based only sixteen Dakotas on the airfield of Wunstorf, at the western end of the centre corridor, with the object of hauling about 65 tons a day. The Russians must have considered it quite a joke when they learned that the Western Powers were now planning to attempt to meet the needs of the entire population of West Berlin by an expanded airlift. It required little imagination or mathematical skill to estimate how vast a transport fleet would be needed to maintain more than 2,100,000 people at even bare subsistence level.

The U.S.A.F. launched 'Operation Vittles' on Sunday, 26 June 1948, initially by plucking semi-retired aircrew from their desk jobs and putting them aboard C-47s (Dakotas). On that first day 80 tons of flour, milk and medical supplies were ferried from Wiesbaden Air Base to Berlin's Tempelhof Airport, 3 tons at a time. Soon, more men and aircraft flooded in, from as far afield as Texas, Alaska, and Hawaii. By 20 July the Americans had boosted their maximum daily lift to 1,500 tons, using 54 four-engined C-54s (Skymasters) and 105 C-47s.

Meanwhile, Operation Order No. 9, issued on 30 June from Headquarters No. 46 Group, R.A.F. Transport Command at Watford, England, set out the British intentions:

1 Following on the dislocation of the surface communications from the British Zone of Germany to the British Sector in Berlin, the latter will be supplied completely by air.

2 The airlift into Berlin is to be built up as rapidly as possible to 400 tons per day and maintained at that level until 3rd July, 1948. Therefrom it is to be increased to 750 tons per day by 7th July 1948.

3 In Phase I up to 3rd July inclusive, Dakotas of 46 and 38 Groups operating under the control and direction of Air Headquarters, British Air Forces of Occupation (Germany) will provide the 400 tons per day lift.

The additional capacity for Phase II was to be provided by four-engined Yorks, evolved from the wartime Lancaster bomber and with an average payload of 8 tons over this distance.

Readers will note the matter-of-fact use of the words 'will be' in the first paragraph of the Transport Command Operation Order. As the airlift *had* to work, to keep the Western Allies in Berlin, then it would do so! And it did.

Having dropped the original British code-name of 'Operation Nicker' in favour of the more appropriate 'Operation Carter Paterson', a further change soon seemed advisable. The Russians, considering the whole affair a bit of a joke, pointed out that the real Carter Paterson was a well-known British removals company. Use of its name must therefore imply the intention to remove as much as possible from Berlin before the inevitable Allied evacuation. 'Operation Vittles' was soon partnered by 'Operation Plainfare'.

As the months passed, with no lifting of the blockade, the aircraft became more numerous and varied. Twenty-five British charter companies contributed everything from Tudors, each adapted to carry 2,500 gallons of fuel oil, to Hythe flying-boats which operated in to Berlin's Havel Lake, side-by-side with Coastal Command Sunderlands. New in-and-out routes along the corridors were devised to ensure the safety of packed streams of aircraft flying non-stop schedules at different heights and speeds. Loads included such unlikely air cargoes as coal and salt, which, if not watched carefully, would quickly corrode any aluminium alloy structural members with which it came into contact. The flying-boats brought out 1,113 undernourished children for treatment in West Germany.

Children who stayed in the city had their own special airlift. Known as 'Little Vittles', it was started by a U.S. Military Air Transport Service (M.A.T.S.) pilot, Lieutenant Gail S Halversen, in July 1948. At his suggestion, youngsters gathered each day near the end of the Tempelhof runway to collect sweets and chewing-gum parachuted down to them by knotted handkerchief and pieces of torn clothing.

Potatoes and eggs for their mothers travelled in dried or powdered form. This prompted a cartoonist in the beleaguered city to produce a drawing depicting the arrival of a stork at the

left
Having proved their ability
to survive in combat areas,
even after damage to their
rotor blades, helicopters
became standard vehicles
for surprise attack and
assault. Some operate from
naval carriers; others, like
these Anglo-French Pumas,
serve ashore.
Ministry of Defence

below
Increasing aircraft
performance has demanded
continuous improvements in
operating techniques for
carrier-based types. The
supersonic F-8 Crusader
fighter of the U.S. Navy had
a variable-incidence wing
which could be tilted
upward for take-off to
increase its lift. The ships
from which it operated
acquired steam catapults,
angled flight decks, mirror
landing aids and other
refinements.
LTV Aerospace Corporation

To share development costs and ensure the largest possible market, many modern aircraft are developed as international projects by two or more countries. One of the most successful is the Anglo-French Jaguar, which has a speed of Mach 1·5 and a five-ton weapon load. *British Aircraft Corporation*

home of a young couple, to deliver a packet labelled: 'Dehydrated baby; soak for 20 minutes in warm water.'

It was good to joke, even though the whole business was deadly serious. Thirty-one Americans and eighteen British airmen lost their lives in seventeen fatal accidents. Others had narrow escapes, as when the retired Air Vice-Marshal Don Bennett, former leader of the R.A.F.'s wartime Pathfinders, took off with the elevator control locks of his Tudor in place and had to make a seemingly endless circuit and landing with only the trim-tabs available for pitch control.

In mid-April 1949, what became known as the Easter Parade of 1,398 aircraft delivered 12,940·9 short tons of cargo into Berlin in a single day. On the return journeys, goods manufactured in the city were carried westward. It began to look as if the airlift could go on for ever, and the resulting experience and prestige were clearly more beneficial to America and Britain than to the Soviet Union. On 12 May the blockade was lifted. The airlift continued until 30 September, to build up stocks of food and supplies in the city.

By the time it ended, cargoes flown into Berlin totalled 2,325,000 short tons—1,783,000 tons by American aircraft, 542,000 tons by British aircraft. At peak strength, about 225 American C-54s and 140 British civil and military aircraft were airborne each day, with only one mid-air collision during the entire fifteen months. Lessons learned—apart from the political and strategic ones—included the fact that 68 of the big C-74s that were used for a period by the U.S.A.F. could have done the same work as the 178 C-54s operated in the summer of 1948, with fewer flights, fewer men, less fuel and less maintenance. M.A.T.S. and its successor, the Military Airlift Command (M.A.C.), have progressed to steadily larger transports ever since.

For the first time, a major threat to world peace had been overcome by unarmed aeroplanes. The next confrontations were to be very different, beginning a pattern of dirty, bloody, and pointless campaigns with political rather than military motives, of a kind that produce no solutions to problems and no victors.

The war had left South-east Asia in a state of turmoil. Encouraged equally by the wartime Japanese, the Soviet Union, the United States and Communist China—all with varying motives—peoples everywhere decided the time had come to throw off the yoke of their colonial masters. An early result was the guerrilla war in Indo-China, which ended in defeat for the French, and encouraged those who organized successful campaigns in Cyprus, Algeria and Cuba.

A major Power caught up in such warfare fights at an immense disadvantage, with one hand tied behind its back. To deploy its most powerful weapons—particularly when its national strategy is based on nuclear bombs and missiles—would be like using a 100-ton press to crack the proverbial nut—except that in this case the 'nut' would have to be found amid a hundred others who look the same and may or may not be friendly. A man may work in the fields by day and be a guerrilla at night. Guerrilla armies, fighting in familiar surroundings, can 'melt' into jungle or villages whose inhabitants are too frightened to point them out. They can live sparsely, and move without all the complex vehicles and accoutrements of a modern first-class army. They can often count on the supply of modern weapons, food and shelter over the adjacent borders of countries prepared to support insurrection, but not to become fully involved.

With so much in their favour, it has become accepted as almost inevitable that the guerrillas or 'freedom fighters' must always win. That they did not win in Malaya in 1948–60—the longest continuous campaign by armed forces from Britain since the Napoleonic Wars—owed much to air power, working closely with small ground forces, highly skilled in jungle warfare.

When a State of Emergency was declared in Malaya in May 1948 (shortly before the start of the Berlin Airlift), the British forces set in motion 'Operation Firedog'. Troops of the Seaforth Highlanders moved up-country to await developments; and on 1 July two squadrons of fighter-reconnaissance Spitfire FR.18s, each reduced since the war to eight aircraft, together with a squadron of Dakotas and members of the

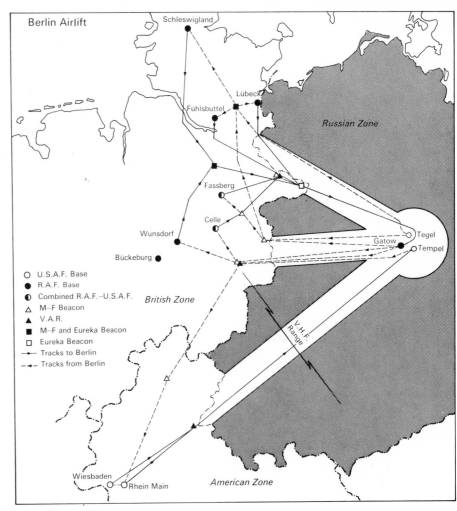

Berlin Airlift

Schleswigland
Lübeck
Fühlsbuttel
Russian Zone
Fassberg
Celle
Wunsdorf
Tegel
Gatow
Tempel
Bückeburg
British Zone
V.H.F. Range

○ U.S.A.F. Base
● R.A.F. Base
◑ Combined R.A.F.–U.S.A.F.
△ M–F Beacon
▲ V.A.R.
■ M–F and Eureka Beacon
□ Eureka Beacon
→ Tracks to Berlin
-◄-- Tracks from Berlin

Wiesbaden
Rhein Main
American Zone

opposite, top
Spearhead of the R.A.F. force serving with NATO in Europe, the vertical take-off Harrier demonstrates its performance and hitting power by loosing a pack of rockets during a high-speed pass over a target range.
Ministry of Defence

opposite, bottom
When the U.S. Navy and U.S.A.F. wanted a potent new attack aircraft with a 7½-ton weapon load, LTV designed a short-fuselage development of their F-8 Crusader, with a fixed wing and Rolls-Royce Spey engine, and called it the A-7 Corsair II. This photograph shows a U.S.A.F. A-7D, seen through the cockpit canopy of another aircraft of the same type.
LTV Aerospace Corporation

R.A.F. Regiment, moved into Kuala Lumpur air base, two miles south of the federal Malayan capital. A squadron of Beaufighters followed in August.

Before long, reports began reaching the troops that Communist guerrillas were attacking rubber plantations and murdering everyone they could find there. Spitfires were called in to look for the culprits, who did not worry overmuch about aircraft that passed above their camps at a height of 18,000 feet. However, the photographs taken at that height revealed the camps clearly to experienced photo-interpreters. When the Spitfires were seen for the second time by the guerrillas, they were not at 18,000 feet but skimming the tree-tops, seeming to blast the camps with cannon and machine-gun fire from all directions at once.

There were few visible signs of the effectiveness of such strikes; another method involved the Spitfires' waiting to ambush guerrillas flushed out of the jungle by troops, into areas of tall grass known as *Palang*. The Communists were adept at carrying off the body of anyone killed, and removing all traces of a successful attack.

For the 'Firedog' forces, it was sufficient to know that they were keeping their elusive enemy on the run, and apprehensive every time an aero-engine was heard. Gradually the air-ground cooperation was extended, and jungle forts were set up in advanced positions for use by patrols and tiny garrisons. From 1950, Dakotas and Valettas parachuted food and supplies weekly, daily, or even hourly on to small dropping zones (D.Z.s) near the forts, or to troops and police hunting the guerrillas. Also in that year, there was an important new development, when Dragonfly helicopters (British-built Sikorsky S-51s) of the R.A.F.'s original Casualty Evacuation Flight arrived in Singapore and started the experimental pick-up of wounded and sick troops from jungle clearings, for rapid, comfortable airlift to hospital.

The Dragonfly was not the first rotary-wing aircraft to serve with the R.A.F. As far back as 1934–5 it had taken delivery of twelve Cierva C-30A Rota Autogiros, and aircraft of this type had equipped No. 1448 Rota Calibration Flight based at R.A.F. Duxford in the Second World War. Their task was to help calibrate the vital Chain Home radar stations round the British coastline, for which task they were each fitted

with a special radio transmitter and an aerial at the tail. They proved so indispensable that the unit had logged 9,141 flying hours with only fifteen aircraft when disbanded in 1945.

By then, both the R.A.F. and Fleet Air Arm had followed the example of their U.S. counterparts, which had acquired examples of the Sikorsky R-4 helicopter (known as 'Hoverfly Is' in the United Kingdom) for evaluation under varying climatic conditions and from platforms on ships, as potential submarine-hunters. The 'casevac' Flight in Malaya was, however, the first helicopter unit employed by the R.A.F. in a combat area. It proved extremely effective, in extending the mobility of ground forces and saving the lives of casualties.

A typical operation involved evacuation from a small jungle clearing of a seventeen-man patrol of the Cameronians, exhausted and sick after twenty-nine days in a swamp area, and complete with a rare captive terrorist. To reach them by any other means would have taken thirteen days.

By the end of November 1954, the Dragonflies of No. 194 Squadron had completed nearly 6,000 sorties, evacuated 675 casualties, and transported more than 4,000 passengers and 84,000 lb of supplies. They had spent hours calling on the terrorists to surrender, by means of voice-broadcasting equipment, and had carried spray-gear to spread destructive chemicals over the terrorists' crops. They had even given a hint of future helicopter gunship development by providing a platform for a soldier with a Bren gun, who caught a party of guerrillas unawares and fired a good long burst at them from the air. After such exploits it was no longer necessary to convince

The strangeness of the initial stages of the Korean War is underlined by this photograph, taken at a U.S. F.E.A.F. base in southern Japan. As he takes off to fly into action over Korea, Captain Johnnie Gosnell waves farewell to his wife and children.
U.S. Air Force

215

the Air Ministry or War Office of the potential of 'choppers', even when they were joined by a rival, in the shape of the remarkable five-seat STOL (short take-off and landing) Scottish Aviation Pioneer aeroplane, able to take off in seventy-five yards and land in sixty-six yards.

Pioneers were inspired by the Fieseler Storchs used everywhere by the wartime Luftwaffe. Rommel relied on one for getting him from place to place in Africa. Another rescued Mussolini from a prison on a mountain-top regarded as inaccessible.

In Malaya, Pioneers showed that they too could fly into impossible places, using tiny rough airstrips at the forts they visited regularly. They ferried troops, tracker dogs and supplies, as well as helping out with casevac. Nor were they the smallest and lowest-powered aircraft used in 'Firedog'. In fact, the 145-hp Auster air observation posts logged an incredible 139,733 flying hours during the Emergency, nearly four times as much as any other type.

At the other extreme were Lincoln four-engined bombers of the R.A.F. and Royal Australian Air Force, which regularly carpeted huge areas of jungle with anti-personnel and high-explosive bombs when guerrilla bands were believed to be concealed in specific areas. The Australian No. 1 Squadron alone dropped over 33,000,000 lb of bombs in this way, and flew more than 2,000,000 miles. Most of the bombs were simply swallowed up by the trees, but on 15 May 1957 they did account for an infamous Communist leader known as 'Ten Foot Long' and four of his henchmen.

Altogether, thirty-one different types of aircraft played their part in the twelve years of 'Firedog'. Even Sunderland flying-boats logged 958 sorties over the jungle, carrying 200 fragmentation bombs each time. By the end, the original Spitfires had given way to jets; and the first-generation Vampires, Venoms and Meteors had themselves been superseded by Canberra jet bombers and Sabre fighters. One

band of guerrillas were so terrified when the Sabres produced a supersonic bang over their hiding-place that they dashed out, straight into a waiting ambush.

As in most wars of this type, the two sides never really saw each other *en masse*. There was not even a proper end to the fighting. The guerrillas simply disappeared, leaving the Federation poorer by £120,000,000. The R.A.F. had lost seventy-six men killed and four wounded. It had gained vast experience of a new kind of warfare and had pioneered many new techniques.

Meanwhile, more than 2,500 miles away to the north-east, in Korea, America and its United Nations allies had fought a far more costly three-year war which nobody won. It began before dawn on 25 June 1950, when the Communist-backed North Koreans crossed the 38th parallel, which had been established as their frontier by an end-of-war agreement in 1945, and attacked the U.S.-backed South Koreans. The two sides were unevenly matched. Spearheading the Northern invaders were squadrons of Russian-built tanks. In support was an air force of 132 combat aircraft, consisting mainly of Ilyushin I1-10s for ground attack and Yak-3, -7 and -9 piston-engined fighters, all of Second World War vintage but flown by well-trained and determined pilots. The South Koreans possessed only sixteen training and observation aircraft.

The U.S. Far East Air Force had large numbers of combat and transport aircraft in the Pacific,

with the Fifth Air Force almost on the doorstep, in Japan. Its aircraft were mostly obsolescent types like F-80C Shooting Star jet interceptors, F-82 Twin Mustang double-fuselage piston-engined all-weather fighters, B-26 Invader tactical bombers, and C-54 and C-47 transports, but were still better than anything in Korea. Farther away, in Guam, the Twentieth Air Force had two squadrons of B-29 strategic bombers. However, at that stage the F.E.A.F. was quite unprepared for war; its Japan-based F-80 jets lacked either the range or armament to provide support for ground forces in Korea, and, in any case, its immediate task in such a situation was limited to evacuating U.S. nationals from the actual or potential combat area.

Care had to be taken to do nothing that might involve a confrontation with Russia, which had ended America's nuclear monopoly by exploding its first experimental atomic bomb in the autumn of 1949. Unfortunately, when air cover was provided for the evacuation, it led to brushes with North Korean fighters, and on the 27th three Yak-7s from a formation of five which attacked Kimpo Airfield were shot down by American F-82 pilots. That day, however, intervention was legalized by a U.N. Security Council recommendation that 'Members of the United Nations furnish such assistance to the Republic of Korea as may be necessary to repel armed attack and restore international peace and security in the area'.

opposite, bottom
Towards the end of the Second World War, designers began to think in terms of transport aircraft tailored specifically for freight-carrying. Their drawings showed large sideways-opening doors, on the nose or at the back of a fuselage pod between twin tailbooms, for easy loading and unloading. On their C-82 Packet and C-119 Flying Boxcar shown here, Fairchild made the loading door removable, so that supplies and even vehicles could be parachuted out of the back in flight. This C-119 was photographed while air-dropping 4 tons of food, ammunition, fuel and medical supplies to U.N. troops in Korea.
U.S. Air Force

below
Cruising off the coast, U.S. and British carriers were able to provide powerful and rapid support for the U.N. ground forces throughout the Korean War. These bomb-laden Corsairs are about to take off on a strike from an unidentified ship.
U.S. Navy

It was to be the first major test of whether the United Nations concept would work in a war that produced–even resulted from–divided loyalties and conflicting ideologies. Before long, it led to British, Australian, Turkish, South African and other nationals fighting alongside the Americans and South Koreans against a clever, ruthless enemy with the two biggest nations on earth as its allies.

Within a month, the U.N. forces had been pushed back into a small area round the port of Pusan, in the extreme south-eastern corner of the Korean peninsula. By then, their enemies were almost without air support, as the Northern air force had been reduced to about twenty-two aircraft. In contrast, whenever a North Korean unit broke through the thinly held perimeter defences, a quick call to the Fifth Air Force produced a close-support mission from Japan to deal with the infiltrators. It was almost unreal for the pilots involved. Often, as they went into battle in their heavily armed F-80s and F-82s, wives and children waved farewell from the side of the runway at Itazuke.

Further support for the U.N. ground forces came from U.S. Marine and Navy squadrons based on escort carriers and the fast attack-carrier U.S.S. *Philippine Sea*, cruising just off the coast. Such operations were to be maintained throughout the war by a succession of U.S., Royal Navy and Royal Australian Navy carriers. They established a new approach to the close support of ground forces, reconnaissance and blockade, which was to be adopted in subsequent areas of conflict–Suez, Cuba and Vietnam.

As summer turned to autumn in that first year of the war, it seemed as if the fighting might soon end. B-29s, moved up to Okinawa, made such a thorough job of eliminating supply routes, marshalling yards and industries feeding the Northern Army that the latter fought itself to a standstill. Finally, its troops even attacked empty-handed, hoping to collect arms and ammunition from the dead as they went forward.

General Douglas MacArthur, wartime conqueror of the Japanese and now U.N. commander, launched his master-stroke on 15 September. Supported by Corsair fighters and Skyraider attack aircraft from three U.S. carriers, and Seafire and Firefly fighters from H.M.S. *Triumph*, the U.S. 5th Marines stormed ashore at Inchon, half-way up the west coast of the peninsula, and began pushing for the southern capital of Seoul. Kimpo Airfield was taken on the 17th; two days later three squadrons of Marine Corsairs flew in to support the ground force. They were followed by a stream of C-54 and C-119 transports, bringing in supplies, fuel, ammunition and equipment, and flying out casualties.

Around Pusan, the main U.N. force had begun its breakout on the 17th. In front of the U.S. 2nd Division, a single concentrated air strike with napalm killed 1,000 of the enemy as they tried to retreat across the Naktong River. Ahead of the advancing U.N. troops flew the little 'Mosquitoes' –adapted T-6 (Harvard) trainers whose purpose was to search for every sign of enemy movement on the ground, call in a strike force of fighter-bombers or 'heavies' to deal with it, and, when necessary, mark the target with smoke rockets. This type of operation–one of the innovations of the Korean War–evolved eventually into the role of forward air control (F.A.C.), and became one of the key missions in Vietnam.

Before the end of September 1950 the North Korean Army was all but annihilated, and the Fifth Air Force transferred its tactical fighters and bombers to airfields in the south, together with Mustangs of No. 77 Squadron, R.A.A.F. Indecision as to whether war with China or Russia could be risked by a U.N. advance over the 38th parallel was settled when the Northern authorities refused a call to surrender. Despite a warning from Premier Chou En-Lai of China that his forces would aid North Korea if that country was invaded, MacArthur was authorized to occupy the North and unite the country.

In an effort to do so quickly, he dropped 2,860 paratroops and over 300 tons of equipment into strategic areas forward of the main advance, using 71 C-119s and 40 C-47s, which subsequently followed up with delivery of further troops and equipment. Then, on 25th October, a South Korean division approaching the Yalu River, marking the border with China, was halted by two Chinese divisions. Over the previous ten days, there had been skirmishes between U.S. and Chinese aircraft and anti-aircraft guns along the Yalu. On 1 November four Mustangs narrowly escaped when they were pounced on by six sweptwing jets bearing red star markings. The MiG-15 had made its combat début, and the war entered a new and grimmer phase.

What began as an act of sheer aggression by one small State on a weaker neighbour now threatened to precipitate a world conflict, with all that might imply in a Nuclear Age. Indeed, as a U.S. Army study made clear after the war, it might have been to America's advantage to take the big risk and use atomic weapons at that moment. As recorded by one historian of the war: *The time to employ such weapons against enemy forces with really devastating effect would have been in November and December 1950, when United Nations forces were in full retreat from the north before a massive Chinese onslaught. For example, on the night of November 24th/25th, 1950, there was a dense assembly of 22,000 enemy troops at Taechon; one 40 kiloton bomb, fused for an air-burst, would have killed or injured some 15,000 of them. A few weeks later, six 40 kiloton bombs bursting over 95,000 Communist troops in the Pymgyang-Chorwon-Kumhwa area would probably have wiped out half of them; while on the last night of December up to 40,000 of the 100,000-strong enemy force poised for an assault along the Imjin River*

would have been destroyed by six 30 kiloton air-bursts.

Whether, in fact, such use of atomic weapons would have been justified is open to question. Once these devices are accepted as a normal means of warfare, it is impossible to say where the limitations might be set. As it was, the war continued much as it had begun, ending with both sides back along the 38th parallel, with 3,000,000 dead and nothing settled. The F.E.A.F. alone ended with a total of 720,980 sorties flown; total U.S.A.F. losses were equivalent to a quarter of its June 1950 first-line strength. The U.S. Navy suffered 814 aircraft losses in 167,552 sorties, the Marines 368 losses in 107,303 sorties. Of 1,050 North Korean and Chinese aircraft destroyed in the air and on the ground by the U.N. air forces, 792 were MiG-15s shot down by American F-86 Sabres, of which 78 were lost in air combat.

By establishing a marked superiority over the MiG, the Sabre helped to offset the growing gloom with which less-informed people in the west viewed the re-equipment of the Soviet Air Force. None the less, there was much to be learned from the fact that this lightweight, sweptwing fighter, with a basically British engine, had a better rate of climb than the F-86, a tighter turning circle, higher ceiling, and was faster above 35,000 feet. Against these advantages, an example supplied by a North Korean deserter revealed a tendency to enter a snap roll and uncontrollable spin in a too-tight turn. Fore and aft stability was not good, and

directional snaking occurred at high speeds. U.S. pilots would have been first to admit, however, that their real advantage came from better training and the MiG's lack of a radar gunsight.

Many other lessons on the future of aerial warfare and strategy came from Korea. The value of the attack carrier could no longer be disputed. Nor could the worth of helicopters for transport into otherwise inaccessible front-line areas and for casevac, which reduced the deathrate for wounded troops to the lowest figure in military history. Korea was, in fact, the war which established the helicopter as a front-line military type.

The proven superiority of sweptwing fighters led to quick replacement of all the old 'straightwing' types in U.S. service, and the long-delayed decision to order Hunters and Swifts to replace the R.A.F.'s Meteors and Vampires. Heavy casualties among the B-29s led to their urgent replacement by B-47 Stratojets by mid-1955; in the same year the big B-36 began giving way to the mighty eight-jet B-52 Stratofortress. To enhance their mobility and rapid deployment, Strategic Air Command's fleet of flight-refuelling tankers was expanded and re-equipped with special versions of the Boeing 707 jet airliner.

Finally, in an effort to ensure that no sudden invasion like that of June 1950 would ever again catch the U.S. off guard, Clarence (Kelly) Johnson of Lockheed was given a secret contract to develop a clandestine reconnaissance aircraft designated the U-2. The results of this move were to be both fascinating and frightening.

The Push-button Age

There are two basic kinds of warfare today. The first, possible at any moment in any one of a hundred potential trouble-spots in the world, goes by many different names, depending on its scale, whether it is a civil war or international conflict, and on whether it is waged by disciplined military forces, guerrillas or 'freedom fighters'.

In this category is the organized, full-scale but non-nuclear, international war of the kind fought between Israel and the Arab States in June 1967 and October 1973. A local conflict of this kind, fought by well-equipped armed forces in receipt of help from major Powers, is normally brief and costly, ending when one or both sides run dangerously short of men or machines.

At the other extreme in this first category is the racial, opportunist or ideological rebellion, like that of the Mau Mau in Kenya in 1952–6. Pitting primitive weapons, terrorism, subversion, voodoo, the ability to use every scrap of natural cover, and sheer fanaticism against modern weaponry, the inevitable losers know that time is on their side in an era of decolonization.

Between the two extremes are the big and bloody Vietnams, drawing in other nations willing to suffer for causes that seem just but may be equally rotten on both sides. There is no winner in this situation, and the sole benefit that anyone derives is the ability to test new weapons under genuine combat conditions.

The second kind of war, for which only the United States and Soviet Union can attempt to prepare–with China aspiring to rival them, and Britain and France in supporting roles–is the full-scale nuclear exchange. The likely contestants know that their strategy must be based on *preventing* this one; if it ever started, there might be nobody left to say 'I've won.'

When the Mau Mau, a Kikuyu secret society, began their rebellion to take back land from the white settlers in Kenya, the only support available for the British ground forces came from Harvards piloted by R.A.F. flying instructors. Learning from the 'Mosquito' units in Korea, these men evolved an even more aggressive variant of the trainer by mounting a machine-gun in the starboard wing and hanging racks of eight 20-lb anti-personnel bombs under the wings. Supplemented later by detached flights of Lincoln heavy bombers and Vampire ground attack jet-fighters, the Harvards played a major part in flushing the terrorists out of their forest hide-outs, so that they could be rounded up. Added to experience in places like Korea, these operations started a search for an ideal counter-insurgency (C.O.I.N.) combat aircraft that has not yet ended.

If an aircraft is to work closely with ground forces, it must be able to go where they go, operating from short, rough airstrips. It must also be simple enough to be refuelled, rearmed and serviced in forward areas without needing any equipment or supplies that cannot be air-dropped. This simple specification has produced several light aircraft that are not so very different from a fixed-undercarriage family two-seater, but which carry a heavy load of bombs, guns, rockets and napalm. None has yet entered large-scale production, as air forces have found it easier and cheaper to arm and armour retired trainers such as the T-6 (Harvard) and T-28.

In places where the enemy does not possess modern anti-aircraft guns and missiles, it has proved equally practicable to use retired first-line combat aircraft like the U.S. Navy's Sky-raider, which served with distinction in Vietnam. But the modern guerrilla can often acquire shoulder-fired missiles, like the American Red-eye and Russian SAM-7 Strela, which are easy to carry through difficult country, can be fired from cover, and are horribly effective at the below-3,000 feet altitudes where C.O.I.N. aircraft usually fly.

For this reason, the recent tendency has been to choose heavily armed versions of jet trainers, like the British Strikemaster (evolved from the Jet Provost) and American A-37 Dragonfly (evolved from the T-37). With a speed of 450–500 mph and 3,000–4,000 lb of weaponry, aircraft of this type are ideal for smaller air forces, as they are inexpensive and can often double as trainers; but they are not STOL aircraft.

In an effort to combine the best of both worlds, the U.S. services ordered the OV-10 Bronco, a twin-turboprop, twin-tailboom design able to carry up to 3,600 lb of ordnance, fly at up to 281 mph, and take off and land in 740 feet with reduced load. In Vietnam the OV-10s gave good service in an F.A.C. role, but have not been bought widely for C.O.I.N. operations.

None the less, they pointed the way, and the U.S.A.F. decided in 1970 to hold just one more design competition, with the prospect of orders for at least 2,000 of the winning type. Fairchild Industries hit the jackpot with the A-10A, powered by two quiet, economical turbofan engines. These enable it to take off from a forward airstrip carrying four 500-lb bombs, 750 rounds of ammunition for its big 30-millimetre gun, and enough fuel for a 200-mile round trip at over 300 mph, including 30 minutes of fighting. The pilot sits in an armour-plate 'box' and the fuel-tanks are so designed that they should not explode or catch fire when hit by air or ground fire.

However, the U.S.A.F. has decided that it will order only prototypes until a detailed programme of evaluation flying proves the A-10A better than the 700-mph, non-STOL A-7 Corsair II attack-craft. This has been in service for years and proved itself outstandingly accurate in Vietnam in dive attacks on small targets with conventional bombs.

In any case, both the R.A.F. and the U.S. services believe that, eventually, an improved version of the British V/STOL (Vertical and Short Take-Off and Landing) Harrier might be far better than anything else, as it is the only combat aircraft in service in the mid-seventies which combines the go-anywhere capability of a helicopter with a dive-supersonic speed and weapon load of 5,000 lb.

The snag with the Harrier, as with most modern front-line military aircraft, is its price. The version currently in service costs about $2,000,000. An A-7 is nearly as expensive. The F-4 Phantoms used by the U.S.A.F. and U.S. Navy for close-support missions in Vietnam cost anything from $2·23,000,000 to $4·58,000,000 each, and the F-105 Thunderchiefs worked out at $2·39,000,000. Little wonder that the R.A.F. and French Air Force tried to cut costs by ordering the tiny but potent Jaguar, built in partnership by their two industries. The resulting aircraft does everything expected of it, with a speed of Mach 1·5, a maximum weapon load of 10,000 lb and, in its British form, a highly advanced automatic (inertial) navigation system, and a laser rangefinder and marked target-seeker for use with homing missiles. But it has ended up much more expensive than a U.S.A.F. F-4D, A-7D or F-105D. That is why most foreign air forces are buying the American F-5E Tiger II, with a smaller payload, lower performance and much less equipment, but costing only $1·33,000,000.

Before discussing other types of aeroplane, it is important to study how experience in Vietnam evolved whole new classes of military aircraft

and proved conclusively the need for sophisticated equipment in localized, non-nuclear warfare in the seventies.

Vietnam was a tougher, dirtier, more frustrating war than Korea. Instead of large conventional armies, in well-defined positions on something resembling a front line, the enemy – Viet Cong guerrillas and North Vietnamese regular troops – infiltrated, fought a quick and extremely efficient action, and then withdrew into hiding. To sort out members of the Viet Cong from relatively peaceful villagers in daytime was almost impossible. The innocent often suffered, not least when transport aircraft sprayed defoliating chemicals over forest and countryside, denying cover to terrorists but robbing already hungry villagers of food.

Defoliation was used extensively in Vietnam. Where it was not practicable, as along the Ho Chi Minh Trail – leading from North Vietnam, through Laos to the South – an electronic warfare technique code-named 'Igloo White' helped to locate enemy personnel and supply convoys.

Basically, it involved 'sowing' sensors of various kinds from the air along a stretch of track or road believed to be used by the Viet Cong or North Vietnamese. These sensors were so designed that they transmitted a signal whenever there were people or vehicles near them. The signals were picked up by an aircraft orbiting far enough away to be in no danger from the enemy who had been 'spotted', and were passed on by the aircraft to an Infiltration Surveillance Center (I.S.C.) in South Vietnam. There the information from the sensors was fed into computers and analysed by skilled personnel. If they considered it worth while, a strike force of Phantoms or other attack aircraft was then given the precise location of the target and scrambled to deal with it.

Sensors used in the Igloo White project included Spikebuoys, 66 inches long and working in the same way as the sonobuoys dropped into the water from maritime patrol aircraft to 'listen' for submarines. The Spikebuoy buried itself in the ground when dropped from a Phantom, leaving only its antenna (aerial) above the surface, and 'listened' for passing traffic. The smaller Acoubuoy did the same job but was designed to hang from trees after being parachuted down.

Used even more widely, Adsid (Air Delivered Seismic Detection) also buried itself, except for its antenna, and then waited to pick up ground vibrations from passing traffic. Acousid passed on both sound and seismic signals.

The aircraft principally used to relay data from the sensors to the I.S.C. were specially equipped versions of the big Constellation piston-engined airliner, designated EC-121R. As such machines, with a large crew, are costly to operate, the U.S.A.F. experimented with Beechcraft QU-22B Bonanza light planes, equipped for signal relay under its Pave Eagle programme. It

was hoped eventually to fly these in pilotless form, leaving them to orbit for many hours until relieved by another QU-22B; but the end of U.S. involvement in the war put a stop to the project.

Electronic devices of other kinds did play a much greater role in Vietnam than most people realize. For example, Phantoms equipped under the Commando Bolt programme were able to make accurate blind-bombing strikes against targets located by 'Igloo White' sensors at night or in bad weather. Some devices reported the presence of enemy personnel by 'sniffing' their body odours; and Black Crow was an airborne sensor which could detect the ignition system of a truck engine even when the vehicle itself could not be seen.

The aircraft which carried Black Crow – the AC-130 version of the Hercules transport – was itself a highly successful product of the war. Its development can be said to date from 1965, when some very strange, dark-painted versions of the thirty-year-old C-47 (Dakota) transport arrived in Vietnam, and went into service eventually with the 4th Air Commando Squadron. Designated AC-47D, each of these aircraft carried three Minigun multi-barrel machine-guns in its cabin, with a combined rate of fire of 18,000

In Vietnam, as in Korea, it was discovered that the pilot of a slower piston-engined aircraft often had a much better chance of finding a ground target than the pilot of a jet. For this reason, the U.S. services made extensive use of the Douglas Skyraider for attack duties, loading the veterans with huge weights of bombs, rockets and other weapons to supplement four fixed 20-mm guns. The aircraft were later handed over to the Vietnam Air Force.

Perhaps the most advanced
combat aircraft in service
anywhere in 1974, the
R.A.F.'s Harrier has a
turbofan engine fitted with
four rotating nozzles. These
enable it to take off and land
vertically like a helicopter
to operate as a STOL
aircraft with a heavier
weapon load. It is
supersonic in a dive and
carries 5,000 lb of weapons in
its initial operational form.
The U.S. Marine Corps
operates Harriers from
both shore bases and ships.
R.A.F. Germany

below
To protect aircraft like this
U.S.A.F.E. F-4 Phantom
from attack with non-
nuclear weapons, N.A.T.O.
is installing a total of 370
TAB VEE (Theatre Air Base
Vulnerability) shelters on its
airfields in Europe. Held
partially open in this
photograph, the steel-
armoured doors weigh
several tons but are carefully
hinged to balance each door
so that it can be opened and
closed by one man.
U.S. Air Force

rounds a minute. Armourers were carried to re-
load the guns, which were controlled by the
pilot and arranged to fire through the doorway
and two windows on the port side.

In action, the AC-47s were directed to the
pinpoint position of a suspected Viet Cong hide-
out. There they began a slow orbit, dropped
flares to illuminate the ground if it was dark,
and opened up with their guns in such a way that

the banked orbit produced a concentrated cone
of fire on the target. Their official name was
'Spooky', but the troops who saw them in operation preferred 'Puff the Magic Dragon'.

Having proved the effectiveness of the AC-47
gunships, the U.S.A.F. decided to see if larger
aircraft would be more effective. First results
were the AC-119G Shadow and jet-boosted AC-
119K Stinger. The 'G' carried four Miniguns, a
flare-launcher, a powerful searchlight and
armour protection for the crew. The 'K' added
two 20-millimetre cannon, side-and-forward-
looking radar, and a forward-looking infra-red
sensor to detect anything hot on the ground.
'Hot' may be misleading; some infra-red seekers
are so sensitive that they can easily pinpoint the
body warmth of a man over a considerable
distance.

Bigger still is the AC-130E Hercules gunship,
with four 20-millimetre multi-barrel guns, four
Miniguns and all the equipment of an AC-119K.
Nor were these the only gunships used in Vietnam, for this war saw the helicopter change from
peaceable transport and casevac aircraft to one
of the deadliest of battlefield killers.

The process began in the earliest period of the
war, in 1963, when Bell HU-1A (Huey) helicopters of the U.S. Army were fitted with two
machine-guns and tubes for sixteen 2·75-inch

Similar armament was fitted to later versions of the Huey; and even small observation helicopters like the Hughes OH-6A Cayuse began carrying a single gun on the port side of the cabin. It was but a short step from there to Bell's AH-1G HueyCobra, the first specially developed gunship 'chopper'. To save time and keep down costs, it was built round the same power plant and rotor system as the UH-1. A new fuselage, only 38 inches wide, presented a small target for ground fire and housed a crew of two in tandem, with the co-pilot-gunner in front. An under-nose turret could house either two multi-barrel Miniguns, or two 40-millimetre grenade-launchers, or one of each. Pylons under the aircraft's stub-wings could accommodate either seventy-six rockets in four packs, or a mixture of rockets and Miniguns, or a 20-millimetre gun.

Development of these aircraft in Vietnam began in the autumn of 1967, and was so successful that the U.S. Army alone had ordered 1,078 before America withdrew from the war. In April 1972 several pre-production AH-1Q versions, each carrying eight T.O.W. wire-guided anti-tank missiles, were sent to Vietnam for evaluation. By 27 June, in seventy-seven combat launches of the missiles, they had achieved sixty-two hits on specific targets, and had destroyed thirty-nine armoured vehicles, trucks and howitzers. None of the helicopters had themselves been hit by hostile fire.

Helicopters assumed in Vietnam a combat role that will be perpetuated in the advanced attack helicopters that will follow the Huey-Cobra. They were also responsible for much of the ground-force deployment during the campaign. Largest of the troop-carriers used in quantity by the U.S. Army were the 33-34-seater Boeing Vertol CH-47C Chinooks, which also hauled back to repair bases a total of more than 11,500 disabled aircraft, valued at more than $3,000,000,000. Also used were the Sikorsky CH-54 specialized flying-crane, with a payload of $12\frac{1}{2}$ short tons, and the CH-53/HH-53. Versions

air-to-ground rockets, for use while escorting H-21 troop-carrying helicopters. Experience had shown that the Viet Cong often heard the distinctive sound of these aircraft approaching, and would lie in wait until they were near or on the ground, putting down their troops, before opening fire. The armed Hueys ensured that any guerrillas in the region of a dropping zone 'kept their heads down' or risked losing them.

AC-119 gunship in action at night. By encircling the target—in this case an enemy mortar position in Vietnam—the pilot of the gunship can ensure that the heavy fire from his four side-firing Miniguns forms a cone centred on the aiming point. The light pattern at the top of the photograph was produced by the aircraft; the descending lines are tracer bullets registered on a time exposure.

above
Most advanced anti-tank
helicopter in service, the
U.S. Army's Bell AH-1Q
TOW Cobra has an
undernose gun turret and
eight launchers for TOW
wire-guided missiles under
its stub-wings. The missiles
are aimed by stabilized sight.
Bell Helicopter Co.

right
DC-130A Hercules carrying a
pair of Teledyne Ryan
Model 154 remotely piloted
vehicles (RPVs) under its
wings. Launched in mid-air
from the DC-130A, the RPVs
contain advanced, self-
contained navigation aids to
guide them to distant
targets. Over the target they
can take up to 1,500 large
photographs on each
reconnaissance. Special
infra-red sensors enable
them to detect vehicles,
personnel or anything else
that gives off heat, even if it
is hidden.
Teledyne Ryan Aeronautical

of the latter were used as transports for up to thirty-eight combat-equipped troops and, with smaller HH-3s, as rescue craft of the W.A.F. Aerospace Rescue and Recovery Service. Whenever a U.S. pilot, or other aircrew member, had to eject from a crippled aircraft, a signal was transmitted to the nearest A.R.R.S. base, or to a U.S. Navy ship carrying a SH-3G Sea King somewhere off the coast. If, as was often the case, the pick-up had to be made in enemy territory, under the noses of hostile troops, the 'chopper' would be given a fighter escort.

After the signing of the peace treaty with North Vietnam, which ended America's part in a war that has never stopped, RH-53Ds towing elaborate minesweeping gear helped to clear areas of sea near Hanoi that had long been hazardous to shipping. But, at sea as on land, helicopters could themselves add to such hazards in any future conflict. There are few combat vessels of any modern navy which cannot carry at least one helicopter armed and equipped to find and attack surface vessels or submarines. Some small carriers, like the Soviet Navy's *Leningrad* and *Moskva*, are designed specifically to operate such aircraft, which are expected to be replaced eventually by V/STOL jets of the Harrier type.

Looking even further ahead, it may be that many of the categories of aircraft which fought in Vietnam, and all the other post-war conflicts, will be superseded one day by highly complex pilotless aeroplanes, controlled by operators seated in front of electronic consoles on the ground, in a ship or on board another aircraft.

A first hint of such activities came in 1965, when the Chinese claimed to have shot down eight pilotless American spy-planes, and exhibited the remains of several of them in Peking. Gradually, such aircraft became known as R.P.V.s (remotely piloted vehicles) to distinguish

A crystal-clear photograph of a North Vietnamese anti-aircraft site taken by a U.S. remotely piloted vehicle (RPV).

A modern fighter costs so much money that it must often display an ability to perform several duties equally well. This Phantom FGR Mk 2 of No. 6 Squadron, at R.A.F. Coningsby, is surrounded by a selection of the rockets, air-to-air missiles, bombs and other external loads that it can carry. It can also be fitted with an underbelly reconnaissance bank containing cameras, side-looking radar or other sensors.
Ministry of Defence

Among the major post-war
successes of the French
aircraft industry was the
delta-wing Mirage III fighter,
of which more than 1,200
were bought by sixteen
nations. To follow it in the
seventies, the French Air
Force ordered the Mirage
F1, seen here, which reverts
to a swept wing and
conventional tail unit.
Compared with the Mirage
III, range is doubled,
manœuvrability improved
by 80 per cent, and take-off
and landing runs reduced.
Dassault/Breguet

With costs and size continually
increasing, the U.S.A.F. decided to
investigate the possibility of producing
a comparatively inexpensive lightweight
fighter (LWF). It ordered prototypes of
two very different designs for evaluation.
First to fly, on 20 January 1974, was the
General Dynamics YF-16, seen here,
which has a 25,000-lb thrust turbofan
engine, weighs a modest 17,500 lb fully
loaded, can fly faster than Mach 2, and is
armed with a 20-mm multi-barrel gun,
two 'dogfight' missiles and other external
weapons.
General Dynamics Corporation

them from the simple jet-powered target aircraft from which they had been evolved.

Best known of the targets was the Teledyne Ryan Firebee. Launched from a surface ramp, or dropped from a mother-plane, this little machine was designed to fly a remotely controlled course for more than an hour, at heights up to 60,000 feet and speeds up to 707 mph at lower altitudes. It required little imagination to visualize such an aircraft, with extended wing span, more fuel, a more sophisticated guidance system and a camera, flying reconnaissance sorties over places like China, where piloted aircraft would be made to feel very unwelcome.

Not until the Vietnam War was almost over for America was Ryan allowed to issue photographs showing similar R.P.V.s being operated from Bien Hoa air base by the U.S.A.F.'s 100th Strategic Reconnaissance Wing. A diagram identified twenty-six different models, mostly evolved from the Firebee but including two of quite different configuration, with enormous wing spans. It transpired that the Model 235, then under construction, was known as 'Compass Cope R' and was intended to replace the big RC-135 jet reconnaissance transports that fly regularly in the Arctic to monitor missile launches from Russia's northern test site.

The other large R.P.V., Model 154, was clearly operational, as photographs showed it leaving Bien Hoa at nightfall under the wing of a DC-130E Hercules director aircraft, and being retrieved in mid-air by helicopter afterwards. Other pictures showed the DC-130Es carrying Model 147 R.P.V.s with an incredible variety of nose, wing and tail shapes. These, clearly, were the means by which America was able to collect crystal-clear photographs of North Vietnamese anti-aircraft sites, learn the frequencies of Soviet-built early-warning and missile-guidance radars, and carry

out a variety of other clandestine reconnaissance and electronic intelligence gathering missions. But they represented only the Wright biplanes of the R.P.V. era.

By 1974, Ryan had already flown R.P.V.s in simulated dogfights against Phantom fighters, which were consistently outfought, and had dropped bombs and guided missiles from others, scoring direct hits on ground targets. More incredible still is the long-nosed BGM-34B 'pathfinder', which carries a low-light-level TV camera to find its target, and a laser designator to mark it. With such equipment, it can lead a flight of missile-carrying R.P.V.s, and direct their weapons at the target with great accuracy. This is,

bomb dropped from an aircraft; the Americans were only planning to do so (presumably because their 'bomb' was still far too cumbersome to go into an aeroplane). To help down the coffee and brandy, he added, 'I am quite sure we shall have soon a guided missile with a hydrogen bomb warhead that can fall anywhere in the world.'

One year earlier, in their annual Aviation Day flypast at Tushino Airport, Moscow, the Red Air Force had displayed a total of sixty-five sweptwing strategic bombers of three types. Four of them were jets, identified subsequently as Myasishchev Mya-4s in the same class as the U.S.A.F.'s B-52. Seven of the others were huge turboprop-powered Tupolev Tu-95s, which could fly 7,800 miles carrying 11 tons of bombs and soon proved to have a top speed of 500 mph. These, clearly, were the vehicles for Russia's nuclear weapons. What else was being developed secretly? In particular, did the Soviet Union really have intercontinental ballistic missiles (I.C.B.M.s) with nuclear warheads under test?

Once again, the peace of mind and security of the world seemed to depend on some form of aerial reconnaissance to provide full and precise knowledge of progress being made. But this was a time of peace and it could be construed as an act of war to fly a reconnaissance sortie over another country, especially when East-West relationships were already touchy.

President Eisenhower of America, the former wartime Supreme Commander in North Africa and Europe, had offered an alternative to his Soviet opposite number at a Summit Conference held in Geneva in July 1955. In essence, his 'Open Skies' plan proposed that America and Russia should exchange detailed maps giving the precise location and inventory of every military installation, aerodrome and missile site in their respective territories. Having done so, they would then permit frequent, unhindered aerial reconnaissance flights over their country, to reassure each other that the information remained comprehensive and accurate.

Eisenhower explained that a single U.S.A.F.

indeed, the stuff of which science-fiction films are made.

So, finally, we come to the big war, and its 'ultimate weapons'.

What might be regarded as the countdown to Armageddon began on 1 November 1952, when an American test explosion in the Pacific caused an island to disappear, leaving in its place a hole 1 mile in diameter and 175 feet deep. Seven years earlier, the 'Little Boy' atomic bomb dropped on Hiroshima had weighed 9,700 lb and had been equivalent to 20,000 tons of TNT (hence its rating as a 20-kiloton weapon). This November 1952 explosion was measured as the equivalent of 5,000,000 to 7,000,000 tons of T.N.T. (5–7 megatons). It was clearly produced by a thermonuclear device–the so-called 'hydrogen bomb'.

If that first test sent a shudder through the world, worse was to come. On 12 August 1953 the Russians, too, exploded a thermonuclear device, and rumours began to circulate that they were ahead of the U.S.A. in the nuclear race. Premier Nikita Krushchev confirmed this in April 1956. At a luncheon given by the Birmingham Chamber of Commerce, he told his English hosts that Russia had been first to explode a hydrogen

RB-47 Stratojet could photograph 1,000,000 square miles of territory in one three-hour flight at 40,000 feet. If anything observed was felt to require a closer look, it could be done through the medium of low-altitude sorties. As an example, he showed his audience a photograph of an aircraft being serviced on an airfield, taken during a 525-mph overflight at a height of only 60 feet. The rivets on the aircraft's wings could be counted. He assumed that the Red Air Force was equally competent.

Knowing the Soviet Union's tradition of secrecy at that time, Eisenhower could not have been surprised when the Russian leaders refused to agree to 'Open Skies'. Two years later, after the Suez campaign, they even cancelled the annual Aviation Day displays, which had, at least, given a glimpse of progress being made in military aircraft design. It did not matter by then.

Unable to get Soviet collaboration for their reconnaissance project, which was designed to 'ease the fears of war in the anxious hearts of people everywhere', the Americans had gone ahead on their own. The late fifties produced rumours, and even a few photographs, of a unique U.S.A.F. aeroplane which proved to be a product of Kelly Johnson's highly secret 'Skunk Works' at Burbank, California. Known as the Lockheed U-2, it was said to be a very long-range reconnaissance aircraft, designed in such a way that it could cruise at around 80,000 feet (out of reach of most fighters and missiles) and extend its already long endurance by gliding periodically with its motor switched off.

The truth of these allegations was revealed on 1 May 1960, when a shocked world learned that an American aircraft had been shot down by a missile near Sverdlovsk, in the heart of the Soviet Union, during a thoroughly illegal reconnaissance flight. Its pilot, Gary Powers, had been taken prisoner, and proof of his 'crimes', in the form of photographs of Soviet military installations, had been found in the wreckage of the aircraft, which was of course a U-2.

In the light of Russia's indignation and scorn,

President Eisenhower had to promise the Soviet leaders that reconnaissance flights over their territories would be stopped immediately. It must have seemed a painful step to many people. As the man who then headed America's Central Intelligence Agency commented later, the capability of the U-2 'could be equalled only by the acquisition of technical documents directly from Soviet offices and laboratories'.

However, Kelly Johnson had already begun planning an even more capable replacement for it. Known at that stage as the A.11, this futuristic, needle-nosed machine, built almost entirely of titanium and fitted with two immensely powerful turbojets, was to evolve into the SR-71A – a strategic reconnaissance aircraft with a cruising speed well above 2,000 mph and a ceiling of more than 80,000 feet, making it the fastest, highest-flying aircraft ever put into service.

What was not explicit in the President's promise was that it applied only to the Soviet Union; elsewhere, the U-2 and, later, the SR-71A would continue their peace-keeping vigil.

The importance of maintaining U-2 reconnaissance became clear in 1962, when an over-

above
Seldom photographed, this operational-type Lockheed U-2 special reconnaissance aircraft demonstrates how it touches down on its tandem landing gear and one of the turned-down wingtip skids.
Robert D Archer

below
One of the photographs taken by American reconnaissance aircraft which confirmed that the Soviet Union was sending strategic weapons to Cuba in 1962. This ship, the freighter *Kasimov*, has crated fuselages of I1-28 twin-jet bombers on its deck.
U.S. Air Force

Boeing B-52 Stratofortress eight-engined strategic bomber launching a SRAM short-range attack missile. A single B-52 can carry twenty SRAMs, each able to carry a nuclear warhead more than 100 miles at high altitude or 35 miles at low altitude. In this way the bomber itself need never approach within range of the close defences of the targets it attacks.
The Boeing Co.

flight uncovered new installations in Cuba which soon proved to be sites for Soviet long-range nuclear missiles, aimed at America. The world came to the brink of nuclear war as the two super-Powers confronted and threatened each other. In the end, Mr Krushchev agreed to remove both the missiles and I1-28 jet bombers that had been delivered to the island. Peace had again been preserved by unarmed aircraft.

The fact that the U-2s could no longer be used over Russia was of diminishing consequence. Eisenhower knew that it would not be long before reconnaissance satellites would supply all the information on Soviet military installations and movements that the West could possibly need.

Under the Strategic Arms Limitation Talks (S.A.L.T.) agreement signed by the two super-Powers in 1972, the use of such satellites has not only been legalized, but has become the designated means of ensuring that neither side ever exceeds the number of I.C.B.M.s or anti-I.C.B.M. defensive missiles that it is permitted to deploy. Their ability to do this is shown by the fact that the huge camera in the U.S.A.F.'s 50-foot-long, 25,000-lb Big Bird satellite can identify objects

1 foot in diameter from an orbital height of over 100 miles.

Satellites and strategic missiles are not really part of the subject of this book, which is concerned with war conducted inside Earth's atmosphere by aircraft. There was a period in the mid-fifties when it seemed that missiles might supersede almost all kinds of combat aircraft, leading the British Government to suggest, in the 1957 White Paper on Defence, that it would not be necessary to plan for any more fighter aircraft after the Lightning or bombers after the Vulcan and Victor. It was a disastrous piece of muddled thinking from which the R.A.F. had not yet fully recovered in 1974, despite the purchase of Phantom fighters from America and a stop-go-stop process which is leading past the wrecked hopes of the TSR.2, A.F.V.G. (Anglo-French Variable-Geometry design) and F-111K to the M.R.C.A. (Multi-Role Combat Aircraft) developed jointly with Germany and Italy.

In fairness, it might be added that no nation can be certain any longer of what it needs to protect itself from one or both kinds of modern war. The M.R.C.A. was conceived as a small, low-cost design that can be used by the R.A.F. as a replacement for the Vulcan and Buccaneer in overland strike and reconnaissance roles, the Phantom for air defence, and the Buccaneer for maritime strike. The new Luftwaffe and the Italian Air Force hope to use it to replace the Mach 2 Lockheed F-104 and the Aeritalia G91 for battlefield interdiction, reconnaissance and air superiority (keeping enemy aircraft of all kinds out of a particular area); and the German Navy plans M.R.C.A. reconnaissance and strike duties against sea and coastal targets.

All the experience of seventy years suggests that it is stupid to expect one type of aircraft to replace everything from a four-engined strategic bomber to a 1,450-mph interceptor. However, the M.R.C.A. is a remarkable concept, based on the use of variable-geometry (swing-wings) to combine the best features of a straight wing for optimum control during low-speed take-off and landing, and a swept wing for high-speed flying, above Mach 2.

The U.S.A.F. demonstrated the potential of variable geometry with the F-111 in Vietnam. After a disastrous early history, this aircraft performed miracles during the final stages of U.S. involvement. Its crews learned to trust the terrain-following radar which piloted the aircraft completely automatically, at a height never more than 500 feet above the ground, as it went through and over mountainous country. Approaching Hanoi, still under electronic control, it 'skiied' down the side of the last high mountains and, keeping below the height at which radar could detect it, usually managed to deliver its bombs and be on the way home before the air-raid sirens sounded an alarm.

North Vietnam had very advanced defences, but those of the super-Powers would be even more

difficult to penetrate. A comparatively small and simple attack bomber would almost certainly be brought down if it were not accompanied by aircraft packed with electronic jammers to confuse and blot out the early-warning and missile radars searching for it. Such E.C.M. (electronic counter-measures) devices were developed and used widely in Vietnam, leading to unidentified bulges, blisters and pods on a variety of aircraft, such as 'Wild Weasel' Phantoms. In addition to jamming radars, such aircraft could often launch Shrike and Standard A.R.M. missiles, which homed automatically on enemy radar transmitters.

All kinds of other missiles form essential armament on modern combat aircraft. Bombers and attack types can carry everything from powerful rockets, steered by joystick into their target, to 'smart bombs' which home on to laser signals 'bounced' off the target by somebody on the ground. Simplest of the missiles carried by interceptors are infra-red 'heat-seekers' like Sidewinder and the Russian K-13, which home on to the hot engine exhaust of their quarry. Most advanced is the radar-guided, self-contained Phoenix carried by the U.S. Navy's swing-wing F-14 Tomcat. In its final pre-service test, a

Phoenix intercepted a tiny Firebee drone, which had been 126 miles away from the Tomcat on a collision course when it was launched. Both the Firebee and the Tomcat were flying at supersonic speed, at different heights, and the missile climbed above 100,000 feet during its trajectory.

Such is the capability of the modern interceptor, and it helps to explain why the U.S.A.F.'s next strategic bomber, the big variable-geometry B-1, is so complex that the planned fleet of 241 would cost over $14,000,000,000.

Is it all worth while? One answer is that, having ended the most terrible war in history in 1945, the atomic bomb, by its mere presence, has prevented a third world conflict ever since. Another answer was given in Vietnam, where the U.S.A.F.'s massive December 1972 'Linebacker II' bombing campaign against targets in the North quickly changed talk into action which ended the war for America. The ability to end a period of fighting by such operations is often more valuable than being able to wield only a nuclear 'big stick' that would leave a wasteland dead to all life for a thousand years.

top
More and more combat aircraft of the seventies are being fitted with variable-geometry wings ('swing-wings') like those of this U.S. Navy Tomcat fighter. Take-off and landing are slower and easier to control with the wings spread; fully swept wings are more efficient at very high speeds. Armament of the Tomcat includes Phoenix missiles capable of intercepting any aircraft yet built.
R L Lawson

above
Most formidable weapon yet displayed in public is Russia's huge SS-9 long-range rocket. The standard version can carry either a single 25-megaton nuclear warhead or one containing several independently targeted H-bombs. Another version puts its warhead into a low orbit, from which it can be directed down at any time on to a specific target area. Yet another can launch satellites able to intercept and destroy other satellites.
Tass

Bibliography

P W Brooks. *Historic Airships*, 1973
J M Bruce. *British Aeroplanes, 1914–18*, 1957
J R Bushby. *Air Defence of Great Britain*, 1973
S Child and C F Caunter. *A Historical Summary of the Royal Aircraft Factory and its Antecedents 1878–1914*, 1947
W S Churchill. *The Second World War*, 6 Vols, 1948–53
M Clark. *Calculated Risk*, 1951
C Dollfus, H Beaubois and C Rougeron. *L'Homme, L'Air et L'Espace*, 1965
C H Gibbs-Smith. *Aviation: an historical survey from its origins to the end of World War II*, 1970
A Goldberg. *A History of the United States Air Force, 1907–1957*, 1957
J E Hodgson. *The History of Aeronautics in Great Britain: from the earliest times to the latter half of the nineteenth century*, 1924
R Hooke. *Philosophical Collections*, 1679
R Jackson. *Air War over Korea*, 1973
F T Jane, C G Grey, L Bridgman, J W R Taylor. *Jane's All the World's Aircraft*, 1909–74
J de la Ferté. *The Fated Sky*, 1952
F C Kelly. *Miracle at Kitty Hawk: the letters of Wilbur and Orville Wright*, 1951
D Mondey. *Pictorial History of the U.S.A.F.*, 1971
A Price. *Instruments of Darkness: the struggle for radar supremacy*, 1967
W Raleigh and H A Jones. *The War in the Air: being the story of the part played in the Great War by the Royal Air Force*, 7 Vols, 1922–37
D Richards and H St G Saunders. *Royal Air Force, 1939–45*, 1953–54
H Schliephake. *The Birth of the Luftwaffe*, 1971
G Swanborough and P M Bowers. *United States Military Aircraft since 1908*, 1971
G Swanborough and P M Bowers. *United States Navy Aircraft since 1911*, 1968
J W R Taylor. *Aircraft, Aircraft*, 1967
J W R Taylor. *A Picture History of Flight*, 1955
J W R Taylor. *Combat Aircraft of the World*, 1969
J W R Taylor and G Swanborough. *Military Aircraft of the World*, 1973
J W R Taylor and P J R Moyes. *Pictorial History of the R.A.F.*, 3 Vols, 1968–70
J W R Taylor. *The Royal Air Force*, 1965
J W R Taylor and D Mondey. *Spies in the Sky*, 1972
J W R Taylor, T H Michael, D Mondey. *The Guinness Book of Air Facts and Feats*, 1973
J W R Taylor and M Allward. *Wings for Tomorrow*, 1951
O Thetford. *Aircraft of the Royal Air Force since 1918*, 1971
C H Turnor. *Astra Castra: experiments and adventures in the atmosphere*, 1865
R Wagner. *American Combat Planes*, 1960

Acknowledgments

Her Majesty's Stationery Office:
From *Aviation: a historical survey from its origins to the end of World War II* by C H Gibbs-Smith. Reprinted by permission.

Cassell & Co Ltd and Houghton Mifflin Co:
From *History of the Second World War* by Winston S Churchill. Reprinted by permission.

Ian Allan Ltd:
From *Air War Over Korea* by Robert Jackson. Reprinted by permission.

Hugh Evelyn:
From *Historic Airships* by P W Brooks. Reprinted by permission.

The Hutchinson Publishing Group Ltd and Curtis Brown Ltd:
From *The Fated Sky* by Sir Philip Joubert de la Ferté. Reprinted by permission.

Air Force Association:
From *History of the United States Air Force, 1907–1957*. Reprinted by permission.

The Clarendon Press:
From *The War in the Air* Vol I by Sir Walter Raleigh.

Index

239